LONGTHROAT MEMOIRS

Soups, Sex and Nigerian Taste Buds

LONGTHROAT
MEMOIRS

Soups, Sex and Nigerian Taste Buds

Yemisí Aríbisálà

Abuja - London

Published in 2016 by Cassava Republic Press
Second Edition, Second Reprint, 2019
Abuja – London

A CIP catalogue record for this book is available from the National Library of Nigeria and the British Library.

ISBN (Nigeria) 978-978-953-514-0
ISBN (UK) 978-1-911115-26-7
eISBN 978-1-911115-27-4

Distributed in the UK by Central Books Ltd.
Printed and bound in Great Britain by Bell & Bain Ltd, Glasgow.

Stay up to date with the latest books, special offers
and exclusive content with our monthly newsletter.
Sign up on our website:
www.cassavarepublic.biz

Twitter: @cassavarepublic
Instagram: @cassavarepublicpress
Facebook: facebook.com/CassavaRepublic

Fún eni tí ó n se nkan tó yi gbi… tó le koko… tìre ni gbogbo nkan àti gbogbo ìyìn.

Also for Jeremy Weate, the Folfallarum who stuck closer than any blood sister and asked for nothing. You are the man.

Contents

Nigerian food belongs to the Nigerian. This is more than a noteworthy recommendation for its intrinsic sumptuousness. It is not gastronomically illustrious, not yet given its due. It is good-hearted, fundamentally starchy and soupy. Delicious as a tangible morsel of food sanctioned by the senses, journeying over the pink rug into the gut, it is also a multifaceted cultural treasure trove full of intriguing stories. It is misunderstood, atrociously photographed; it might yet rule the world. It isn't all just swallow and soup.

end of my explanations. Close friends and family concluded I would be writing recipes when I told them I would be writing about Nigerian food. A major Nigerian newspaper refused my offer of a column on Nigerian food stories because they didn't want recipes for jollof rice and egusi soup and beef stew. This was the extent of the stretch in the fabric when I proposed the existence of a person called Nigerian food.

In the late months of 2008, at the suggestion of Ebùn Feludu, a colleague from my days at *Farafina Magazine*, tall-as-a-soursop-tree vegan Jeremy Weate called from the brilliant but short-lived Lagos-based newspaper *234NEXT* to offer me a food blog. Lagos and Abuja were both turning the corner into the thick of an exotic-restaurant trend. In Lagos, you could already eat the cuisines of South East Asia, North America, the Middle East, North Africa and three European countries in one weekend if you were determined to do so. And you wouldn't have to move outside of the 9 km² of land area representing Irù/Victoria Island. I know for a fact that Weate was thinking *perambulating attractive woman with cast-iron stomach doing the rounds of local restaurants and bukas.*

I, however, did not fit the persona. Rather than eat out, I was worrying about dissecting food in my one-window (that didn't count as a window) kitchen. I was all but living in there, cooking three meals a day from scratch, using the nuts and bolts of my superficial relationship with Nigerian food. It was drudgery, not a love affair. I was nothing more than a home cook with children who had food sensitivities and intolerances. My son's condition was so dramatic that he could only eat food in the colours of the Nigerian flag; nothing orange, red or yellow, no carrots, tomatoes or red corn, and nothing processed. Since I am the parent with some identical food sensitivities, it made sense that I was paying for the recalcitrance of my genes in that kitchen. My stomach was so very sensitive it could barely digest a bowl of white basmati rice. (I have since then discovered that white rice is number two on my list of food intolerances.) If I ate out, I expected to fall ill; it had almost become a foregone conclusion.

It was therefore a near-impossible luxury for me to leave home and sit in a restaurant or buka for thirty minutes on most days. I was nothing in the vicinity of gorgeous nor did I possess hair that moved with the flow of the restaurant air conditioning. Like most mothers of very young children, my daily style was unbathed and frazzled in flip-flops, with stray bits of garlic up the front of my dress, all my nerve endings relocated to the tips of the hairs on my arms, one minor preschooler infraction away from losing my mind.

I'm not the ideal Nigerian epicurean either. I thought people would size *me* up and legitimately demand, 'Well what do you know about Nigerian food *really*?' Because writing a good modern book of Nigerian recipes (as they assumed I'd be doing) would take someone empirical, focused and experienced, as well as willing and able to travel. It is easily presumed that I am not empirical, focused or experienced, nor particularly ambulatory in my relationship with Nigerian food.

There are others who fit this bill perfectly. Or who have a wholesome respect for boundaries before creativity is allowed in the door. My imagination is always ahead of real life.

I don't have a head full of measuring cups or a grasp of the indigenous technicalities of small and large mudu: 1 Abuja mudu equals 9 milk tins, 1 Calabar mudu equals 12 milk tins, etc.

I don't have the instinctive intelligence to decode and approximate cigarette tins to Derica tins to ounces and pounds and vice versa. I have never had a head for measuring anything not in mudu or ounces or cigar tins. I lack the quickness that converts an ounce to a shaky hill on a tablespoon and does so accurately. The first map of Nigeria that I ever drew put the states where I wanted them, and I had to pretend I was not crushed when my mother said I could not put Kaduna in the east just because I felt it should be there.

Writing about food in the way that I do involves noting the influence of food on life and life on food and attempting to weave an accurate cultural landscape. Anything representing efficiency and structure, or measuring cups, are only allowed in my loom because of their nostalgic quality, because of the charm of the national trend of carrying old tins around and insisting they stand in for more precise measures. Measuring food in Nigeria stands out in its unsystematic nature: it is large Derica versus small Derica. It clashes with the necessary standardisation of 'measuring'. I would not be true to the personality of our food if I was caught up in pounds and ounces, yet I do not see how anyone can write a contemporary Nigerian cookbook that could join the global dialogue without acknowledging pounds and ounces or cups.

There is also the matter of my incongruous appearance. There is a portly hoariness that Nigerians take for granted when visualising the Nigerian epicurean or that person who claims she has an intimate relationship with our food. In the same way that a Nigerian politician with a shirt-stretching belly and some grey hairs will command involuntary respect and an almost immediate presumption of competence over his slimmer, younger-looking colleague, you must unequivocally look the part. And, as if it isn't enough to live an age and look the part, one must bring the ability from the other side, from

4

beyond the womb. We call these people who cook from beyond the womb 'olowo síbí': literally, 'hands of spoons, spoons for hands'. You have to be the appropriate alchemical container for the gift of cooking.

In the estimation of many Nigerians, I don't look as if I have been around as long as I have in fact been. Nor do I possess a prima facie reverence for institutions of Nigerian cooking. The true Nigerian epicurean must cook within the boundaries exceptionally well. Such a purist who would never go as far as to declare ogbono in otong a genuine soup, only an aspiring rogue of a soup. Nor have I begun to travel the length and breadth of Nigeria, studying all the recipes belonging to over one hundred and eighty million people.

A better means of describing my relationship with food would be to consider my rejection of what people say when you have a bad dream: 'Don't take it too seriously. What did you eat last night?' For someone like me, trivialising my dreams as a symptom of dinner would not be in any way comforting. What I ate last night is as significant and as tangible as my dreams. My dreams are as tangible as what I am eating. Neither of them can safely be taken for granted. Life seen through the prism of food has more colours, not fewer.

Similarly, sex is redeemed when expressed though the language of food, as I explain in 'The Snail Tree'. It is exactly like the palate: personal, unequivocally owned, in my mouth (my mouth not anyone else's). It is many things I am under no pressure to put into firm imagery. I can harness food when talking of sex and no one would feel I was judging their own experiences, assaulting their sensibilities or being false. If I said sex was a bowl of yam pottage and described the cooking of the dish, I would have my foot in the door and most likely elicit a smile from the listener. Suggestions and suggestiveness might mean the same thing. The words would do their own work of creating imagery, yet there would be no tussle for technicalities. It would not be pornography, Western liberal dictates, communal metaphors for sex, or glossy magazine drivel. It would be immensely more than drab titillation, despite a generous helping of repression, but certainly not a recipe.

Not that I have anything against recipes. I give some and suggest twists in the use of time-honoured ones. But I have always wanted to do other things, like deconstruct the Christmas stew. In many other countries, Christmas meals must be complicated, sophisticated and dressed up, otherwise people feel that Christmas has been taken for granted. The Nigerian Christmas stew is 70 per cent psychological fare and 30 per cent gastronomical fanfare. The desperation to mark Christmas in some special way remains relevant. Give the villager roast turkey dressed with the most expensive ingredients in the world and he will still just want his Christmas rice and stew. The psychological and gastronomical balance adds up to the same 100 per cent no matter what.

The context is especially significant. It is Christmas fare because it is cooked around midnight on Christmas Eve and the aroma wakes everyone in the house (or at least filters into pleasant dreams) and welcomes home those who felt the need to greet Christmas Day in church.

The rice is Uncle Ben's parboiled rice. It's imported, but the prestige given to Uncle Ben's rice, which isn't at all special, is peculiarly Nigerian. I think we might still find the kindly black man's face on the orange box reassuring. The meat in the stew is the tough old layer chicken that wandered the village all year. All in all, a simple meal, yet Christmas embraces it as the best fare of the year. Christmas will never be Christmas without plain, simple rice and stew. This is a uniquely Nigerian story.

I have written about the dog-eaters in 'Eating Dog', not only to describe a room where people eat dog meat, but to showcase the normalcy and ardour with which they eat it. Would I be writing with sincerity if I didn't talk about how that normalcy scandalises and shames the rest of us self-righteous meat-eaters, voracious devourers of goat, pig and cow? If I had a recipe for dog, how many people would attempt it? Yet in Calabar, dog meat is the pinnacle of gourmet food. People sit around on Sunday afternoons in Calabar Municipality and eat dog with nothing but ageing, frothy palm wine. The dregs of the palm wine and dog meat are recommended for the new bridegroom.

So many Nigerian perceptions of food and relationships with food traverse the borders of spirit and body. Cooking itself is a holistic exercise that can never exclude the spiritual. That which you eat enters your whole being, finds its way into your soul and touches your dreams. That which you cook is informed by everything about you: your mood, spirit, environment, temperament. Many Nigerians will decline a meal prepared by someone whose spirit they do not trust, although a few will eat that food to confirm their lack of trust. Restaurant meals don't count because the food is being cooked for/aimed at the stomachs of many people, not one person. A man will request a meal from a woman to prove her ineligibility for marriage. Steamed foods are rated the perfect medium for these compulsory analyses, as depicted in a story about a wedding in Calabar.

In the tale, the bridegroom is very highly placed and everyone is coming to the wedding. In order to be able to feed all the guests, the cooking is organised in a large open field, the kind of field big enough to play a professional soccer match. Women are apportioned different meals on the menu. This being Calabar, the carte du jour is elaborate, to be cooked with fine-tuned expertise. There are women in charge of large cauldrons of seasoned ground beans steamed in thaumatococcus leaves (moin-moin). All the cauldrons go on the firewood at about the same time, but when everyone else's pot has been taken off the fire to cool, the moin-moin in one set of women's cauldron is still bizarrely unsteamed, uncooked.

A machete is inserted in the pot among the parcels. The insertion of the machete is a spiritual remedy or investigation, if you like. When all the material possibilities have been seen to, one seamlessly moves into the metaphysical. All of these steps, by the way, are taken in the most casual way. No one is in the least impressed ... not yet.

After the machete has stood among the wraps of moin- moin for long enough and the cooking still isn't progressing, the women around that pot unequivocally become suspect. Think of the cauldron that we call Agbárí Ojukwu sitting on a fire for hours, the firewood under the pot burning ferociously; the skin of the cauldron blackening before your eyes. The cauldron keeps requesting sips of water to be poured into the gaps between the wraps of moin-moin. This performance of thirsty licking of water and gyrating flames continues, but every time the supervisor comes round to open a wrap of moin-moin for inspection, as soon as he carefully peels back the thaumatococcus leaves, the beans spill out uncooked.

Organising this kind of cooking for a grand wedding ceremony, where catering is needed for thousands of guests over days of celebrations, requires a random rallying of women from different cooking establishments without real cuisinal formality; without requesting CVs of cooking experience or something akin to cordon bleu recommendations. Loose or otherwise, these cooks are chosen by familiarity and word of mouth. They arrive, and if their wrappers, fingernails and hair are clean, they are given the job. However, the supervisor of the whole enterprise must constantly keep her eyes peeled, not only for the lazy worker who wants to disappear among the activity and collect an easy day's wages, but she must especially look out for the container of malice who feels slighted by the extravagance of cooking for a whole city, or the peripherality of the labour producing the meal to the glory of the events. There are no foolproof methods of detecting malevolence or malfeasance but as surely as a meal cooked in anger will give the eater a stomach ache, so is a person with ill will in her heart or mind incapable of creating a pot of perfectly steamed moin-moin. If a woman has a spiritual problem – call it a 'quirk' if you like – the food will respond negatively to her. It will fight her and the outcome of the cooking will indicate that there is something lurking.

In the end, the women whose moin-moin did not cook are paid off and sent home. Everyone present will agree that the revelation was unpremeditated, procedural, and therefore as empirical as the fact that water boils at 100°C. The leap between the spheres is like stepping over a narrow puddle. The preparation of the meal has revealed more than the ability of its cooks: it has revealed their hearts. You don't want these women's hands on your food, their spirits hovering over something that will go inwards and inform all your insides. There is a question mark over their character, or they're dabbling in something dark.

Similarly, there is a cross-cultural Nigerian belief that there are two pure elements that will not respond to malice. Both can overpower their handlers and refuse the infusion of poison: water, whose lucid innocence will immediately out the poisoner; and palm oil, which is regarded as 'ero' – a red elixir and powerful remedy for poisoning, and even more significantly as a remedy for malevolence.

I write about the power of nostalgia in relation to eating snails in 'Letter from Candahar Road'. The love of snails practically drips from an old letter I found in my grandparents' trunk, from Bísí Omotárá in London to Mrs Fáníyan in Ososàmì, Ìbàdàn on 27 January 1966. My love of snails predates and overtakes the discovery of the letter. In the beginning of 2013, I ate peppered snails every single day for three months, and in the process I broke the bank. In that fifty-year-old letter, I can visualise the longing stretching across continents like resilient snail mucilage. I had to call an uncle to confirm how long it takes boiled then fried snails, cooked with plenty of fresh pepper, suspended in a container of groundnut oil ... how long will they take to travel by ship between Lagos and London? Two weeks, they sail the seas, spending a day in customs. In expectation of these very snails, Bisi Omotara, longingly writes:

Bíì kí igbin yen ti dé ló ń se mí. Àfi bí eni pé nko je igbin rí ló ń se ń wùn wá je. Olúwa aláànú yíó bù sí àpò fún yin o ...

She is not only counting the days till the snails arrive; she is moved to say a prayer that the pockets by which the snails were purchased be deepened. Amen.

Snails are a powerful yet cloaked sexual symbol. Like oysters in paler, more exhibitive cultures, snails and their mucilage, their resemblance to the labia minor, and their fat-skinned duskiness, are unwritten Nigerian sexual theology. Periwinkles are snails in other parts of the world. Here they are not. Snails have faces; periwinkles do not. Snails turn up in the encyclopaedia of demonic food; periwinkles do not. Snails are tools of bewitchment; periwinkles are not. If you stopped the average man on the street and asked him what the difference between a snail and a periwinkle was, he would answer that a snail is a snail and a periwinkle is a periwinkle; simple as that. But what a question! There are social graces or possible disgraces attached to sucking a periwinkle out of its shell in a public place. Periwinkles have their own orthodoxy, their own protocol of eating. Their classification as not-snails is based on these parameters, not on the denial of biological terminology or character.

I once cooked a pot of afang soup that was overwhelmed with water. It was in April, at the beginning of an apathetic rainy season. It was flooding in a gentlemanly fashion in the streets of Calabar, a town that usually floods with such angst that adults get carried away from the middle of the street by floodwaters. The heat was like the heavy blanket used for sweating out malaria.

Anyone who has cooked afang soup long enough, anyone whose opinion on afang soup must be respected, anyone who can claim to be knowledgeably writing a recipe for afang soup, must first understand that the liquidity of afang heavily depends on the diminutive waterleaf. Then they must understand that this leaf is a pretender. What it does is gather up all the rainwater and transform it into petite elliptical leaves and tiny purple flowers. Once in the soup, the waterleaf regurgitates all that water, recreating the flood right before your eyes. Why does it do this? It could very well be because diminutive men always have something to prove; flooded soup is a warning not to take the size of the waterleaf for granted.

The Nigerian epicurean would never, ever allow a pot of afang to flood. The housewife who cannot read a line of a recipe; the 8-year-old who needs to stand on a stool to reach the kitchen sink; the teenage girl already successfully cooking pots of afang completely unassisted: they all understand, at a back-burner level of thinking, the balance of water, palm oil and floods hidden in waterleaf. It is commonsensical that if it is raining and flooding outside, then the quantity of waterleaf for afang must be reduced to keep the flooding out of the pot of soup. *Commonsensical!*

And yet Nigerians don't talk about their food. Even if people don't realise it, even if many Nigerians themselves don't know it, Nigerian food is the most endearing, enduring topic in the world, especially because we have gone so long without talking about it. The relationship of the nouveau middle-to-upper-income-earning Nigerian and their food is a mixture of love, snobbery, the passion that results from the snobbery, and social repression. It's like loving fat women but being compelled to marry a thin one to keep up appearances; it makes the clandestine meets with the fat one all the more scorching. Nigerians will sit in restaurants in every part of the world, in Lagos, and in Abuja, and eat sushi, fugu, Peruvian ceviche and piure. They will eat it all with an open mind, a fierce worldliness and a sexy congeniality, and then they will go home and bring out the amala and ewedu and crown the night with sighing, with tears in their eyes, and noses weeping beads of sweat.

But we won't start a public discussion with those who do not know our food intimately; a discussion that will open the door to some painful, uneducated remark about the fat mistress. This is the seeming nonchalance with which we regard our food, the Nigerian reticence that began to melt with my *234NEXT* blog. I think perhaps it is a way of keeping that which is sacrosanct just so by not tainting it with words.

I can still write a million expositions and a few recipes on Nigerian food and make the world – and even Nigerians – wonder. I blogged about Nigerian food at *234NEXT* for close to three years, and in that time only scratched the surface of what our food is about. I think the person on the street has stopped keeping count of tribes and local government areas and languages and dialects within languages; imagine millions of people divided along those endless lines.

Think of the variations of pepper soups and banga soups or all the different names and different ways of fermenting locust beans. The species of yams is the subject of endless debates on who owns the best-tasting tuber; one could very well be at it for a lifetime. A species of mushroom called 'okokobioko' by a Boki man in Obumatung Kakwagum in Cross River State is called 'ekpazara' an hour and a half away in Adadanma, Yakurr. Twenty minutes away from Kakwagum in Okuni, it is called 'olobo'. We are still in the same state, and more interestingly the locals from all these villages are referred to by the sometimes derogatory title of 'Atam'. Or 'Mbon enyung enyung'. Travel high up into the hills of Obudu cattle ranch and you will find weather reminiscent of winter in Northern Europe: low hanging clouds, dense fog, coral sunsets and fair-faced Fulani. Come down the hill and the layers of clothing will have to come off. In the time it takes to travel up the hill in a cable car, you might as well have left one continent and arrived on another.

I am often amazed that, in 2016, people still try to take Nigerian food and squeeze it into this all-encompassing title of 'African food'. I can guess that the rest of the world is seeking a kind of exotic simplification: condensed Fágúnwà, a working summary, an effective way of getting the feeling across that Africa will fit in your handbag as a commodity, a book, a piece of cloth or a gourmet bottle of shittor. However, I wonder why Nigerians themselves agree to the use of the term. The British and the French would feel their food was being belittled if you tried to lump them all under the term 'European food'.

I don't know Congolese food. The Congolese man on the street probably doesn't know Nigerian food. This table where all of us 'Africans' are seated eating the same food just doesn't exist. And the idea of it is so unsophisticated that one just wonders.

I refer to the recipes in Michael Barry's book, *Exotic Food the Crafty Way,* as a case in point. Published in 1996, the book took an exotic culinary world trip that included Jamaica, Japan, Argentina and Afghanistan. In his culinary sojourn, Nigerian food didn't exist, and if it did, it had no international identity. So, his Nigerian recipes were an attempt to interpret intimate conversations for a public Western hearing. In that year, every family in Nigeria converged in front of the television one evening a week to watch Maggi cooking programmes. The shows ran for almost two decades. They were all about the how-tos of cooking Nigerian meals, even if not about the personality and rationale behind Nigerian food.

The instinctive connection of 'Nigerian' with 'soup' and 'stodge' is a lazy stereotype. I lived in Calabar for five years and have not yet fully understood the intricacies of Cross Riverian food. Nigerian food is often stodgy and soupy. But it is also misunderstood, atrociously photographed, not yet given its due. It's a multifaceted cultural treasure trove full of intriguing stories. It might not be gastronomically illustrious but it is energetic and good-hearted. It belongs to one of the most fascinating personalities in the world: the Nigerian. Needless to say, it is delectable. The Nigerian soup is a living, breathing, evolving being.

Now on to the meet.

A Bowl of Aloof Nigerian Soup

To declare an interest from the start, I'm a soup man myself.
Michael Barry

I have an old copy of Michael Barry's cookbook and its ambition appeals to me. The clout for writing *Exotic Food the Crafty Way* is proclaimed in the book's introduction: Barry was half Welsh, half Indian and widely travelled, with a broad-minded palate.[1] He was born Michael Bukht. He became a famous BBC chef and household name, but only as Michael Barry, not Bukht.

His book presents Jamaican rice and peas on one page and an Indonesian rice cone on the next. You'll find Venezuelan black bean soup followed by pea soup from Barbados.

It's an inadvertently prescient, rudimentary index pointing to the rambling cosmic cookbook that is the Internet. If a bowl of West Indian callaloo and crab soup walked past, you might recognise it because Michael Barry had told you about it. His Nigerian groundnut chop was my first attempt at a groundnut anything. It was delicious. In retrospect, it did almost everything a groundnut stew should. You would, of course have to eschew the word 'peanut' because only the most pretentious Nigerian would call a 'groundnut' a 'peanut'.

---

[1] Michael Barry, **Exotic Food the Crafty Way** (Norwich, Jarrold Publishing, 1996).

If you dry-fried your groundnuts with love and vigilance; if you refused to cut your stewing beef into tiny 1 cm cubes (because no self-respecting Nigerian does any such thing); if, instead of chopping your onion 'quite fine', you blended or ground it up with the 450g of ripe tomatoes and fresh hot peppers, then Barry's sketch of groundnut soup might acquire a familiar wonky smile. Groundnut soup does not originally come from the Yorùbá; it is more accurately ascribable to the Edo, although the Edo and Yorùbá own common ancestry. It was not cooked in our house when I was growing up, and that is my explanation for having to resort to a book when I was looking for something 'exotic' to cook for my husband. I'm too ashamed to address the irony of cooking Nigerian food from a half Welsh, half Indian man's cookbook.

I'm intrigued that, in Barry's introduction to the technicalities of the recipe, he mentions that colonial and postcolonial novels deride the gorgeously hot-buttery groundnut soup. That is something I am still attempting to engage with. Perhaps the problem was with the writers of the novels and not with groundnut soup; no one who has tasted its exquisite creaminess would dare think it worthy of derision.

Barry's Nigerian River Province chicken soup is the second attempt at Nigerian food in his book. The recipe is so fascinatingly confused in its interpretation that it makes me wonder if Nigerian recipes are inaccessible to the outsider and have been so for a long, long time, or if outsiders generally believe that our food is unsophisticated, without a concrete identity, and can just be made up as one goes along. Imagine a country the size of Nigeria, and it is possible to presume that you could throw anything into a pot and it would immediately become Nigerian food, perhaps just because a Nigerian cooked it.

'Nigerian River Province chicken soup' is, I suppose, cooked in the Nigerian River Province, wherever that is.

Combining the words 'Nigerian', 'River' and 'Province' to describe a place 'in Africa' must give the foreign reader an immediate burst of irresistibly colourful imagery enhanced by the titillating expectation of learning about food cooked in such a place. I assume it's more effective than simply saying 'Bayelsa soup', for example. Similarly, a Guyanese in-law of mine who lived for some time in the United States assured me that North Americans did not want to hear that wax print fabric (made in Holland) does not uncompromisingly represent the 'African'. The imagery of that rippling, colourful fabric peremptorily gets the juices going.

The name of Barry's Nigerian soup reminds me of something that used to happen often when I was in school in Wales. I would introduce myself to a new acquaintance as 'Yemisí' and seven times out of ten I'd end up having the following conversation:

'Yesimi?'

'No. Yemisí.'

'Mmm. That's a nice name. How do you say it again?'

'Yemisí. Like in tonic sol-fa mi re mi.'

'Is it like "Yemí"?'

'No that's a different name.'

'Isn't it interesting that it is Yemisí and not Yesimi. You would expect that the "s" would come before the "m" somehow. Do you have an English name? ... It's just that it's a little difficult to say. You know it is pretty ... interesting ... I met this Nigerian chap the other day and he had a Nigerian name, but then he had an English name also. His name was Fred.'

'Really!'

'And he said most Nigerians have a Nigerian name and a Christian name.'

'I only have one name and it is both Nigerian and Christian.'

'How do you say it again?'

'Yemisí.'

'So pretty ... like Yemeni ...'

In the introduction to the recipe it says that the River Province soup is eaten very thick with a kind of bread made from cassava. I had gone through the book many times before it dawned that the cassava bread was probably gari or ebà.

I have heard of gari/ebà being referred to as dumplings, never as bread. 'Dumplings' is a passable compromise in helping the outsider's mind adapt to the idea of Nigerian gari. It is at least like saying that condoms become balloons when you blow them up. There is as much truth in that statement as a dose of B6 in a B complex capsule. But saying that gari is bread by any stretch of the imagination ... Well it just isn't.

'Nigerian River Province soup' presumably contains the following ingredients: finely diced chicken, peeled and chopped tomatoes, one heaped teaspoon of chilli powder, washed or frozen spinach, peeled and chopped onions, palm oil (which, according to the recipe, can be replaced with ordinary cooking oil), cooked peeled prawns, etc.

There is a spirit of compromise inherent in Barry's recipe that could not exist in the context of a real Nigerian dish. The very idea of Nigerian soup containing diced chicken has something deeply contradictory about it. Any Nigerian soup worth its salt must contain meat visible from the other end of the room. Using diced meat could be misinterpreted as putting on airs when you should just admit that you cannot afford meat. If you served soup with diced anything to guests, they would immediately begin to wonder whether you were trying to hide something. And even if there was nothing to hide and the soup was just meant to be fashionable, the guest would be convinced it was the worst sort of affectation. This is the truth even if most Nigerians hold meat in such high esteem and would rather have it present in every dish. In many cultures within Nigeria, meat is being successfully substituted with crayfish, mushrooms and dried bean sprouts, among other ingredients.

Once you get your mind around all these stumbling blocks in Barry's recipe – Frozen spinach! Peeled and chopped tomatoes! Chopped onions! Any replacement for palm oil! A teaspoon of chilli powder! – you soon realise that the problem is that Barry is familiar with soup from many parts of the world, but knows next to nothing about Nigerian soup. Furthermore, I suspect a Nigerian called 'Fred' is lurking in the background of this recipe. He is a good-hearted fellow asked to help bridge the gaps in comprehension, availability of ingredients, and even in culture, but he is so eager to please that he has pushed the boundaries too far.

Barbara Page-Phillips, an elderly friend who gave me the use of half of her home, Claysgarth in Somerton, Somerset for a writer's retreat, showed me a treasured Nigerian recipe from her meticulously-kept box of recipes. Barbara taught me how to make my first vinaigrette. She demonstrated the diplomacy needed in grilling a filet of sole until I learnt it perfectly. Her Nigerian recipe was written out for her by a Wilson Bodisei – a man from Ijaw, Rivers State. A *Nigerian River Province man.*

Barbara had typed the recipe on the same page as recipes for Yorkshire curd tart and cream cheese tartlets.

The Bayelsa delicacy that I believe Wilson was translating is a plantain pottage whose name is so maligned we can't decide whether it is 'kekefiaye', 'kekefieye' or 'kekefiya'. This isn't unusual, because we aren't dealing with an English word; Nigerians are attempting to speak Ijaw in English. Also 'ekporoko' and 'okporoko' are both valid translations for stockfish, depending on where you are from.

There is no excuse for the inclusion of tomatoes in the dish and it could be argued that you can't make this particular plantain pottage without bush basil. In 2013, I had to get help interpreting the recipe. The person I consulted took a double take and said this must be that famous Bayelsa dish. The soup predates the birth of the Nigerian state called Bayelsa.

The straw that broke the camel's back was Barry safely concluding, with Fred's help, that Nigerian River Province soup 'should have the consistency of a good thick minestrone'. It's a lot like Bukht becoming Barry to be more palatable to BBC viewers.

So the fundamental, burning question becomes: what is Nigerian soup? Or, for the long-suffering Nigerian whose culinary culture has been forever grossly misunderstood and really knows only one soup: what is soup? It is certainly not a diced chicken and frozen spinach affair.

First, back to Barry, who joyously declares:

> I'm a soup man myself. I find the variety of textures, ingredients, flavours and, dare I say it, liquidity, of the world's soups a never ending source of pleasure and discovery. I've given a small selection

of my great favourites here ... like the Singapore Laksha or the Nigerian River Province Chicken Pot [which] are in fact meals in themselves ... Soup is something that can be said to separate cultures and communities ... Some are meant as a prelude to other dishes ... Some are meant to stimulate the appetite ... What they all have in common is that they are easy to make and very economical.[2]

The 'soup' Barry has in mind – the type that is affordable, easily made and eaten with bread – is an entire world away from our own. There is nothing economical about Bayelsa soup, nothing easy in the preparation of afang soup. Soup is eaten with gari, fufu or rice. Lumping Nigerian soup under Barry's selection is like describing sushi as rice and fish eaten all over the world.

The mixed wires are lethal; it is not Nigerian if we do not recognise it as Nigerian. One cannot understand Nigerian food without understanding the *ankara,* the *cloth* of the soup. Nigerian soup is like the Yorùbá language: more sophisticated than English (which is the child of rape of Frenchmen and Germans) and superior to French, which is by far superior to English. Our soup is like that living, breathing, complex, door-behind-door-behind-door language, plus context, plus particular context plus individual flair plus fascinating expressions plus a few English words (like a can of tomatoes) allowed to those people who *we know* can't find fresh tomatoes or speak Yorùbá very well. Mind you these are only a few words; it's allowance, compromise, not influence.

---

2 Barry, *Exotic Food*, 9.

Nigerian soup does not even have a contemporary in French cooking. It is a global individual. It has a face, a look. It has as a fundamental, flowing premise like blood running through its veins: palm oil. And unlike Barry's suggestion, 'that oil' cannot be replaced by 'any oil'. Our soup is a tree with many branches. There are branches dedicated to flavour and if you follow one, you might have processes spanning days or weeks in commitment to getting one stunning detail in a pot of soup. A case in point is the dawadawa or irú (fermented locust beans). This is just one ingredient but many purists will not eat soup made without dawadawa.

There is the green leaf or vegetable that cannot, and most definitely should not, be frozen spinach. There is afang leaf unwound from its symbiotic partner in the bush. There is afang leaf grown in town and snubbed by the bush afang. There is the pumpkin leaf that, in one unique language, is called 'ibok iyep' (red blood corpuscle) for its nutritional powerhouse status. There are leaves used for flavour and aroma, bitter herbs for complexity, heat and mere aftertaste. There are the choices of meat, and effort is required to get even one kind of meat in a variety of about five in a pot of soup. The options may include stockfish from Norway, grass cutters (cane rats), snails, goat, stingray, periwinkles, etc. There is the extra-special addition of mushrooms: fresh, fermented in banana leaves for months, or smoked over wood fires. Or perhaps pieces of desiccated unripe pawpaw, bean sprouts, and bitter-melon seeds processed into faux-meat.

There are pots of soup tailored to the palates and digestive systems of children; soups cooked for men to send them sexually suggestive messages; soup to help the bridegroom perform his functions on the wedding night. I have to be frank and tell Mr Barry that he has never met any soup that resembles the Nigerian soup!

In contrast to Barry's presumptuous exotic Nigerian recipes is the *Maggi Family Menu Cookbook* (1986), one of my most treasured cookbooks. It's the third in a compilation of recipes from the television series that every Nigerian family with a TV watched from the late 1970s to the mid-1990s. With this book, there is no hesitation, only supreme confidence and authority. Apart from the nostalgic value of this dog-eared, stained, torn and otherwise much abused book, I am reassured by the fact that in it otipi is otipi, ukazi agworoagwo is what it is and obe-korowó is uncompromisingly prepared with dawadawa, bushmeat, smoked fish and korowó (snails).

If you get lost – and you will – there are two pages of pictorial representations of everything from isamagwa to guinea corn sprouts. There is also a glossary where you will understand that 'ebearenmowu khor' is the Beninese term for tea-bush leaves or bush basil, also called 'nchanwun' in Igbo and 'efirin' in Yorùbá. In English you could say the leaf is a unique cross between basil and mint. Those who attempt to define it in English either call it local mint or local basil being fully aware that it is neither. If you are looking for the thinly sliced dried unripe pawpaw for that unusual Yala soup, you will not find it posing as 'papaya'. You would call it 'kiquabana' and the name is only really familiar to the owners of the soup in Yala, Cross River State.

Unlike Barry, the writers of the *Maggi Family Menu Cookbook* understand that some things cannot be translated without catastrophe and need the greatest care and respect. Sometimes with a choice of two or three descriptive words. The translated subject will never become English. It will always be like that

Nigerian mother who has come for her daughter's graduation, standing in the tube station in aso-òkè worn on top of woolly jumpers. Believe me, her name will never be Mrs Earl Grey.

We are talking about a form that is played with, recreated, enhanced and reduced daily by millions of people in a vast eclectic entity that feels more like a continent than a country. And yet that form is so similar in particular aspects, we immediately recognise it wherever we see it. The number of ingredients available to create our soup is undocumented, but the oil, flavour enhancers, leaves, herbs and meats are similar. The accompanying gari, fufu and pounded yam are well loved. The mode of starting with one ingredient and ending with another is near rote.

Nigerian soup may seem aloof at first, but once given its due, it will immediately make itself friendly at the very least. You would know it even if you did not have every ingredient available to cook it. If Nigerian ingredients were so easily replaced by others, we would not need entire Nigerian food sections in London's Brixton Market, or customs officers at the airport collecting bribes to turn a blind eye to dried afang wrapped in old newspapers and hidden in underwear bags.

It's possible that I have been phenomenally unfair to Michael Barry and unduly finicky about Wilson Bodisei's recipe. If a Nigerian took pizza, made the base out of yam flour, littered the top with wara (local cottage cheese), balls of bitter melon, ground peppers and meat, shouldn't he be commended for his creative interpretation? There are enough people who know what pizza is to cry foul when the interpretation goes too far, or when it tastes nothing like pizza or when the maker of the pizza is claiming that Nigerian pizza is how it is made in Naples.

Most people around the world have no clue what Nigerian food is. It is what Michael Barry says it is. It is what Marcus Samuelsson in *The Soul of a New Cuisine: A Discovery of the Foods and Flavors of Africa* (2006) says it is. Perhaps it tastes like Pierre Thiam of Senegal's cooking in his restaurant in Brooklyn; he cooks jollof rice, okro and black-eyed beans after all. It is buried in Frances Case's passing references in *1001 Foods You Must Taste Before You Die* (2008). (The book says ogbono soup is fiery and I wonder why on earth the authors chose that description. Fieriness is not a characteristic of ogbono soup as pungency is not a distinctive feature of egúsí soup.)

We did not make it into the August 2012 *Newsweek*'s '101 Best Places to Eat in the World' (chosen by no less than fifty-three of the 'finest chefs', if you please), nor did we make it into *National Geographic*'s *Food Journeys of a Lifetime: 500 Extraordinary Places to Eat Around the Globe* (2009). Googling 'Nigerian chef' offends my browser: it pouts and spits out women in blue headties cooking on YouTube. 'Nigerian food' brings up ubiquitous bowls of jollof rice, mounds of pounded yam and egúsí, fried plantains, puff- puffs and kikife/kikifieye/kikifiya etc. I'm hungry but not inspired; the owners of the blogs are plagued by a unique restlessness. They talk a little bit about Nigerian food and a lot about food from other countries cooked by Nigerians. They all go down the same road and eventually lose interest. Our food belongs to a personality that animates its eating, but you can't tell by looking on the Internet that she is so fascinating her food can't not be.

There is a logic to our food that cannot be guessed. The Yorùbá say that you must ask the owner of the face before you slap it. It is an awkward proverb about presumptuousness: if you presume that a person would like to be slapped across the face, you would most likely be wrong. What it is saying in this context is that first you get familiar with the face, and then when you tap it in foreplay, nobody is offended. Or you should ask if the face would like a slap and have a definite 'No' to go by. I would hate for Barry to get away with his Nigerian River Province chicken soup and bread or with suggesting that our food can be simplified and reformulated/recast/ reconstituted into something else, something it is not.

River Province chicken soup is certainly not Nigerian soup.

How to Make Meat

I am at the old woman's condiment stall, buying uyayak pods (tetrapleura tetraptera) with bitter kolas to keep snakes out of the house, when something behind her catches my eye.

'What is that?' I ask.

'Usu,' she responds absentmindedly, gathering the pods into a bag.

Why do I bother asking these sort of questions when I always get those sorts of answers? 'What is Usu?'

'Usu … Usu!' She turns around to reach for the soil-covered, nodular tuber, and my eyes grow round from shock.

'Where is this from?' I ask, attempting to keep my voice from expressing excitement. She is putting all my things in one place and can't seem to do that and hold a conversation at the same time. She stops what she is doing, catches her breath and explains that it is like a mushroom. You take a bit of it, put it back in the ground and it grows. 'Just like that!'

I know she doesn't mean 'just like that'. I'm staring at her with amazement because of the striking similarity between what she is nonchalantly holding in her hand and what those odd white men on the BBC Lifestyle channel rapturously refer to as a truffle: a very expensive mushroom that you cannot put back in the ground to grow just like that. Of course, if I start to ramble on about wild fungi and how one fist-size truffle can cost over a thousand euros, and how it is documented that you absolutely cannot commercially grow truffles, she would forevermore treat me like a *market-crazewoman*, the worst sort of *crazeperson*, so I keep my cool, buy a small, cleaned piece and ask her what she would cook with it, if she will cook it. I am already treading dangerous ground standing around asking questions.

She says she will. She won't infuse oil with it or frugally shred it on top of her meal. We are in a market in Calabar but there is no market for this usu; there is no need to think about whether or not it is commercially growable or if it is the most expensive food in the world. It is just a mushroom that Igbos eat, so the mental partitioning that the locals apply to her wares when they approach her stall has relegated the usu's value to next to nothing. Achi, ofo and ogbono have more market value than the usu.

In Calabar, it is not unusual to run into world-renowned delicacies pretending to be nobodies: strawberries up on the plateau at the Obudu Cattle Ranch; sole peddled out of old basins on Hawkins Street; lime-green and red rambutans hawked on little girls' heads in May. And now usu, which might be the tartufi bianchi, one of the most expensive, luxurious foods in the world. Perhaps I should say nothing about it so that Calabar is not overrun by trifolau with specially trained pigs hunting for truffles. As far as we are concerned, the blood of the market is the home-cook's list – tomatoes for stew, afang for soup, periwinkles for soup-character, plantains for porridge. There is no categorisation of tomatoes or onions or species consciousness. No one will pay for it. Sometimes on a Thursday you will see Chinese traders, who we have to thank for the erratic visits of fresh beetroot sprouts and purple cabbages, but the market's mind-elastic will only stretch so far.

The condiment woman is more like a traditional medicine practitioner than a businesswoman. She has to be on intimate terms with at least one forest. It is how she knows you can ask trees for directions and that you never go up a palm tree without a bitter kola between your teeth. There are herbs under her counter that must not be exposed to daylight. When she says you can put the mushroom back in the ground to grow, she is talking like a genuine trifolau with knowledge of a special grove in a secret place. The place where the usu will grow is not anyplace that you know or can reach, so what value is that information to you? Nothing.

She recommends combining usu with egúsí to create a meat substitute. A beloved, triumphant meat substitute, not one in the fashion of tofu-pretending-to-be-chicken, or those vegetarian sausages you might see in La Pointe supermarket that have a sort of I'm-sorry-I'm-not-meat air about them. I am amazed by this suggestion because we like to stereotype ourselves as unrepentant carnivores who can't bear the sight of our meals sans animal flesh. Yet here is a local substitute that we would happily eat in soup.

Hand-shelled egúsí is ground with the usu in a blender and then pounded in a hand mortar until the oil begins to separate from the seeds. A blender speeds up the process but cannot apply the necessary pressure to extract the oils from the egúsí. Even the pounding of the seeds must be vigorous because it is fundamental to removing all of the oil, and all of the oil has to be removed to change the texture of what is left behind – a thorough combination of ground seeds and usu. The successful pounding and the separation of the oil leaves a smooth beige mound. This processing is the same as pounding egúsí for the ntutulikpo soup but with the added dimension of taste and texture from the usu. Salt, pepper and onions are added if the eater desires. A large pot of water is kept boiling on the hob. The mixture is cut into equal sized pieces, shaped as desired and cooked in the boiling water until the meaty texture is attained. This boiling typically takes thirty to forty-five minutes.

There is something about boiling that doesn't quite agree with me: I keep thinking of all the flavour and nutrients being drowned. The egúsí and usu mixture should be steamed in thaumatococcus leaves, but boiling is the only way to create the texture of meat, the only way to create something that can texturally hold its own in a pot of soup as a meat substitute.

The Purist's Pot of Soup

I'm no purist when it comes to food. Anyone who knows me well could confirm that I have a problem doing as I am told. It is a venerable problem that prevents me from, amongst other things, following recipes to the letter, keeping within boundaries that old cooking hands swear by, or cooking one dish the same way over and over. I love the rebelliousness of the smell of cumin seeds frying in palm oil. Many pots of ogbono soup that I cook have leeks in them, as well as onions and turmeric and ginger and garlic and, worst of all, paprika. My response to anyone scandalised by this is that, as long as the soup has the fragrance of dawadawa, the depth of first-grade palm oil, the umami of shine-nose fish and the sweetness of ground ogbono, it is ogbono soup.

There are, however, those things about which I am particular, about which there can be no compromise. My okras must be tiny and stubby, nothing like a 'lady's fingers'. They must be newly harvested and prickly to the touch with the fresh, minuscule petals that are a sign of recent harvesting. They must leave fine, cactus-like needles in your fingers. Their seeds must burst between the teeth. Urban dwellers categorically cannot buy such finicky delicacies in the city. They are our just rewards for waking up to the singing of birds, breathing clean air and being regarded as backward country hicks.

There are those dishes I am happy to cook with some degree of fastidiousness because I am fascinated with the ingredients, and because the diversity in just one pot satisfies my restlessness. I have to register my amazement at the number of condiments in Nigeria. Every day it seems I discover something new, from region to region. In Cross River State for example, one can cook a pot of soup in Calabar that has ten ingredients in it, while in Boki in Northern Cross River, those ten ingredients will be completely different in a similar pot of soup.

Dawadawa can be the subject of a whole book: from the roasted, ground variety in flat circles, to whole, brittle beans moulded into charming spheres; from slippery, fresh, grey-faced dawadawa, to well-dried versions with the aroma of endless days of lazy smoke fires.

I was recently introduced to a variety of condiments that I have never before set eyes on, and my tutor interjected her lesson with astonished laughter because it was clear that I did not understand the basic anatomy of a pot of 'native' soup. If I did, I would never desecrate it with things like turmeric and paprika. The purist's pot of soup is, after all, spoilt for choice with ingredients. There would definitely be palm oil in it, and dawadawa of whatever choice and variety. There would be fresh hot peppers and a thickener, whether ogbono, okra, ofo, yam, egusi or ground sesame seeds. There will be meat in the form of ponmo, beef, crayfish, 'ice-fish' (frozen mackerel, which I hate in soup for the very reason people love it in soup; because it disintegrates and disappears leaving behind a strong fishy aroma), dry fish and/or stockfish. Not last and certainly not least, is the green leaf that can be ugwu, bitter leaf, scent leaf or uziza leaf. The list goes on ...

Then, there are those ingredients to which I have only just been introduced, such as dried green pawpaw. It's harvested, left in the sun to slowly ooze out its white milk, then cut up, its firm beige flesh sliced thinly and sun-dried until it has the appearance of dried mushrooms. It's usually added to beniseed (sesame) soup. What is its function in the soup? Nutrition and meaty texture.

If I had been asked if sprouts were a part of the Nigerian diet, I would have arrogantly answered that they were not. Until, to my surprise, a friend who had just gone and come back from Northern Cross River State handed me long, black desiccated petals: white-bean shoots, sprouted in soil until the shoot comes up about one to two inches, then harvested, the bean shell discarded and the sprout sliced open, cleaned and sun-dried. These also add textural character to the soup.

Imagine the sophistication and deliberateness of the palate that can distinguish dried pawpaw and dried bean sprouts in a pot where there are strong flavours of palm oil, dawadawa and stockfish.

For five years I lived in Calabar, Cross River State, in the centre of probably the most vibrant food culture in Nigeria. There, the sophisticated palate was not an elitist preserve. The farmhand from Abakaliki spending a few months in Obumatung village in Kakwagum is a food connoisseur with a virtuoso sense of taste, far and above the Lagos food snob's.

She will be harvesting cassava in the field on an ordinary day; a mild day with a cooling wind that makes conversing about anything desirable, and laughing easy. She will stumble on mushrooms. The conversation will come to a reverent halt. The mushrooms rightly belong to Mr Michael Odok, the owner of the farm. It is not finders keepers. He has warned his workers that mushrooms found while working must be handed over to his wife or his daughters. One must understand what esteemed delicacies these mushrooms are. What would you do? The likelihood is that the okokobioko (oyster) mushrooms are quickly and expertly picked and folded into the farmhand's wrapper. They won't be eaten immediately. They'll be wrapped up in banana leaves and allowed to dry naturally. They'll be watched over every day to make sure there is no trace of rot on them. Over time, they will become like soft leather, their flavour and aroma will intensify, their umami deepen. The farmhands are experts at preserving mushrooms till their return to Abakaliki. There they will cook up something so delicious you can only imagine it. The mushrooms are hoarded, and dried with a unique smell of ageing banana leaves and delicious mustiness, and anticipation like stolen treasure. They, not meat, are the highlights of the soup marking the worker's return home.

A woman's wrapper is taboo; not even the farmer's wife can broach the subject, so the stolen treasure is safe from the owner's reclaim. The real sacrilege is to imagine that one would go to all that trouble to steal and preserve okokobioko, then turn one's nose up and be purist about the mushrooms, about the cooking. The purist would put them in groundnut soup, and make them disappear. He is an ingrate and has stumbled on the mushrooms one day while he was taking a walk. Or he found a basket of them in the market and bought a handful while people walked past, oohing and aaahing at the sight of them. He is of no account and should, in fact, be flogged with a long curling cane if one is at hand. The gourmand like the Abakaliki farmhand will shop for fresh tomatoes and one well-examined onion. She will cut them up and tease them in fresh vegetable oil over a lick of flame. She will meanderingly cook these two ingredients until instincts tell her they are ready for the weight of gold, for the long anticipated mushrooms. She will turn off the fire under the cooking and litter the gentle red motion of cooked onions and tomatoes with aged mushrooms, inhale, then reach for slices of boiled old yams to spread into mash.

I have nothing of the experience of an Abakaliki farmhand, but this is what I would do. I would flex every muscle of smitten imagination to cook and eat those mushrooms. If there is any religion in the vicinity of that kitchen it will most certainly be under-the-influence, celestial church style trance-like religion with dancing and singing and whistling and thanksgiving. Conformity would never be my chosen response to the spontaneity of once-in-a-year, chanced-upon, stolen mushrooms.

Perhaps it is the soup gone urban that has lost its way and become a tired, uninspired idea. The urbanite has no recourse to nature's sleights of hand, or the presence of mind to keenly discover them. Poor him: if he finds food treasures, they've already been abducted and trapped under cellophane. There is a price tag and if he steals them, he ends up in Panti police station. With great empathy, we leave him to his purist pot of soup.

My Mother, I Will Not Eat Rice Today

This is why I live in Nigeria: it is the natural habitat of intense chromatic visions, of masquerades acrobatically tumbling, knocking heads together. They live next door, these masquerades. They are my neighbours, so I'm not regaling you with unverifiable stories, although verification adds nothing. You can see something with your unborrowed eyes, walk away from it and swear afterwards you were hallucinating. Your mind will refuse to frame it and hang it on the wall.

There are no frames of reference for many of the visions here. Life is as devoutly raw as a morning at the abattoir. There has to be a principal coping mechanism, among a range of ancillary coping mechanisms: colloquialisms for the cryptic. You must, at the very least, attempt to create a neat filing system, and have palm oil handy for the wheels of its animation. You must do something with what you see, otherwise you will never retain even the most basic malleability fundamental to living here. All the stories that fled other parts of the world, rejects from pristine, sophisticated, 'normal', 'abnormal', or blatantly evil space; all the bats hanging between night and day, facts that confound good and bad fiction, every eccentricity under the sun: they all live here.

This is their country of origin, or they have joyfully naturalised. They are the Efiks of Cuba writing to His Majesty, the Obong of Calabar, Edidem Professor Nta Elijah Henshaw VI: 'We're coming home!'

If you are a writer, this is *your* country. A match made in heaven for your hard-working imagination. If my mental Lycra holds up, this is the country of my dreams.

1

A ram goes for a ride and ends up on jollof rice

On Eid al-Adha there's a man who's paid for two passengers on the back of a careening motorcycle in traffic. He has with him a ram sitting in an affectionate posture in his lap. The ram is calm, reassured by the tension of its owner's embrace, by the balm of warm shirt, skin and marinating sweat that represents the driver's back. You can see that the ram is fully convinced of the agreeableness of their destination, and of its humanity acquired by association, by being the third traveller on a motorbike, its right-to-ride paid for like everyone else's.

It's on its way to a furiously boiling pot placed over firewood at the back of a house on a quiet residential street. A handful of bay leaves already dance on the face of the boil. Immaculate MSG, Ajinomoto crude enough to bleach an artisan's shirt cassock white, discreetly dissolves at the bottom of the pot. After boiling, the ram will proceed to frying in an Agbárí Ojukwu until all that is recognisable are oily threads of gamey meat. It will be served on red jollof rice perfumed with wood smoke, fresh hot peppers and deliquesced tomatoes.

The two – rice and fried meat – will be packaged in pink Styrofoam containers, secured with rubber bands, and sent out to the neighbours in honour of the Muslim holiday. The especially esteemed neighbour will get theirs delivered in gleaming Pyrex dishes covered in new dishcloths, snuggled in a basket (all of which must be returned).

The two men and the ram weave past a smiling traffic warden, the driver waves, and the world glides as if on film.

Evocative of outdoor cooking: jollof rice

3 cups parboiled rice

6 medium tomatoes (more sweet than tart)

½ cup water

3 Scotch bonnet peppers (fewer if you don't want it hot)

1½ red onions

2 small cloves garlic

5 teaspoons vegetable oil

2 tablespoons tinned tomato paste

6 small or 3 large red tatase peppers, seeded and chopped

1 teaspoon dried thyme

1 teaspoon salt

3 dried bay leaves

1 teaspoon white pepper

6 cups home-made stock

Necessary equipment: a cast-iron pot that burns gracefully.

Put the tomatoes, one onion (reserve the rest for later), peppers and garlic in a blender with a little water. Blend until you get a thick, smooth mixture. Add drops of water until you reach your goal. Put the vegetable oil into the cast-iron pot and let it heat up. Add the blend and allow it to cook at moderate heat for about 15 minutes.

Wash the rice as many times as needed to get the water clear. Drain all the water with a colander. Add the tomato paste, stock, salt, white pepper and thyme to the cooking blend. Stir well and add the rice, making sure it is well coated with the blend. Make sure the distance between the settled rice and your blend is over an inch and a half to allow for sufficient swelling of the rice. Add the rest of the onions, thinly sliced. Place the bay leaves on top of the rice. Close the pot tightly to keep all the heat and steam inside and turn the heat down completely. Allow the rice to steam for about 15 to 20 minutes. Let the bottom of the rice burn into a layer that makes the rice fragrant. Turn the fire off and let the rice rest.

2
The spectres on the bridge

We drive across Lagos' Third Mainland Bridge on a harmattan morning. The windows are wound down. The lagoon's tide is out. The water is a grey, tarred road you can walk. There is a receding green path of water hyacinths beguiling the eyes and mind to somewhere serene and beautiful. Remains of fog visibly swim in and out of the pores of air you are breathing. There is a cotton slip hanging in shreds from the sky, and behind it the sun is already undressed. It's going to be a hot day.

Spicy sawdust smoke hurries towards us from Oko Baba sawmill. The aroma is strongest just before we start to turn and descend the bridge into Herbert Macaulay Street and Yaba suburbia. The nose welcomes the invasion as part of the landscape. It might even suggest outdoor cooking. Local olfaction collapses the astringency of smoke into the idea of fresh air, as if that were possible. If you inhale the air it tingles, slapping all the nuts and bolts into place, but don't breathe in too deeply, mind.

If you look right as we ascend the bridge at Adéníji Àdèlé you'll see the morning spectres like corpulent birds perched on the railings of the bridge. My mind involuntarily conjures up Billie Holiday percolating perplexity at the form and abnormality of daytime apparitions, simmering, threatening to warp the container of reason. Not strange fruit, but strange birds: One, two, three, four of them on the bridge's railings, hands dangling, knees in the air in one direction, stark naked bottoms in the other. They are there with the routineness of men in their toilets, doing what men do in toilets, but down into the water below. In the still-distilling morning light, this organic levitating lavatory changes definitions: of a toilet, of privacy, of man, dignity, the fear of heights, the unease we consciously invest in distancing that which we eat at one end from that which we excrete at the other. It closes the distance we put between what shocks us and what we have confirmed as unexceptional and routine.

The picture is set regardless of my sensibilities or yours. You might think that film is supple while we, the viewers, remain stationary, that we should define reality, yet it is the spectres' opinion that counts here. We who are driving in our cars, we are the elastic reality rushing along in defiance of gravity. The spectres, birds, men, are as grounded as their breathtaking backdrop, and it is the first time I have seen this kind of adaptability displayed just by sitting, squatting, perching: the form of a man rounded into the plumpness of a bird. The spectres regard us calmly. They see our craning shock, our grimaces. They read our number plates, judge our velocity. All we see is a blur of crude satire.

On the other hand, Lagos knows how to primp and sashay on bridges, new skyscrapers, tall swanky things. It has $1,200-a-night hotel rooms; overestimated real estate on anxious hairlines of land arbitrarily reclaimed from the sea; fragile, sand-filled peninsulas anchored on the grace of God. From my flat I can see the lights on a dredger on the lagoon. It's been sucking up sand for months, and now its lights are comforting in the distance, like a house on the water.

Amazingly, Lagos simultaneously quarters homeless men between land and lagoon, without social amenities. They are not homeless in a depressing textbook way; their homelessness means freehold ownership of an expansive house without walls. They own the title deeds to *all* of the outside of *all* of the big houses and mansions, and they do with it as they please. They are rugged, and their spectrehood grants them all kinds of unconventional entitlements, like leave to use the moving tide as a toilet from perches on the highest points of a bridge-railing that might stretch five kilometres before the bridge curves. If the filing system of your mind is all-inclusive and disorganised like mine, then the bridge might stretch on infinitely.

If words cannot bear the weight of what you see, then *you* will have to change your mind about what you see. The editing will be subliminal; if you let it, it may pass under your skin, enter your nostrils without any hint of a quarrel, like the aroma of Makoko and Oko Baba sawmill. Burning, suffocating sawdust will painlessly keep company with hunger pangs, nostalgia, routineness, freshness, and the natural movement of food from one end to the other. Everything will be natural. The timing of the process will be effortless and unmetered. There's a footnote that life is short. Like I said before, you might opt to fight what you see because it makes no sense at all, but I advise you not to do this. If you let the water wash over a large stone long enough, I assure you that it will become a crocodile, naturally, and the makeover won't take a lifetime. This is the way to live here in Lagos: to accept the passage of masquerades in and out of the fabric of life as they will, using men as bridges.

3
A hill of fingernails

I am sitting on a bench in the British consulate at Wema Towers on the Marina, waiting my turn to be interviewed for a UK visa. For some reason, I lean over and look under the bench. There are a few of us sitting on it and we've been intermittently sitting and shuffling along on our bottoms when ordered to do so by officious security guards. Whenever someone gets up to go to an interview window, we clean up their space with the seats of meticulously ironed trousers and Sunday-best skirts. I look under the bench and there, collected into a tidy hill, are clipped fingernails, as if a roomful of people had been instructed, as they entered, to cut their nails and submit them to a man who piled them under the bench. I right myself and decide that I'm imagining the hill of fingernails …

Every single colloquialism I possess is of food, like the jollof rice that you cannot cook anywhere else in the world, because you will not find the necessary environmental redolence anywhere else: no firewood smokiness, no accurate hit and temperament of locally grown hot peppers. This isn't Maya Angelou's red rice. It isn't the original Senegalese Wolof rice. It is its own person.

If you do not want to cook, there is Ghana High jollof rice. There is only one old consulate-building-cum-open-air-buka called 'Ghana High' anywhere in the world. It is on King George V Street; Boyle Street behind you, Berkley Street ahead and to your right. That whole area has something about it, a niche for what we Yorùbá call 'ìpápánu' – snacks, 'mouth-toys'. You might miss it if you don't know. It's fried-food heaven. It's got gurudi, kuli kuli, chin-chin, freshly roasted groundnuts, oranges with spitting-green skins, and the ugliest, creamiest bananas in the world. Underfoot are reams and reams of salty brown groundnut skins accumulated over days and weeks. In Ghana High's untidy frontage you can buy a bowl of jollof rice. The steam will be like levitating ghosts and every grain of rice will be single-minded as if it was individually cooked. Under the rice, there'll be an indecent pooling of bright orange oil. In the lunchtime queue, men in dress shirts and Paul Smith ties will giggle in 97°F heat, vowing that no matter how well their wives cook, this is the jollof rice worth the repercussions of infidelity.

There is lyricism everywhere: in the grime; in old benches and fracturing concrete; in the haughtiness of fat servers with faded wrappers who treat you worse than contemporary French consulate officers; in the pasta salad, with bleeding red onion rings and fresh tomatoes with exploding seeds. The salad is so delicious you will eat it with intensity and suspicion, not enjoying it in the least because you'll wonder what right it has to be so delectable, so uppity, in a place like this.

There will be one woman there whose job description is owner of the pot of beans. She will have perfected the cooking of honey beans to a doctorate. On a Sunday, if you steal into the SIO Towers on Boyle Street, and look across into the compound of the old consulate, you might see old men donning white wrappers secured on one shoulder, praying up kitchen gods. They'll perambulate the grounds, incanting as they walk, infusing the walls, ceilings, benches, leftover firewood, pots and cooking cauldrons with the proposal that Ghana High jollof rice is the 'sweetest' jollof you'll ever eat. Like the fingernails under the bench in the modern consulate, the men's incantations are an antidote, carried out to ensure that people buy Ghana High food. They are leaving nothing to chance.

4
If you leave, where will you go?

Where will I go? This is the million-naira question that desertion of this land of overwhelming visions and misogynistic masquerades oppressively poses. Where else will you find puff-puffs now-now fished out of roiling oil on Lagos Island before 7:30 a.m.? They are the sacrosanct reason people turn 'CMS-Marina side' to the axis of their journeys. Those puff-puffs are handed to you in old newspaper, so that the combined aromas of food and the pica-fragrance of newsprint are the first premise of the addiction to the route. The stories on the newsprint are all terrifying shades of truth and half-truths…

An Igunnukó with a panpipe made from millet stalks arrived last night, playing an air that lured 234 young virgins away. Its unique instrument had four holes on six single-tone millet stalk flutes all bound together. The Panpiper was last seen on 24 October 1966 at a frantic Zaria train station, on a crowded platform that reeked of fear and blood. He was holding a bag of heads belonging to girls called Ada ...

Peppered puff-puffs with the aroma of newsprint

250g plain flour
2 teaspoons bread yeast
¼ teaspoon ground nutmeg
1 pinch ground dried Cameroonian peppers
3 pinches salt
Granulated sugar, depending on sweetness required
Lukewarm water for mixing
Vegetable oil for frying

Mix the flour, ground nutmeg, powdered yeast, sugar, salt and pepper in a bowl. Using your hands, add the water in small quantities until you have an even mixture. Use warm water if you want the mix to rise faster. Keep mixing until the batter is smooth and coats a spoon. The mix should be thicker than pancake batter. Cover with aluminium foil, sealing the lip of the bowl with the foil to make an airtight environment. Leave to rise for 45 minutes. The puff-puff batter must have risen and must have air bubbles on its surface. Pour at least 3 inches of vegetable oil into a pot, leaving room at the top for the oil to spit. This is necessary for spherical puff-puffs. Fry until golden. Fish the puff-puffs out of the oil and put them directly on the front page of today's newspaper. Dip in freshly ground Scotch bonnet if desired.

The sweet smell of flour, sugar, and yeast fermentation, of fried, sweet, bad things modulates all feelings of powerlessness, I promise you. The overworked oil scandalises your digestive system and makes you want to go back to sleep, but you are in transit to the office, where you can get a mug of Nescafé from that dated tin that surely only houses Nescafé in Nigeria and nowhere else. You'll hurry in case the puff-puffs lose their crust of thin, tan skin, their hot pillow elasticity on the inside. There is nowhere else in the world you can buy this kind of motivation because they are not croquembouches, not doughnuts, and even if they were, even if you could buy them as street food in some other country in the world, you wouldn't find the necessary punctuation of old newsprint flavour. You wouldn't find the satisfaction of taking out an Ìgunnukó with puff-puffs. There is a distinct way that Nigerian newspapers behave; what about the necessity of that ingredient?

5
My mother, I won't eat rice

My mother's friend brought home a little naked boy from Lagos' Iddo Market. She watched him, came home and conjured him up for the sake of a shameful cultural joke, because we had all subliminally agreed before that day that derision was due to that which was south-western and rural. I'm ashamed to admit that the boy's accent, his chosen words, the way he spoke the words, and the subject matter of his quarrel with his mother in the market that day indicated that he was from Ìbàdàn, or Oyo, or Òsogbo, or Ìgbájo. No, actually, you could state with confidence that he was from Ìbàdàn. In the context of the joke, Ìbàdàn quintessentially represented those parts we all originally come from, backwaters where we escaped, by a hair's breadth, the accent, the chosen words, the derision of those who had escaped ahead of us. We escaped the jokes about what other people are eating and how it makes them 'bush' – local champions. These kinds of jokes were only funny because relief was being expressed in the laughter.

I am from Kúdetì, Ìbàdàn.

When I was a child, non-Ìbàdàn relatives and friends would come over to the house and force my siblings and me to participate in a call-and-response ditty that every Yorùbá-speaker knew to use in mocking the Ìbàdàn indigene. Many Ìbàdàn indigenes still can't say 'sh' and 'ch' sounds. They replace them with a sibilant 's'. The non-Ìbàdàns would come through the front door and buzz with excitement and amusement at making us sing back the lines of the response of the song, and you wondered about the so-called elevation of adulthood. The malefic song went:

Call: *Omo Ìbàdàn kíni sóò re?* (Ìbàdàn man, what's the show?)

Response: *So súo* ni (The show is sure)

Call: *Kí lo fi jókòó* (What are you sitting on?)

Response: *Cusin siar* ni (A cushioned chair)

Call: *Kí lo je lánoo?* (What did you eat yesterday?)

Response: *Eran síkìn* ni ... (Chicken)

And on and on it went until you were asked what time you arrived and you responded, 'Sis sarp' (Six sharp). We obligingly dropped our 'sh' and 'ch' sounds and pretended to possess the 'inferior' pronunciations for the amusement of the adults. The song made you feel self-conscious and eventually contaminated. Subconsciously, you resolved not to be Ìbàdàn. It was how many of us ended up laughing at toddlers in the marketplace and taking sketches of them home to make jokes about them.

Like many toddlers in the market, the boy was naked for the unambiguous reasons of comfort and a child's incontestable entitlement to nakedness. He was wearing nothing but a string of coarse, recycled beads around his hips and black kohl around his eyes. His legs were toothpicks, his stomach happily spherical and taut. He stood with his calves pushed all the way back until his thin legs were curved into impossible arcs. One more degree of bend, and they would go no further; he would break clean into two picks and a torso.

The boy was giving his mother a stern warning in the most articulate terms. He was warning her that he wouldn't eat rice, no, not today! He was standing next to her, singing it without drawing breath, projecting the sound right into her ear. She was bent over her wares, her expression as placid as if the boy wasn't even there, as if there was a grain of possibility that she didn't know him. It was clear that he was a naturally voluble child and his mother had developed a device of shutting his sounds out in order to carry on with whatever needed doing. He persisted, his small fists fixed on his naked hips. He was back at the beginning of the request, going over it not like a broken record, but a very sound one. His voice was uninflected, like something coming out of a battery-powered toy or like a drill held to the brainpan.

Ìyá mi, mi o je'resì! Ìyá mi, àní mi ò je'resì. (Mother, I *said* I won't eat rice today.)

Mother was ignoring him, so he stood his ground, repeating himself, then persisting with ultimatums: *Ìyá mi, t'ésù ò bá ní se o lonìì ... àní mi ò je'resì. Oka ni ngó je* (Mother, if you do not want to see the wrath of the devil today ... I said I won't eat rice. I will only eat àmàlà).

The boy would do anything for his bowl of àmàlà (desiccated yams ground into a dense white flour, made into a lightweight grey mound using boiling water, strong arms and an omorogùn) with ewédú and a splash of pepper stew. He would risk the smack that would surely soon fly out of his mother's reticence. This was how you knew for sure that the boy was from Ìbàdàn. The Ìbàdàn must have their àmàlà every single day, served with ewédú (boiled jute mallow leaves beaten with an ijábe until you have a thick, dark-green, mucilaginous soup) and gbegìrì (liquified, skinned cooked beans); a combination called àbùlà.

His exasperation at his mother and the threat of bringing in the devil to settle the matter were both justified because of the universal understanding that little boys, with their drinking-gourd stomachs, need their starch and soup doled out at regular intervals throughout the day, starting with fist-sized fufu and soup first thing in the morning. If the staple pins in the stomach are not straining, then a boy is not full. And fullness is a little boy's entitlement, like the entitlement to unflappable nakedness. The fullness in question is achieved easily enough by filling the gourd with bowls of beans and corn or slabs of boiled yam and pepper stew; complex starches, not rice, nor cheap Chinese noodles nor fried plantains, not girls' food nor bird food. Every good mother of every respectable little boy knows these facts. He was not the one being troublesome here; it was his mother who was being difficult and unreasonable.

The boy did not use the word 'àmàlà' though. He said 'okà' and when that word is spoken, nine times out of ten it is from the mouth of a native of Ìbàdàn.

Before Lagos even had the presence of mind to search out the word 'swankiness' in a dictionary, there was Ìbàdàn. In the meanest of agboolé (homesteads), in the deepest archives of retrospection in the quarters of Ìbàdàn outlaws who robbed you on horseback, you would never find the degeneracy of going to the toilet in the sky.

Before Lagos became, in Akin Adésokàn's words, the 'cosmopolitan, showy, shallow, culturally bastardised, elegant and ruthless'[3] home of Uncle Ben's rice-eaters, Ìbàdàn personified cultural sophistication with over a century of pedigree. It was a disobedient, sprawling entity that metamorphosed from rowdy military cantonment to a place called the butt end of a gun because it was where warlords retired and died without any cause whatsoever to fear for their safety. It was from the soil of Ìbàdàn that the cocoa house, the tallest building in tropical Africa (Ilé Àwon Àgbe – The House of Farmers) grew, still signifying the scientific and cultural sophistication and agricultural wealth of the western region of Nigeria. I eternally choose to rendezvous with Akin Adesokan on the grounds of the Dùgbe Market with its:

airy "smell" of *láfún*, the cassava flour, of *iru*, fermented locust seeds used as condiment, and of dried meat, called *kundi*; Gege with the whiff of butchered-animal entrails in its air;

---

[3] Akin Adesokan, 'Ìbàdàn, Soutin and the Puzzle of Bower's Tower' in *African Cities Reader* edited by Ntone Edjabe and Edgar Pieterse (Cape Town: Chimurenga, 2010), 64.

Bodija redolent of ground peppers, hen-coops and thawing mackerels; horny danfo drivers letting go of their libidinal frustrations on their horns, like 'Trane on tenor sax.[4]

Also, what would the city be without 'Ìbàdàn', J.P. Clark-Bekederemo's light-filled postcard drawn with nineteen luminous words? The enduring, clichéd postmodern poem preposterously redeemed Ìbàdàn from the barbarians' point of view, rescued it as just one point of light from the nonsensical derision undermining the genetic self-confidence of children to the point that they grew up wanting to be known as Lagosians and rice-eaters.

If red meat is a colloquialism for brain evolution and Mediterranean olive oil a colloquialism for longevity then this okà, àmàlà with àbùlà, the punchline of the scorn poured on the Ìbàdàn is the food that has nurtured every violent rabble-rouser, every pedigree-conscious intellectual, every subversive politician in the south-west of Nigeria from Sàngó, the third Aláàfin of Oyo and god of thunder and lightning through to Adégòkè Adélabú and Làmídì Adédibú. It is in honour of the almighty okà that the Olóòlù, one of the most dreaded Nigerian masquerades, wields an ìgbako.

This is why I live in Nigeria and brave the masquerades: because otherwise I would be convinced to disregard the backwaters in rationalising who I am. I would believe slapstick sketches of how the Olúbàdàn was deposed from his palace by a clan of rats who lived on eko leaves that his unhygienic household had refused to throw away; I would believe that

---

[4] Adesokan, 'Ìbàdàn', 70.

this is a real story exemplifying the intrinsic insalubriousness of the Ìbàdàn man.

I would not comprehend that ravishing singer-songwriter Sade Adu was born without fanfare in Ìbàdàn and probably spent her first years wandering around naked, demanding her àmàlà and gbegìrì too. The narrative of cultural appropriateness, sophistication, intelligence and eating what suits the image would have been my lot too. I would have paid my dues in singing inane ditties and gained no wisdom in the singing. I would have been some desperate diasporan fighting my way back to Nigeria for superficial bowls of acceptance. I would have agreed to have my psyche mutilated in order to fit into Lagos. And I would have given up all that dignity just for the privilege of driving my fancy car past a view of birds perched on Third Mainland Bridge railings.

If I lived in Kiev, I would miss out on the sense of communality that settles like calm in my mind when I open the door and get my own jollof rice topped with ram in my own pink Styrofoam package, the container lips held together with my own rubber band. That ram is the very same one that sat on a bike and believed it was human, the one that filled our space with its bleats, its blood disfiguring our street, turning it into an informal abattoir. Flies gathered over the next days but we bore it because we all ate the meat. Anyone who got no ram is entitled to feel slighted, to plan his revenge against the owners of the backyard where the goat was slaughtered. This street, with the veil of concocted smoke, drying goat blood, crooning highlife from someone's radio, is Nigerian. If I leave, I won't find the capsule anywhere else in the world. I would not be a real Nigerian writer. No one would trust me with their secrets, their depths of nostalgia, or the mucilaginous connections between nostalgia and food. I would not have heard the rumour that in a south-western Ondo town at 6 p.m. every single day, a spontaneous xylophone of mortars and pestles from every house in town is formed, an inadvertent percussionist choir generated from the pounding of yam into suppleness for dinner. They say it is all white noise to its residents, but to a stranger it is an unnerving strain that never ever repeats itself.

By the way, at a remembrance party for one of our grandparents in Ìbàdàn, my siblings and I noted that we were some of the only people being served rice. It was what we requested, but we found ourselves on the fringes of the party, because I suppose anyone who would choose rice over àmàlà and àbùlà just has no clue about good food. Selah.

Bones of Choice

In uncomfortable minutiae do I recall details of the teeth grinding brought on by white people telling me that 'Africans have such good strong teeth'. For me it was a hint that I was smiling too widely and needed to close my mouth, that there was too much light in the face of the person to whom I was speaking

On a good day I answered, 'Really?'

'Yes, really,' the owner of the conviction said, a little less enthusiastically. I guess I was expected to grin wider and say, 'Oh thank you very much indeed.'

The response in my head was, 'All the better to eat you with my dear!' How I wished I had said that, and then stirred together the stereotype of good strong African teeth with the accusation of African cannibalism. What I wanted to say was that I didn't know who this African was, nor did I know the continent where every single person living on it had good strong teeth. I was only a Nigerian after all, and not a well travelled one at that. I often wondered what the relevance of a whole continent of people with good strong teeth was in the mind of the person who believed in its existence. I sometimes wanted to respond to the gaffe with the notion that it has something to do with a contrast between white teeth and very dark skin like mine, but in the end I thought it was more important to get it across that a black person who could be from anywhere on the African continent might not take it well if you said that Africans have good strong teeth. Surely it was the kinder way to go.

Not that I wanted to be kind. I wanted to laugh slow, diabolic laughter to go with my wolfish grin made up of African dentition. The problem was that the people who brought up African teeth were trying to pay me a compliment. They were often like Florence Hook and Joyce Dowding: two sweet old ladies from the URC church in Somerton who made it a late-life calling to dote on me, the only black person in sight in Somerton, Somerset in 2000. One of them gave me a punnet of lovingly cultivated cherry tomatoes from her back garden. The other one offered me small black mints from a tin that had the word 'Negroids' on it and got a sharp, brisk nudge from the former.

Instead of responding to 'Africans have such good strong teeth', I ground my teeth and briskly wiped my face and voice clean of any amusement or willing participation in the discourse on Africans and teeth.

I have a British cousin called Sayo who went to school and told her teacher that my mother ate bones without any meat on them. My mother and her mother are sisters, so she was talking about something she had seen *kòrókòró* ('with your own two eyes'). There was no lie there. The teacher could not contain her curiosity, and when my aunt came to pick Sayo up she asked if it was true.

My aunt was furious at both the teacher and Sayo. At the former for being so titillated by the intelligence on bone-eating that she broke her default English reserve to pry, and at the latter for not understanding that she wasn't supposed to be playing soccer for England and giving stupid busybody oyinbos more anecdotes about Nigerians to share at tea while exercising their delicate teeth on scones and strawberry jam.

The answer to the teacher's question has not changed. My mother eats bones, as do I, my brother, and many other members of my family. There is, of course a discriminatory art to eating bones. You don't just pick up any bone to chew, as the teacher would assume. The clear problem with her reaching for African stories was her guaranteed inability to stick to an ungarnished one. She couldn't be trusted. What was a good story without the chiffonade arranged on the dish? In her shoes, among friends who barely interacted with black people, I doubt I could resist embellishing the imagery of Sayo and her African family sitting down to their dinner of bones with their bared, buffed teeth.

The bones of choice are those of the bird we call 'local chicken' or free range. The next best and more widely available choice is the old layer, or country fowl, who doesn't really wander free, but has some level of freedom in a chicken house in a family farm in Òshogbo or Akampkpa.

In London's Brixton Market, or Peckham Rye Market, they are called 'don't-cut-my-leg chicken' because Nigerians want them with the legs on, with the head and everything on and intact, no vital organs missing. These birds are lean and tough. The fat on them isn't white; it's the colour of turmeric. They don't roast or grill. You must boil them for about ninety minutes, and in order to produce a bone worthy of eating, the boiling must be patiently done with the skin of the chicken on and a blend of spices. At least, that is the way I like to boil my don't-cut-my-leg chicken: with cumin, coriander, anise seeds, black and green cardamom, black pepper, cinnamon and whole cloves, red hot peppers (the aromatic kind), some garlic and ginger (fundamentals in my cooking), sea salt, a teaspoon of honey, and sometimes some lemongrass from my garden. Tortuously slow cooking ensures that my mixture of spices and pepper penetrates the very insides of the chicken bones. Cook until tender.

Because we are interested in the bones of the chicken, it has to be cut strictly to the Nigerian anatomical map for cutting chicken. Legs must be separated from thighs, arms separated from wings; the neck, head and feet stand alone; the back must make four pieces, with the bishop's nose on the most auspicious of the four. The breast cuttings are irrelevant. Really. No one cares for their categorical fleshiness.

Any bone worth its salt cannot have any trace of red in it. Red is blood, and this is what discounts the Agric chicken, with its cloying fat and chemically induced weight.

The boiled chicken is left to cool in the stock at the end of cooking, to allow the stock to seep further into the marrow of the bones. This is the reason for keeping the whole stock and whole chicken till the next day, reheating it gently and then, and only then, feasting on it.

And for goodness' sake, no one sits down and grinds bones between their teeth to the consistency where they can be swallowed. The bones that will cook to this degree of softness are not the kind you want to eat. The point is to eat the flesh of the chicken, crack the chicken bones gently between your teeth and suck the delicious stock out, suck it out with the depth of your lungs, and discard the bones. Give them to the patient dog.

There is something in the resounding eating of chin-chin, kuli kuli, koko and gurudi. Many Nigerian snacks are hard on the teeth, and you can hear them being worked in the mouth. Just naming them gives you the firm idea that they are work. I've often heard people complain that chin-chin is too soft, never that it's too hard. My teeth may have suffered some serious abuse and survived the sugarcanes that my grandfather brought from the farm. We tore the back away with our teeth to get to the sweet chaff. Alexander McCall Smith might have been invited to a lagbo lagbo on Lagos Island and seen some strapping lads round up everyone's Coca-Cola bottles and stoically pry them open with bare teeth. Or there might be secret archives of photographs of Nigerians with chewing sticks, cleaning their teeth from morning till noon. Whatever the case, I don't believe I know where these Africans with good strong teeth reside, no better than I know where the court of the Lilliputians is.

Eating Dog

It is my overfamiliarity with the dog that breeds utter contempt for the idea of eating dog meat. Eating some domesticable, constantly salivating animal that smells like a dank rug, eats its own faecal matter, licks its privates and has the capacity to exercise uncanny intuition, is beyond my culinary pliability. It just does not feel right to eat dog.

It does not, therefore, follow that I am one of those people who would sleep in the same bed with a dog, play chess with it and then take it to the south of France on holiday. I have absolutely no desire for dog companionship. I have not even perfected companionship and fellowship with human beings. I've been accused of being misanthropic. Dog-lover is therefore out of the question.

If there is something hypocritical about attempting to determine which animal to eat or not by the animal's intelligence, affability to human beings, hygiene and other random parameters, then let it be so. And, by the way, I have the utmost respect for the moral courage or self-righteousness or strength of conviction or whatever, that it takes for the vegetarian or vegan to say an unshakable 'No' to placing herself at the apex of the food chain and eating everything beneath. Until further notice, however, I am a meat-eater. Not a liberal one, not a very capable one, because I struggle to digest red meat, but a meat-eater nonetheless. An incompetent, apprehensive meat-eater. My sensibilities are easily offended and I still wonder constantly whether, if I'm not eating dog, I should also leave out pork since pigs are said to be the most intelligent domesticated animals in the world, and George Orwell's allegorical *Animal Farm* considers them so intelligent as to be worthy representatives of our domineering, presumptuous humanity.

The reality is that Nigerians eat dog, and it's cooked 'well-well'. Nigerians also eat monkey, horse, camel, deer, goat, snake ... whatever meat presents itself and appeals to us. It is probably more honest and healthy to admit this than to say one eats one meat and not another. Nigerians generally tend to have a straightforward, non-judgemental relationship to meat, and when I say Nigerians, I am intentionally snubbing the 2 or 3 per cent who learning and travelling has made mad. I'm not in the 2 or 3 per cent because I am consciously mad. We have the capacity to view the slaughtering of the animal and eat its meat without fighting off the hovering spirit of Peter Singer. As harrowing as it may be for someone from another culture to be presented with a dish called 'isi-ewu' with eyeballs, brains, tongue and other parts of the goat's head brazenly tossed with vegetables, to us, to me, it is completely commonplace, and completely delicious. I like the eyeballs squishiness especially.

I believe people like myself, who have an urban dweller's hang-ups about eating dog, are a minority in Nigeria. Dog meat is happily consumed in Plateau and Gombe, in Akwa Ibom, Cross River, Abuja and Ondo, and these are only the states that are consistently documented. In Cross River State, where it is a serious delicacy, dog meat is affectionately referred to as

'404'. Why 404? I asked Nsor Nyambi, whose witty exposés on Calabar and Cross River have helped me navigate the culture as well as have a good laugh. 'Because dogs run with speed, like the 404,' he said.

The 404 is the Peugeot sedan ('pijo' in Nigerian lingua franca and 'piyot', soft 't', in Cross Riverian articulation) that my generation caught a passing glimpse of before the more enduring 504. At the time, the 404 sedan was considered fast indeed, and when Cross Riverians were searching for a worthy comparison for the speed of a running dog, 404 was the tongue-in-cheek equivalent. I suppose there is some wicked irony in terming a type of meat *running meat*: running as fast as a car, yet not outrunning the eater.

Dog is not cooked in stews, not in pepper. Like isi-ewu, or suya, it is not an accompaniment to a meal but a delicacy deserving all the attention worthy of a main course. The meat-eater wants to devour it alone or with the uncompetitive blandness of steamed rice. Sit-outs on Hawkins Street in Calabar South and in an area called Adiabo are renowned for their dog meat prepared in special sauces. The Dog Joint on Asi-Abang Street in Calabar is la pointe to eat dog. On a Sunday after church, you won't get parking space anywhere near the faded sangria bungalow with sit-out. You might not get a plastic chair to sit on. Your dog might have to be takeaway. The other popular joint is Atimbo, for bushmeat and palm wine, and Atimbo makes a better attempt at comfort and ambiance.

The Dog Joint has no appurtenances of comfort or pretensions of refinement. No air conditioning, no soft seats, no proper doors, or levelled floors or umbrellas for the sit-out. The canopy for the outside sitting area is made up of overlapping branches of old trees. The main bungalow is one long stretch of unadorned room with a row of plastic tables and chairs on either side. At the head of the room is a long table laid with a colourful rubber cloth. A huge cast-iron basin with its charcoal burnt bottom sits on the table, a pot of steamed rice on one side and on the other, a pot of sauce made of chopped greens and palm oil. The server wears a headscarf and a sneer. Behind her head, a piece of paper Sellotaped to the wall informs you that dog meat cannot be bought on credit.

I went to The Dog Joint on a Friday at 2 p.m. and saw three men sitting outside on plastic chairs with small-stout, big-stout and bottles of Guldar beer on the floor beside their chairs. They were in beginning-of-weekend mode: shirts off, sweat travelling down the tangled hairs on their chests, tipsy, laughing so loud you could hear them three streets away. Their drinks were on the floor because the table was unstable from the force of their laughter and the demonstrative conversation that required hitting the table. Another man was inside the long bungalow, wearing a tie and a white shirt. His own workday was still in progress, as you could tell by the bottle of soft drink and plate of white rice accompanying his dog meat, and by his contemplativeness. There was another man ahead of us at the long table, ordering takeaway. The black nylon packaging sagged from the heat of the dog meat.

I wondered briefly at the absence of women until I was distracted by the sight of a long slender bone in the basin ending in a well-defined dog paw. I turned to the person I was with and asked him, under my breath, whether he would eat the meat we were buying, because I had lost my courage at the sight of the limb. He shook his head briskly from side to side and looked down. We would buy it anyway. We already looked out of place, and we were almost at the front of the queue. Up close, the meat was lean and brown, as if cooked in the cast-iron basin until dry, then tossed frugally in the sauce with greens. I could discern no spices in the aroma of the meat. I could discern nothing exceptional or even inviting about the aroma. For a thousand naira we got five medium-sized pieces, and we were offered a spoon of sauce. We declined. I stopped at Adrian's on MCC on my way home, bought soft white loaves of bread and made a present of the meat and bread to my gardener, Pastor Monday.

On Sunday afternoons after church, women accompany their husbands to the dog meat joint and the men respectfully keep their shirts on. The women order bottles of big-stout, or small-stout in plastic cups imitating the shape of mugs of palm wine. Everything is kept on the tables and not on the floor because there is no raucous laughter and jokes to dislodge the food and drinks.

In parts of Calabar South, street hawkers carry cast-iron pots balanced with rolled cloth on their heads. The pots house freshly cooked dog meat offered for sale with boiled yam. The residents of the streets that the hawkers walk bring out their own containers to buy dog meat. They take the meat into their homes and improvise meals with it. There is usually some white bread to eat it with, or a bowl of drinking gari.

There is no doubt a residual self-consciousness attached to eating dog meat, and it is a self-consciousness that the pietists and the elitists inflicted on the righteous. No one who I have asked if they eat dog has given me a straightforward yes. There are immediate qualifications to the type of dog or the ethicality of the death of the dog. It isn't local dog, it comes from the north. It doesn't eat its own excrement. It isn't a familiar dog, or a pet, or a dog that has been given its jabs. It was put to sleep without hitting it violently over the head with a stick or suffocating it in a bag. It is organic dog that eats wheat or swallow and soup. Dog meat is a cure for malaria. It wards off juju, it improves your sex drive, your instincts, your spiritual awareness etcetera, etcetera. Some people will admit to eating it in the past but not the present. Or they repent and make a counter accusation: it is those Akwa Ibom people or those Ondo town people. Those rare people who admit to eating it must do so with a sense of bravado, or mischief, or humour, or sheepishness. And, come to think of it, I don't know a single woman who has ever owned up to eating dog meat.

Àkàrà and Honey

The word 'àkàrà' is soft, seductively broken on the back of that letter 'k' so that as it is spoken, you can conjure up a squish and hushed chew, the compression of air through respiring pores of hot, freshly fried pillows of seasoned, milled beans. No one ever talks about the oil insidiously escaping the reach of the kitchen towel, oozing from the àkàrà directly into every self-righteous resolution on fried foods you ever made. The fact of deep-frying, the oozing of oil, can never be allowed to be a compelling issue in the eating of àkàrà.

I grew up in a place where electricity frequently went out or failed to make an appearance at all ('no NEPA' was how we said it ... is how we still say it). There was hardly ever even the independently generated kind that my children take for granted now. Our generator was this ancient, recalcitrant contraption that had to be wound with a lever, and only my father had the arm to wind it until the coughing turned to the emphatic chugging that generated electricity. He came home late on many nights after we were in bed, so we sat outside after our night baths, doused in methylated 'dusting' powder, indigo batik skies travelling over our heads, stars blinking vigilantly, night breezes tiptoeing around our discussions on what happened to children who whistled in the dark. We listened wide-eyed to the stories my aunty told because she was the undisputed queen of melodramatic twists, of scandal draped in *onomatopoeia*, of alternative endings that morphed according to mood.

My mother was no less mischievous in the telling of her stories. She owned the copyright to the stories of Topo Island, that desperate place where children who don't do as they are told are sent to live after it is established, without any regard whatsoever for their sides to the story, that their parents are sick to death of them and therefore can and should send them to the island for the rest of their natural lives. Each child on Topo Island gets a small coconut and a roasted fish in the morning and has to make it last all day. If she eats it all when she is handed it in the morning, she deservedly starves till the next day.

There was the story of the man with a bottom lip so fleshy, so distended, it swept the ground as he walked. He would go around provoking little children to stare or pass comments at his disfigurement. He knew they could barely help themselves. The child who laughed or grimaced or whispered something under their breath was immediately caught up in the wet folds of his giant lips and swallowed whole.

He always had to say the same words before swallowing, to enhance the melodrama of the swallowing: *Ètè tagìrì gbemì kóló* (Lip, topple the child, swallow him whole with the sound of 'kolo'). The 'kolo' at the end was the coin-in-a-clay-pot sound of the child popping past the cave-opening of the man's throat and landing in the bottom of his stomach.

It was my mother who convinced us that if we sang over and over again, 'He is King of Kings and Lord of Lords, Jesus is the first and last, no man was like him,' the electricity would return and we would go to bed in the soporific embrace of air conditioning. Some nights were so still, so frustratingly humid, you sang just for the distraction of singing. We sang ourselves hoarse one unremarkable evening until suddenly the house lit up. The fan whirred alive, the television resumed the reading of the nine o'clock news, the deep freezer purred, the air conditioning growled and kicked the compressor, and we, on cue with all the children in Pilot Crescent, Pilot Close, Adéníran Ògúnsànà and the tall buildings behind our crescent of houses that we called Onílé Gogoro, chorused, 'Up NEPA!'

That evening's enchantment only ever worked once. On the many nights before and after that, my aunty told her stories until they were faded out by sagging eyelids. I am certain that it was in this outhouse of stories that the outrageous àkàrà, honey and Àjàpá (tortoise) story emerged.

There are two Àjàpá stories that have to do with àkàrà and honey, although the truth is there are innumerable Àjàpá stories that have to do with àkàrà and honey; as many as you like. The secret of the tortoise's endurance is that no one has been able to imprison him with written words. He turns up in every kilometre of life and dreams, leisurely outsmarting the swift hare. He is neatly tucked into black foundations among twenty-four rows of sparkling sleeping fish. If, in the dream, you are walking past a hedge of smooth white stones, and you topple it and fall down into the dark, you will find him there holding up the house of the world, as fresh and unruffled as if he were cast into the mould just today. He swims out of an ocean where he has outlived every creature, a resilient symbol of indestructibility, of shrewdness and wit and outrageous wickedness ... and so he does what he likes and has done so for centuries in oral storytelling.

The particular story that I am talking about is the one in which Àjàpá pays back an offence done to him by the chimpanzee in the most disfigured coin. In typical Àjàpá fashion, he takes time to size his enemy up. Àjàpá is never in a hurry because he is going to outlive his enemy by a few lifetimes. The enemy in question is only a chimpanzee; bigger, faster, stronger, yes, but really only a chimpanzee. Àjàpá goes into his artillery of wickedness and trickery, which would never be complete without knowing how to cook one dish to evil distraction. And Àjàpá can cook many such dishes. No Àjàpá story is told with integrity without references to indolently simmering pots of yam pottage, sputtering like a thick-lipped man talking in his sleep.

He can make moin-moin with seven spirits (elemì méje) of

1. spreading egg yolks
2. fresh prawns
3. cubes of beef
4. smoked fish
5. pinches of corned-beef
6. cooked liver
7. mackerel

His moin-moin with wayward spirits (elemì k'emì) has the freshest, largest prawns, hanging on to life by breathing droplets of water under still-pulsating carapaces. Their determination to live only ends when they enter the stomach. He can also make pounded yam accompanied by mind-bending egúsí soup.

Àjàpá is not only an avid connoisseur; he understands the ins and outs of food: bewitchment, distraction and confusion, tied to the taste buds with okro soup strings. Food has the power to disarm, to buy time to get a few blows under your enemy's armour. He comes up with the luminous idea of àkàrà: fried, fished out of hot oil, then quickly dipped in honey, the crispiness of golden àkàrà arrested in a lucent sleeve of dense sweetness.

In reality, the Yorùbá have no native palate-cache with bytes on savouriness plus sweetness. We have no tradition akin to sweet and sour; nothing like àkàrà, which behaves in the way that a doughnut does, with a hidden reward of jam. There is no culture of jam-eating or dessert-eating at the end of meals, because the Yorùbá adult has an incongruous relationship with sweets and sugar. On the one hand we regard sweet things as legitimate distractions for children. On the other, contradictory hand, they are as potent as poison.

There should really be no cultural agreement in which you give children something that is believed to be deadly, but there exists an interesting island between the two beliefs. It's not a mediator, but rather a précis of all the ideas and fears of the Yorùbá concerning sweet things: Angst Island, like Topo, where the obsessive topic is haemorrhoids, their connection with eating sugar, and the cures for doing so. In reality, next to the ubiquitous Yorùbá pot of stew, there is a pot of boiling herbs in case someone overindulges a sweet tooth.

Anyone who eats too many sweets is going to be plagued with haemorrhoids. There is no middle ground to this middle-ground belief. Like a fashion decision, Western media discussions on food are always running towards and away from dramatic conclusions, and sugar has became deafeningly carcinogenic, and a pointer in Alzheimer's and other diseases. But from antiquity the Yorùbá have insisted on the need to chastise the eating of sugar. The pot of herbs is always punishingly bitter, both a palliative and a seminar.

Honey's classification is inconsistent. It's sugar, but we hold it in high esteem because it symbolises an allegorical sweetness that is more than a sensation in the mouth. In the naming ceremonies of eight-day old children and in marriage ceremonies, honey represents prayers that life will be pleasant in spite of all the unavoidable pain; both sweet and bitter. Honey is acknowledged as nutritionally and medicinally powerful, an indispensable part of traditional medicine and the treatment of skin conditions and burns. Nevertheless, the average Yorùbá from my parents' generation will not agree to dip their àkàrà in honey, and the suggestion of eating one with the other will earn more than a few disdainful looks.

The biggest incongruence of all must be the ceremonial cake we wholeheartedly adopted from the West, but not because we wholeheartedly wanted to eat it. We replicate it, build it up to the ceiling, embellish it with every creative device and make speeches about it. There is no wedding, engagement or birthday celebration in Nigeria that does not have some coiffed, tiered, version of gateau mounted on its own stage and introduced with great fanfare; a centrepiece of the room and of the show, representing our understanding of trends, our money and our good taste. Interestingly enough, the Yorùbá call this cake 'àkàrà òyìnbó', which sounds a lot like psychological distancing. 'The white man's cake, not ours!' the name declares. The cake must have icing: expensive marzipan and meticulously crafted sugar or cream cheese icing and toffee essence whipped to mouth-watering peaks.

But most people won't eat any of it. Check the dustbin bags at the back of the building and you will find them full of scrupulously scraped-off icing. One might see that precious facial expression on elderly Yorùbá women as they scrape icing off cake. It is a revelation: all the contradictions will be visible in every line of grimace. The cake under the icing is eaten with the ghoul of haemorrhoids sitting on one shoulder, and a mental note to drink a shot of àgbo jedí – herbs and roots soaked in original seaman's schnapps – when one gets home from the occasion.

... So this morally grey creature called Àjàpá comes up with a recipe that has made my mouth water like mad for forty years. In his plan to get revenge on the chimpanzee, he prepares some àkàrà, coats them in fresh honey and places them just outside the lion's door. He hides behind a tree and waits.

What has the lion suddenly got to do with this story? Well he is the bullet in the cartridge, and that description has to suffice for now because the procedure of a good story is as legitimate and necessary as that of making a cake. Children instinctively understand this.

The àkàrà is warm in the cuddle of the honey, and the aroma hangs in the air. No, the aroma *distends* the air. The lion is drawn out of his rooms and out of his front door by the weight of the fragrance of àkàrà. He opens his front door and they are there, arranged in a pretty spiral in a basket, hot, glistening and completely irresistible. He picks one up and eats it, and the àkàrà is sweeter than any he has eaten before. In Yorùbá parlance that sweetness means 'deliciousness'; a successful appeal to all the aspects of the taste buds, not sweet as in 'sugary'. The lion cannot resist the genius of sweet and savoury; of hot, peppery and heavy sweetness. He eats another and then another until all the àkàrà are gone. He wants more. Of course he wants more.

Àjàpá comes out of hiding and offers the lion the option of more. Wouldn't he like to know the source of such delectable cakes? Knowing the source means an endless supply. But of course! The lion is so bewitched by the honeyed àkàrà that he is not suspicious of the serendipity of the whole affair; of why Àjàpá the tortoise – manipulative, wicked, crafty – would make him such generous, unsolicited offers. Even the king of animals is not above the mesmerising power of good food. Àjàpá once convinced Aiyékòóto the parrot to give the details of a secret feast in heaven by bringing out of his shell the biggest, juiciest mangoes Aiyékòóto had ever seen. The lion won't wonder where the strings are attached. Of course he wants more.

Easy, Àjàpá tells him: the àkàrà and honey is the caca of the chimpanzee. All the lion has to do to get more honey-infused àkàrà is give the chimpanzee a few well-aimed blows to the stomach. Note 'well-aimed blows'. The àkàrà and honey will emerge from that end where ... chocolate cake comes out.

You can imagine our riotous laughter in the dark as children. I was old enough to be scandalised by the twists in this story, young enough to be delighted by its filthiness, and conscious enough of my size to want the smaller, slower tortoise to win against the bigger, stronger chimpanzee. We were horrified, my siblings and I, yet we laughed. Because you can scrape off the icing and eat the cake, can't you, and allow yourself to enjoy the àkàrà òyìnbó, even if you are feeling guilty: that universal guilt that even òyìnbós who own the cake confess to.

The filthy twist of the story was too precious a gift for a child navigating the world and needing to feel some degree of power when dealing with big, strong, often insensitive adults who can send one off to incarceration on Topo Island because they are fed up. The climax of the story is that the lion strides off, fuelled with the scent of hot àkàrà, and the glutamic high of honey to give the chimpanzee the beating of his life. The beating intensifies because the chimpanzee won't produce honeyed àkàrà. The repeated blows to the chimpanzee's stomach produce nothing but ... chocolate cake!

We never asked if this beating was fair to the chimpanzee. Who cared about degrees of cruelty in the glow of enchanting, honeyed àkàrà? It was superior to the allegiance to adult sensibilities and repugnance. Àkàrà and honey is true to the impossible, irrational sweet things in children's books. It is, in fact, on page 200 of the unwritten universal manual of children's intelligence.

The anatomy is the same: the house in the clearing in the woods built with gingerbread and cakes and windowpanes of clear sugar, belonging to a haemorrhoid of a sight-impaired witch; exploding bonbons swelling like living things in your mouth until they burst into sweet, warm elixir in the land of the Faraway Tree. These overwhelming quantities and varieties of cloying sweetness are just plain delightful in the estimation of a child. Àkàrà and honey is the Yorùbá child's pregnant bonbon and there is no Yorùbá child who cannot relate to a fried àkàrà, the smell of it dancing in hot oil on a Saturday morning, the aroma beguiling you out of sleep. Or of stolen honey, dirty fingers in the jar. If you are caught with your fingers in the jar and given a beating, you are consoled by the honey and plan to be a better thief. Adult cynicism applies well here – the end justifies the means.

But for me, Saturday-morning àkàrà always falls short, perhaps because it is too predictable, because it is relegated to being an accompaniment to something, to ògì or Quaker oats.

Or it is the filling between slices of bread, eaten as a sandwich. There is no flamboyant engineering of umami, no twist, no possibility of a daring collision of savoury and opinionated sweetness. No lion pummelling the chimpanzee's stomach! Oh, for sure, the àkàrà stories taint the mind. When I think of the tortoise's àkàrà, I think, well, why not? Why must it always be the same basic peeled beans blended with water, the same chopped onions, salt and pepper? Why can't I buy a big syringe from the chemist, fill it with honey and stick it up the àkàrà's bottom? My àkàrà with its honey injection is the perfect therapy for PMS: hot, sweet irreverent – a lot like chocolate mousse with Tabasco sauce. Or maybe honey diluted with salt, pepper and a dash of vinegar, used as a dip.

Àkàrà

4 cups black-eyed beans
5 cups water
1 generous pinch grated root ginger
The white length of a medium leek (The smell of leeks always reminds me of cooking beans, and for that reason alone they have earned their inclusion.)
1 tablespoon tahini paste or almond butter (optional)
Dried ground Cameroonian peppers

Soak the beans in clean water for 5 to 8 minutes, then peel them by rubbing them against each other in loose fistfuls. If the beans are soaked for too long, their skins harden instead of softening and become near impossible to peel off. Blend the peeled beans with all the ingredients except the salt until they form a thick milky coat on the back of a spoon. The perfect oil for frying àkàrà is coconut oil, and because I'm not made of money and coconut oil is gold, the frying must be shallow. The use of coconut oil is absolutely necessary for superior aromatics. The salt is added just before the frying commences. This is important in helping the àkàrà to puff up into nice round bellies.

The ladling of imperfect dollops into oil is therapeutic. The hot oil seizes them, pushes them upwards, sealing the edges with needlepoints of quickly firming blend. The frying needs medium heat and is done when the àkàrà are golden, not brown. Àkàrà is a strange creature, and I hope someday someone with a scientific mind will explain why it guzzles so much oil, why, with each successive batch of frying it flattens out in the exhausted oil instead of plumping upwards. As my frying progresses, the idea of àkàrà-coated shrimp always suggests itself, but I am never proactive enough about making àkàrà to have blended beans and shrimp in the house at the same time.

The enemy is palate boredom. After eating a few àkàrà that taste the same, I want some with enough pepper to blow your head off. I want some garlicky, and some with chopped green peppers. In the end, the process is like Aunty Dele's stories: spontaneous, showing a determined aversion to keeping the storyline intact. I eat my own portions standing up, frying and improvising. I wait till everyone has had their fill, then I do what I like with the rest.

Kings of Umami

A straight line is completely antithetical to the idea of good food. The reason why our wholehearted adoption of Maggi is so tragic is that stock cubes are the unimaginative shortest distance between two points. You want a pot of soup to taste delicious, and you immediately reach for the stock cubes. But it is for reasons like this that Nigerian food is losing its lifeblood. Every good cook knows that the soul of soup is in the layering of flavours and it is this layering that old hands, over time, turn into virtuosity. The best dishes take the scenic route to flavour, not only in terms of cooking time but preparation. What is food, after all, without the perambulating, without the longwinded trips to markets, the indispensable journeys to acquire food, the haggling over the ugly grimace of stockfish with the fish seller? All those factors make food more than the mechanics of eating or filling the stomach.

Two close friends once returned from Ebu in Delta State, bringing back a stack of dawadawa from the market in Issele Uku. Each disc of dawadawa was so thick it reminded me, not of split black beans pressed together to make a fresh patty, but my love-at-first-sighting of the insides of Eccles cakes, of the black, moist crowding of raisins.

Yes, the old roads to flavour are still drivable. So perhaps I wouldn't say that imaginatively measured Nigerian cooking has become a closed road; I would say the roads are deserted. You can get on a bus in Ebu where yam farmlands are the bed of the river Niger in the rainy season. The river recedes in the dry season, giving back soil saturated with minerals. The Ebu have a secret twist that accounts for their gigantic yams: keeping them in the soil longer than necessary, and thus harvesting tubers so heavy you get a hernia from trying to carry one. From Ebu you pass through the villages of Ukala Ukpuno, Ukala Okwute, Akwukwu Igbo, Ezi, Onicha Olona, Issele Mkpitime to the market in Issele Uku.

The market in Issele Uku used to be close to where Mkpitime the water goddess lived; her old address before she got it into her finicky head that she didn't like to see people dressed in black. She saw the reflection of mourning clothes in the nearby market, pouted, picked up her river and left. The people who followed her from Issele Uku sought to appease her and named themselves for her: 'The people of the Mkpitime' – Issele Mkpitime.

If my friends had not gone to Ebu and brought me back some fermented locust beans I might be holding a stock cube in my hand, agreeing to the wholesale kidnapping of my palate, my imagination and fascinating stories of perambulation by an unarmed cuboid. I would never have heard of yam farmlands immersed for months in the river Niger, or temperamental river goddesses giving ultimatums, moving from one village to the next, carrying a river as conveniently as a roll of cloth. Nor would I have learnt that you can casually buy a roll of weed around the river Utor, on that informal boundary of a bridge going over it, separating Urhomi and Asaba; a place where people disdain this ridiculous business of state boundaries. The echoes of 'Awa!' and 'Nago!' in the Igala language are proof that this is a single, supple region. You could be in Edo or Delta State, in Kogi or even Benue and be speaking upside-down Yorùbá.

In the same way that the long route to food enriches my experience of cooking, umami needs the layering of flavours and aromatics if it is to have integrity, but it is a little bit more than that. 'Umami' is a word borrowed from the Japanese, and it is best defined as a well-rounded savoury taste. Scientists suggest that certain taste receptors induce salivation and a furry sensation on the tongue, stimulating the throat, the roof and the back of the mouth. They are informally referred to as umami taste receptors, in addition to the sweet, sour, bitter and salty receptors.

In 1908, a Japanese scientist called Kikunae Ikeda isolated the glutamate that is the chemical source for the taste of umami. It is with this knowledge that monosodium glutamate came to rule the world. We can say he created the beginnings of our loss of sophistication, but the Japanese, in spite of chemical alternatives to glutamate, such as Ajinomoto, have not lost their esteem for natural sources of umami, like kombu, seaweed and dashi. They haven't lost the ability to distinguish between the synthetic hit-and-run sensation of MSG and the powerful, bottomless expressions of fermented glutamate. Kombu, seaweed and dashi, along with the almighty miso, remain fundamentals in Japanese cooking.

Throughout the year, Nigerian women from Rivers to Katsina repeat the process of fermenting locust beans as often as favourable dry weather will allow, yet the methodologies of fermentation are not scientific. They work more like strong suggestions. Daughters learn the process from their mothers, tweak it and pass it on to their daughters, each tweak adding individuality in taste and texture. The desired result is not consistency but rather adaptability to the individual or household palate. I think of the endless results not only across Nigeria but across the West Coast. The Togolese make dawadawa, as do the Ghanaians and the Cameroonians. The results are, of course, also affected by weather, soil and other environmental factors. Making dawadawa is similar to the process of making cheese or wine that includes all the romantic connotations as well.

One day, in Calabar's Marian Market, Thelma Bello, a cherished food mentor, eagerly drew my attention to a brown paper package secured with rubber bands. She opened it with a great deal of fanfare, parting some dried, unwholesome-looking leaves. Lost in the leaves and recycled paper was a smear of something; a visual anticlimax. No, worse than that, because the smear had taken on the greenish look of something that needed to be resolutely binned. That greenish tint and an olfactory rudeness – the ominous sneer on the smear – are the recognised personality traits of ògìrì – sesame seeds or castor oil seeds left to the will of fermenting bacteria. The soup-condiment seller in front of whose stall we stood not only sold ògìrì made from sesame seeds; she also sold a variety of fermented locust beans, some flattened after fermentation, shaped into discs like the ones from Ebu, dried and infused with extra aromatics over smoke fires. Others were simply moulded into fresh dawadawa balls after fermentation.

This Marian Market woman's irú/dawadawa was the most expensive I had ever seen. A small ball of the dark locust beans was N100. I also bought a significantly cheaper version, stronger smelling but still bearable, with the same suggestion of dark chocolate and the complexion of rich loam. The insignificant smear of ògìrì was N100, but worked out to be the cheapest of the three as ògìrì is used in very sparing quantities.

I immediately termed the combination of the three condiments the 'Kings of Umami'. I dare any pot of soup not to become gorgeous after crossing their path.

I grew up eating unsmoked or fresh dawadawa. My mother's past might have had diligently prepared dawadawa in it, but the ones that I remember buying with her from Sura Market in Lagos unequivocally showed a nonchalance in preparation. The Yorùbá call dawadawa 'irú'. The unsmoked dawadawa we call 'irú pete'. The dawadawa at Sura Market was sold wrapped snugly in strips of cellophane. It had usually been sitting among other condiments in the market for days on end, the fermentation continuing in the unsavoury, suffocating environment of plastic wrapping. The smell was overpoweringly pungent and drew flies. You had to make sure all the gaps in the window netting were closed when you cooked, otherwise you got an invasion of flies.

It felt marginally shameful cooking with it. It was always, always riddled with fine sand and small stones. It needed to be picked through with methodical concentration, then washed vigorously. You wondered whether the whole 'organic' angle had not been overplayed. You seriously wondered whether you wanted to eat it after all. There was a sense of resignation to the whole usage of the dawadawa that took the joy out of the eating. If the smell was really, really bad, you found yourself giving unsolicited soliloquies on medicinal values and the eventual enhancement of flavour. It was the very last attempt to convince yourself to cook with and eat what I considered substandard dawadawa. As a result, I have an eternal grudge against Yorùbá irú pete. I am convinced that the people who eat it have done so for a lifetime and so feel that there is no alternative to the assault on their senses. I know many people who find nothing at all wrong with this kind of dawadawa.

The smell of carefully monitored fermentation cannot be missed. A friend from Benue State gave me some dawadawa that I worked very hard at loving. I kept it in the freezer thinking that would tame it, but found that every time I opened the freezer door the smell jumped out like a thick-skinned neighbour who always wants to make small talk. The smell wore me out. I realise that for many people the aggressive flinging open of olfactory doors is the experience they recognise. It is the smell of dawadawa from the foundations of their childhood.

There is exquisitely produced dawadawa. I mean dawadawa produced with the concentration that I imagine one uses when making a timepiece, and I'm not exaggerating when I make this comparison. Not everyone feels the compulsion to move at the pace of Lagos, and I have met families who make palm oil or own one stall in the marketplace, and do everything slowly and gracefully, with an integrity that honours tasks that will never create a fortune. I was convinced of it from the moment I met the Marian Market condiment seller, yet she represents only the first rung in a culture of punctiliously fermented beans. Her produce was 'market quality' dawadawa. It was good, but it isn't the stuff kept at home by those who make dawadawa. The quality dawadawa kept to be eaten as the maker's reward is beyond gorgeous.

The Ebu dawadawa, even though it was bought in the market, was prepared so conscientiously that the thickness of the discs was at least half an inch and it was clean enough to immediately put in the mouth and devour. The discs brought to mind every delicious, black, moist sweet thing: the crowded insides of Eccles cakes, chocolate, chocolate cake, Christmas cake, Christmas pudding. This repetition of sweet things is not haphazard. Good dawadawa smells sweet. It might not be the first olfactory door to open, but it is there, the smell of sweetness competing with that of warmth. If the temperature range of 'warm' had an aroma, it would be that of good dawadawa. The warmth is heavy, like the bass in a piece of music. The pungency of fermentation is actually comfortable and mellow in the nostrils. Depending on the dawadawa, you will catch aromas of:

- chocolate and mud
- coffee and humidity
- braised beef
- fermented cocoa beans
- rain-beaten soil.

If the dawadawa has been hung high over fading firewood embers, then you will have the added smokiness to both smell and taste. You will be able to testify that there is a confident mustiness that hangs on to the end of your nose even if the beans have been moved away two minutes before, but there is no overloading of the senses with one strong, bad smell. Never, ever that. The aromatics are just one part of the powerful umami that good dawadawa provides.

The olfactory doors open gently in one's head, one after the other, following the progression of the dawadawa towards the mouth. In the mouth, the dawadawa has the same stick-in-your-teeth chewiness of raisins. If there were such a thing as savoury raisins, this is what they would taste like. Next comes the strong, salty savouriness interestingly similar to a cup of brewed miso. The cavity of the mouth fills with the aroma of fermentation, the slightest hint of bitterness that dissipates quickly, and strong organic meatiness. The aftertaste is fermentation and warm, salty dark chocolate.

As proof of the level of rural sophistication in fermenting locust beans I know people addicted to snacking on dawadawa. One girl in particular could not be sent to sun the dawadawa on the roof in the morning because half of it would end up in her mouth between the door and the sunning.

Since that day in Marian Market, I have felt some lingering sense of irritation and disappointment at the urban disregard for dawadawa and ògìrì. Sometimes I am able to convince myself that the Sura Market dawadawa of my past was not bad because the Yorùbá handling of locust beans is inferior, but because the market is in Lagos, and Lagos itself has an inferiority complex when it comes to fermented foods. Maggi cubes have that neat, boxy indifference that appeals to urban impatience and the control of aromatics necessary to living in close proximity in terraced housing units with small windows and anxious kitchen extractor fans.

I have a two-hour stock that I make regularly to showcase the pure clout of umami my two kinds of dawadawa and ògìrì possess.

The Kings of Umami are, in reality, more than three in number. There is one other king but his citizenship is a bone of contention. He is the air-dried head of cod from Norway that we lovingly call stockfish. He is ugly, argumentative and smelly, but in a simmering pot of stock he becomes a thing of beauty that is forever a joy in the stomach. A good head is worth at least N700, but for a pot of stock I use a quarter of a head, and that is quite extravagant. I once bought a whole stockfish head and brought it home intact. It was an unnecessary hardship. Breaking up a stockfish head is only half as traumatic as attempting to cut up kanda (cowhide) with your bare hands.

The head is more conveniently cut up with a saw in the market. Parts of the stockfish head are rinsed and put in a large, unglazed earthenware pot. A quarter of a smoked catfish head is washed with salt and warm water and added to the pot. The Ebu dawadawa is balanced on the tip of a fork and carefully passed over a small stove fire. It is allowed to catch fire but as soon as it starts to burn, the fire is put out. This is repeated, passing different parts of the dawadawa over the flame. The oils from the beans will come to the surface and the dawadawa will gain a crust. Once this is done satisfactorily, the dawadawa is put in a dry mill and blended until it looks like ground coffee. You really only need half of the thick disc of dawadawa, but my friends who brought it claim that one whole disc per pot is the usual quantity. The pot is filled with water and put on the hob to boil. Salt, ground Cameroonian pepper, one Scotch bonnet pepper and grated ginger root are added to the fish and dawadawa. The tip of a teaspoon of ògìrì is added to the pot, and a generous swirl of palm oil. Once the water begins to boil, the heat is turned down and the pot is left simmering for at least an hour and a half.

After this time, the heat is turned off, the bones are fished out, and the stock is left to cool completely. It is then refrigerated for twenty-four hours and ready to use by the next day.

There is no better way to describe the process of creating umami in this pot of stock than saying that it is a burrowing down into the depths of flavour. The bottom of the pot opens into another realm with layers upon layers of taste and aroma and combinations of tastes and aromas. Once the tongue gets used to this kind of good living, pampering – awakening even – it is near impossible to ever willingly return to just unwrapping a stock cube and depositing it in a pot. Cooking with stock cubes bears no comparison to time, patience, and a lot of perambulating. Absolutely none.

How to Wear A Kitchen

Never dismiss a woman with the words, *Get thee into the kitchen*. Not because of the omnipresence of glistening user-friendly, keenly-sharpened tools gracing the room's counters that are so effective in gutting fish and full grown man. In the kitchen, a woman has unlimited access to cutting tools and to dismissive man's balls. I mean his plates. The full unquestioned power over his guts. She who stirs the soup rules the house, no arguments. Over 70 percent of our immunity to disease is sitting inside our guts at the mercy of the food we eat. She has license to spit in his meals or lace them with arsenic. She has him, innards and all.

Yet that isn't the pressing point. Why bother to go to the trouble of stating the obvious; pointing out the wholesale, no-small-change stupidity of a man who imagines he is demeaning a woman, or putting her in her place by telling her she belongs in the kitchen, belongs in the living room, or in some other vaguely charted room.

The Nigerian president Muhammadu Buhari is proud proprietor of the *Get thees* and the spiteful rudimentary mind that sprouted the words.

'I am sure you have a house. You know where your kitchen is. You know where your living room is. And I believe your wife looks after all that even if she's working' The president says to Phil Gayle of Dutsche Welle news.

'That is your wife's function?' Phil Gayle asks

'Yes, to look after me.' President Buhari says

'And she should stay out of politics?' Phil Gayle clarifies

'I think so.' Buhari says

The podium that preceded this one was on October 14th 2016 where the president stood next to Angela Merkel, incidentally one of those creatures with a vagina that shouldn't be at an international press conference talking politics, but rather in Mr. Sauer's kitchen and living room and other room. The president's head was lowered to place it close to the microphone in front of him. *He-he-he-ing* past his neck wrapped in what looked like a Burberry scarf, the rumoured uniform of English hooligans, aristocrats and other morons. His eyes as mirthless as palm kernels in their shells, he said in response to a query on his feelings about what his wife, Aisha Buhari who had criticised his choice of cabinet members during a BBC Hausa radio interview.

'I don't know which party my wife belongs to [...] but she belongs to my kitchen and my living room and the other room.'

Why bother to address the President's words if their utterance doesn't increase the momentum of potent untruths? If fiction-in-stealth isn't untying the tent poles of the facts. More worthy of attention is the idea that the kitchen is a place where the scorned abide. There is a developing downtrend in social lexicon, maligning snobbery, intellectual desertion and low P.C. value progressively ascribed to the kitchen. Because of all kinds of cultural entanglements, misunderstandings, endless wars of attrition between men and women, because of our politics, our human rights, gender equalising army orders, the kitchen is being falsely implicated in the diminishment of a woman's power. This much needed, loved and utilised room is now outrageously persona non grata.

The corollary to the snobbery is that kitchens are still full of people; full of men in fact, especially paid men. Whether in fancy five star hotels or when you lower the scale economically, the kitchen remains itself - a room of imperative, sacred utility. It is the difference between a wife and a chef. Many starched white employees in high powered Nigerian homes cooking for the residents are men from Akwa Ibom or Togo and Benin Republic. Most women can't afford to hire cooks to attend to the kitchen fires. They can't afford the scrupulous tallying of household denizens versus tasks that nobody likes to do, divided by gender. Kitchen work is hard work, often unfairly allocated to female members of the house. Yes, culturally, women are "still expected" in the division of tasks between gender, to 'man' the kitchen, but there is no diminishment whatsoever in the doing of the hard work. And my personal philosophy is that somebody has got to wash the dirty dishes. The washing of dirty dishes should not be a gender issue.

Many Nigerian women cook their own meals at weekends, freeze them, thaw them according to meticulous timetables after long work hours during the week. At night after transits in snaking traffic, they arrive home and wear the apron and the kitchen with pride. Yes, pride. They cordon off the interference of men. Cooking is a language and the kitchen is a faculty. With two little salt, too much water, a flourish of pepper, discontent, sadness, disgust, can be expressed in the end product and in presentation. The eater without words can hear the voice of the one cooking … made to understand in his gut that there is a problem, and it isn't with the skills of the cook. Vice-versa joy and other similar emotions can be expressed and felt in the virtuosity of the cook's skills.

Sede Alonge in her Guardian piece (17th October 2016) warns that '...behind such statements as the Nigerian president's, that demean and relegate women to positions of servitude, there is a woman or girl belittled. The statements of the most powerful man in the country also have an impact on how millions of impressionable boys will tailor their expectations of women.'

Is there really relegation/belittlement in telling a woman to get into the kitchen or is there an exposé on the size of the person doing the telling? Let's get the facts straight because a Nigerian woman's kitchen is not familiar territory in global lexicography, it can therefore not be concluded on in general terms. The Nigerian woman's kitchen isn't a room in which she can be depreciated. It is a room of power and illumination. The simple act of striking a match bellows "let there be light". Many of the instruments in this room cannot be operated by men. Mortars and pestles and grinding stones aren't about strength in the arms and back as much as conscientiously learnt skill. Competence at using such equipment isn't something that even women like myself can pretend to own.

A woman who enters into a room that houses her tools of alchemy, that lights a fire representing her hearth is entering a place with many rich secrets. The mortar is the vagina, the pestle the penis ... but ... the pounding of yam into supple mound is at the woman's pleasure. She decides pace, force, beginning, end, heat, coolness, yes or no. Being in that room where fires are lit is an apparel of power worn by a woman that money cannot pay for. The room yields its secrets to its owner and not to the paid drudge.

Before the publishing of my book *Longthroat Memoirs: Soups Sex and Nigerian Tastebuds*, two dynamic, very well educated Yorùbá women who are close relatives loved to luxuriate in their snobbery of the kitchen by telling me whenever they visited that it was a shame that I spent so much time there rather than at my desk *getting brain work done*. Since my book ... and the shock of the book's existence has punched many holes in these women's accusations against the kitchen, it is my turn to elucidate why there cannot be a loss of status in the wearing of my kitchen.

My paternal grandfather would use the word d'ana *(light a fire)* to explain all the tasks related to cooking, as opposed to the words we use now se onje which simply, flatly translates as '*cook*'. Instead of talking of a kitchen, he spoke of a place where many diverse fires were lit. I have even taken his old-world Yorùbá usage to signify the menorah like structure of the ovaries, the two moons that spark shrouded fires. The demonstration of those fires of sexual desire and emotions is the powerful legacy of all women. The loss and depreciation of language has perhaps closed access to deeper cultural meaning and power.

Look at Aisha Buhari, all she needed was one match, struck, and you understand how petty, how sore, how incompetent her husband, how naked the emperor. He says she should keep out of politics, but her political projections could not be answered by him in any professional or ethical language beyond that of small mindedness and squeezed laughter. She exposed him and you have to feel sorry for him. Because in the end you don't mess with a woman who has your guts in her hands. If Aisha Buhari has lived with the president for 27 years then she can predict accurately what the perfect

rip-off. They are not sweet. They are pretenders. The yams are tired and shrunken from travelling so far. There is no fresh afang to be bought, no fresh pumpkin leaf. The ogbono seeds are not first-rate; you can smell rejection on them. The palm oil is Ghanaian – enough said. You have to break the bank to buy stockfish although it comes from Finland next door. There are no plantain chips at the 7 Eleven. No Thaumatococcus daniellii leaves for wrapping moin-moin.

The situation is unexaggeratedly desperate. My friend's husband would be beyond embarrassed if he were caught smuggling fried chicken in his luggage but embarrassment at customs is nothing next to his wife's wrath. Isn't she also carrying twelve fried chickens? Won't he eat part of the efo rírò that will be cooked in their apartment on the other side? So what's all the coyness for? No one is taking a taxi to Lwandle and risking a mugging. Any man who is too good to carry ugwu in his luggage must not be too good to eat efo rírò made with kale, and that's as good as any Nigerian adage.

The lady in Woolwich, south-east London, who sells Nigerian food has an attitude. You have to call her 'Sis' and she charges an extra £30 to deliver. You won't get the real ground dried red peppers, won't find any dried Cameroonian peppers, and if you do it'll be good for nothing but keeping weevils out of the beans. No Ìjebú gari; that one is a matter of life and death. It isn't that you can't find beans in the supermarket, it's that you get riled up seeing beans packaged like they're going to get married, branded and arranged on supermarket shelves with prices in pounds sterling. It feels too pretentious to purchase.

My mother still reminisces about loaves of Shackleford bread and *The Mail* newspaper brought in on ships from England in the 1950s, collected at the port by my grandmother alongside her retail goods. Her memories include fresh fish caught from the waters of Jebba, and a whole tin of Titus sardines to go with the whole loaf of Shackleford bread. My grandparents were not rich. My grandfather was a train driver before he retired and became a full-time farmer. They loved to eat. My grandmother owned a stall at Dùgbe Market in Ìbàdàn where she sold metal travel trunks. It was in one of these trunks in the house at Ososàmì, Ìbàdàn that I found a letter from Candahar Road dated January 1966. The letter was from Bísí Omotárá, aka Iya-Battersea, – my grandmother's younger cousin's wife. She'd received news, probably by word of mouth, that my grandmother had sent her cooked snails by ship. The snails were probably boiled, then fried with salt and plenty of hot pepper, and put into a container of groundnut oil. They would have had to sail the seas for two weeks, then spend a day in Legal Quays in London. Bísí Omotárá was waiting for her snails and wrote a letter to my grandmother to catch up.

'My mother', the letter begins. She calls my grandmother 'Mother' because there is an obvious age gap between them, yet even if there were not, the Yorùbá say 'Kò sí kékeré àno' – there is no small in-law, i.e. no in-law so trifling as to be undeserving of a term of endearment. You gave all your in-laws nicknames and terms of endearment, even if they were babies.

'Ìdí-ìleke' (waist with strung beads), if they were fat.

'Opelenge subú l'àwo' (a thin person falls on a plate … and the plate doesn't break), if they were thin.

According to Yorùbá tradition, a wife is lower in ranking than the youngest family member in the house she marries into. In any case, nicknames can only be used by peers and those older than you.

Here is the full letter:[5]

I thank you for your letter received from Mrs Fasoro. We could tell that the letter had been given to her a long time ago. But she apologised about this, explaining that she didn't have an address to post the letter to, otherwise we would have got it sooner. Almighty God who is merciful will continue to be your help. She gave us a little bit of Zorro that she was able to carry with her. She says she put the rest of it on the ship ... If I say I should begin to bless you, it will overwhelm the mood of this letter. Our God of mercy will bring good rewards from it all. We will yet have the privilege and joy of setting eyes on you, on each other. The way I feel is as if those snails should have arrived already. The intensity of the longing to eat snails is as if we have never eaten snails before. God will bless and reimburse your pockets.

It is only God who can help us all bear our problems ... these are things too heavy, too troubling to speak about ... By the power of God we will not be disgraced. How are all my husbands?[6] Please greet them all. Ha! I thank God that the trouble that broke out in Nigeria did not touch our own

---

[5] Photographs of the letter can be found on the first page of the colour photo section.

[6] 'Husbands' meaning my mother and her siblings. Anyone in the vicinity really. As a wife, you called all your in-laws 'husband' as a term of endearment. Sometimes you called a child that as a way of showing affection.

people. We have received news of different high-ranking people who have been killed. My mind was completely unsettled until I received a letter from Brother Isaac yesterday. It was after we got this letter that we were able to 'eat into our insides'. If it was not for Brother Awomolo who first sent us a cablegram on the 21st of January that reassured us ... Our merciful God will be our help. I was so afraid that I became sick. The fear became sickness in my body ... all the people who were killed, like Akintola, The Sardauna (Alhaji Ahmadu Bello), Tawa (Abubakar Tafawa Balewa) and many other people who we could not recognise are being shown on television here. We thank God that this is not the nature of our own ends. We were so moved with pity for those who were killed ... it is really too harrowing to talk about. May God keep Nigeria o. Please greet your sisters and my brother[7]. I am yours truly.

Bisi Omotárá

---

[7] My grandfather.

Okro Soup, Gorgeous Mucilage

Siddhartha Mitter's essay 'Free Okra: Rescuing a vegetable from a slimy stereotype' was all the justification I needed in the world to unreservedly allow myself my first aesthetic bowl of okro soup. You would think I needed no permission to do this, but I live in Calabar and there is no cultural point of reference here for eulogising okro soup or being sentimental about food. Okro is much-loved but handled as perfunctorily and efficiently as an official file. Most Nigerians I know, myself included, are not naturally sentimental people. I imagine that prettifying food feels a lot like being soft when dealing with a child, stroking a dog, crying on Oprah, acting the wimp. I don't know any Nigerian – and this is no generalisation – who allows themselves the luxury of feeling so much, except in Pentecostal church services. Perhaps it's for the simple reason that you would not survive the bombardment of a weekday as a Nigerian if you did.

Siddhartha Mitter is Indian, his family originating from Calcutta and Boston. He paints a picture of the cooking okro in the very first paragraph, which I read over and over because it presents itself like a religious experience:

Indians often call okra 'lady's fingers', and the preparations that came off the charcoal fire that the village-raised cook preferred to the kitchen stove were everything that the name connotes: smooth, delicate and perfumed. Mustard oil infused the okra slices and deepened their flavor. Cumin, turmeric, or chilies added zest. This was okra unabashed and uncut, the perfect offset to a classic Bengali meal of pungent river fish and simple steamed rice. The pods were rich, pillowy, and moist. I became hooked on okra for life.[8]

I have willingly taken a cue from Mitter's defensive reverence, joining him in acknowledging that there is an agenda and language of the enemy; gastronomical bullying anchored in words like 'slime' and 'goo'. I cannot write it better than he does: 'the dishes the coloniser rudely rejected turn into sources of shame.'[9]

My glossy Heritage Publishing *South African Cookbook* describes okro as 'a mucilaginous pod which becomes slimy when cooked and as such is not liked by all.'[10] The cookbook is, of course, being cordial.

Shape magazine is less diplomatic. It has listed 'okra' as number twenty-four of twenty-seven 'Ugly Foods You Should Be Eating'. They are described as '[c]one-shaped' with 'weird seeds inside' and are said to 'help your digestion and colon due to lubricating mucilage.'[11]

---

[8] Siddhartha Mitter, 'Free Okra: Rescuing a vegetable from a slimy stereotype', *Oxford American*, 49, 2005.

[9] Mitter, 'Free Okra'.

[10] 'A Comprehensive Guide to Vegetables' in *South African Cookbook* (Heritage Publishing, 2006), 186.

[11] Ysolt Usigan, 'Ugly Foods You Should Be Eating', *Shape*. Accessed 13 January 2016. http://www.shape.com/healthy-eating/diet-tips/ugly-foods-you-should-be-eating

I am grateful to Mitter for pointing out that these conclusions made by such 'authorities' exclude but in no way negate the opinion of huge tracts of the gumbo, okro, okra and quimgumbo eating world, such as Haiti, Egypt, Turkey, India and the Ivory Coast. From the US he lists New Orleans; Charleston; Checotah, Oklahoma; and Cleveland, Mississippi, even though he qualifies North American enthusiasm by noting that '[m]eandering across the South on a series of okra pilgrimages, I found that okra's marginalization runs deep.'[12]

There are millions of global okro-loving citizens for whom mucilage – the 'draw' – is a fundamental craving, a deeply invested love affair, a genetic imprint. Call it what you like; it's proof that there is no such phenomenon as okro becoming less popular. South Asians show culture-confidence in cooking their 'bhindi' in curries with garam masala, cumin, turmeric and lemon juice. In her cookbook, *The Real Taste of Jamaica*, Jamaican cuisine doyenne Enid Donaldson suggests that 'ochroes' are washed and drained, while one egg is separated, the yolk beaten first, the white added after. The whole ochroes are dropped in the beaten egg, and then into a mixture of cornmeal, flour and salt. They are fried in oil in a heavy skillet until browned lightly, then drained and served hot with salt. The crispy outside texture is balanced by the soft inside texture.[13]

Japanese health researcher, Junji Takano, exhorts us to eat okro raw with mayonnaise or vinegar and pepper.[14] The suggestion should only be taken on board if one fancies the

---

[12] Mitter, 'Free Okra'.

[13] Enid Donaldson, *The Real Taste of Jamaica* (Kingston: Ian Randle Publishers, 1996).

[14] Junji Takano, 'Health Benefits of Okra'. Accessed 20 March 2016. http://www.pyroenergen.com/articles07/okra-health-benefits.htm

idea of a mucilaginous cucumber with exploding white seeds or perhaps if one believes this was the bona fide beauty secret of Yang Guifei, the exquisite Chinese consort of the Tang Dynasty.

It goes without saying that Nigerians are avid okro eaters, mucilage eaters, although the cooking of okro sometimes merits the use of bad words. The cooking I can describe is nothing like Mitter's poetic imagery of Calcutta. There is the big-knife-and-wooden-board approach that you can hear from three houses away. The okro fingers are cut into small pieces, then chopped, then jounce-chopped to within an inch of life. The seeds are pounded with the knife until the personality of the vegetable is extracted from every pristine seed to create green and white surrender. The okro is then cooked in oil and stock with fish, meat and smoked crayfish until you have a pot of goo. It is cooked for close to twenty minutes until it flatlines. It is what it is. It's goo.

In more internal regions of Cross River State, okro is pounded with a mortar and pestle (otong soup) because the goal is to create the highest degree of draw. An in-law from Gboko in Benue State explained that to cook okro soup well, it is necessary to let it 'draw well-well'. The draw must be tight enough to require the snapping of wrist and upper arm to cut up the soup when lifting it to the mouth.

It's called arm-choreography: first a piece of the mound of pounded yam, gari or fufu is pulled off and rolled into a ball. It is depressed with the thumb to form a spoon, and then the spoon is used to scoop the soup. The soup is reluctant or asleep and an effective scoop involves invading the soup with the morsel of pounded yam and pulling away with a brisk tug of the arm. This is no ordinary tug; it is skilfully done so that the soup breaks away neatly without drawing messy patterns all over the utensils and the table.

Our neighbours in south-eastern Nigeria (who, technically speaking, are not our neighbours because when you are in the border towns of Manfe, Ekok, Mfum or Ekang there is no difference between Cameroon and Nigeria, or Cameroonians and Nigerians), hold in high esteem a soup called nkui. On a scale of one to ten of draw soups it is ten and a half, which means it sometimes needs to be cut with 'a something' or separated by holding it and putting pressure on it – just slightly less pressure than squeezing a tube of toothpaste. An attempt to nonchalantly pick it up like normal draw soup, would, in the first instance, require some level of grip on it. It's dangerous to attempt to put it in one's mouth without cutting it into small portions because it can snake down the throat of the eater, gagging them.

The otong soup, in the words of an Efik food purist, is another formal okra soup that is an overstatement of draw. Some people want their ogbono soup cooked with okro to make it more mucilaginous. Each to his own, but ogbono soup cooked like this holds zero appeal for me.

I was brought up cooking okro like an aside in the conversation. You got out the grater, and used the middle section that didn't grate too small. You brushed the okro against the chosen side until you had a pile of grated vegetable similar to but coarser than the one chopped with board and knife, although at least the seeds were intact. You boiled a small pan of water, dropped the fresh okro into it, stirred it to spread it out, added a small piece of potash and a pinch of Maggi, and in eight minutes it was ready. You didn't think too much about it because you were focused on the stew and the mound of ebà or àmàlà and the pieces of meat. At best it had the relevance of a cucumber raita; at worst it only functioned as lubricant to move the ebà along. It was possibly a stimulating island of green refereeing the coarse beige of ebà and the red of stew, but only for those people who think too much. It was never, ever the focus of the meal.

I married into the heavy-handed interpretation of okro soup, with the blanket-like smell of smoked crayfish, and the extended cooking until the face of the soup becomes grey. It was as if the green was an offence; an indication of undesirable rawness.

In 2008, in Lagos, I ordered a takeaway okro soup from The Yellow Chilli restaurant in Victoria Island. It was green and fresh, seeds whole and texturally intact, cooked with just a touch of palm oil for no longer than a few minutes. My first impression of the unprepossessing yellow plastic takeaway container was redeemed by the fat spirit that floated out when it was opened: a big, gamey umami aroma of he-goat meat sliding off the bone. The okro was not chopped fine, blended or grated; it was cut into even tapering Pennette Lisce-like pieces by some unpatriotic unNigerian machine. The marrow in the goat bones was like peppery butter. This was a beautiful, clever, faithful interpretation of a customarily odorous home-cooked meal, executed with respect and love and sentiment. I, the eater, was moved.

It was a one-off. I never met the person who cooked that meal but it was apparent that they were having an emotive day. I wondered if they'd had their wrist slapped for it. I returned again and again but never got that same calibre of food, with the same artistic investment. As if to confirm that the food, the day, my approach, my enthusiasm – the whole package – was a complete aberration, the person who I reluctantly offered a share of my takeaway meal to looked into the container, folded his face like an unironed napkin and said, 'It is too fresh!'

In the competition between my growing-up version and ilá alásèpo, the Cross Riverian one I married into, the latter was the self-righteous winner. It wins because someone has put effort and meat into it. The Yorùbá are gastronomic lightweights who lost because they cook okro in the nonchalant way that produces a characterless green nonentity that cannot legitimately call itself a soup.

My father still eats okro with everything: boiled plantains, boiled yam, steamed rice, àmàlà, ebà – everything and anything. He certainly has no regard for the international snubbing of okro, nor have I ever heard him voice a preference for degrees of mucilaginousness, and my father is a notoriously finicky eater. I therefore gained an obsession with okro as a congenital condition, eating it all the time, some nights as comfort food before slouching off to bed. If I'm feeling ill or gloomy, ebà and okro is the surefire remedy.

Unlike my father, I am particular about how mucilaginous my okro is. The draw must be light. The okro must be cut in big chunks, the seeds intact, retaining their bursting texture between the teeth. The okro chunks must be boiled for barely five minutes in more water than is required. It is not stirred, but allowed to adjust itself. A few slivers of onion, one hot pepper, a grudging spoon of palm oil and salt is all that it needs. No meat should tarnish this meal, but lightly smoked catfish is welcome. The gari for the ebà must be well-fermented Ijebu gari that makes your teeth jump. At the end of cooking, the okro must be green, not muggy.

My congenital okro condition has not only resulted in the eating of okro but in a long-running experiment to see whether okro soup will ever become rave-reviewed fine-dining fare while retaining its integrity: cut up, mucilaginous, yet innovatively conceived, pretty enough to tempt anyone to try it at least once. The obsession is a niggling matter of wasted potential. In Lagos, one will find food designed for the fine diner from every corner of the world, and Nigerians mechanically paying good money for caricatures of these cuisines. But a well-executed bowl of okro soup not cooked with a buka mindset may be a once-in-a-lifetime occurrence, like my Yellow Chilli version, unless perhaps one travels to New Orleans.

Pierre Thiam, the Senegalese-born visionary who owns a restaurant in Brooklyn has taken food from the heart of Senegal and translated it into fine-dining feasts in New York. He sent me his version of okro soup cooked in the restaurant Yolele:

with seafood reminiscent of its New Orleans cousin (gumbo) adding mussels, shrimp, crabmeat and lots of okra and of course palm oil. I would keep the mussels fresh in the shell and add them last to the stew until they open up (5–7 minutes). It presents quite well this way and I serve with rice or fonio (a grain that is considered as the oldest cultivated African grain). Okra is not for everyone but who cares, it's my favorite.

The Nigerian beautification proves most difficult. It was easy to find glowing testimonials in the newspapers about okro soup's two-way lubricating qualities – helping the gari down the oesophagus, and sending it out of the large intestine;

a most commendable quality since alternative medical practitioners believe all disease begins in the colon. More glowing testimonials laud okro's protection of the human body from diabetes, high cholesterol, colon cancer, atherosclerosis, lung inflammation, cataracts and depression. It is loaded with vitamin A, and the contentious draw is due to calcium. It contains folic acid, iron, potassium, protein, and vitamin C. My favourite okro soup morale was in Femi Kúsá's column in *The Nation*: 'Natural Remedies for Sound Body and Mind'. It stated that 'the chlorophyll, blood of the [okro], converts to human blood, leaving behind lots of magnesium to power and calm the muscles, particularly the heart.'[15]

The mechanics of okro turning to human blood has a compelling 'Africa Magic' sound to it. But after reading widely on the proficiency of okro in keeping the body healthy, I still had to conclude that it is like the case of the fear of God not successfully making men good. No matter how therapeutic okro is, I wouldn't eat the village version or expect anyone who has no prior relationship with okro to do so, because in the first instance it is too sure of itself in its unventilated mucilaginousness. *Monkey no fine but im mama like am* cannot be the pay-off line for getting anyone to eat a bowl of Nigerian okro soup in a restaurant. Even more so than most vegetables, because of its textural peculiarity and single-minded global naysayers, okro is going to have to loosen its tie and work hard to become fine-dining fare.

My friend Reme Obaseki, a brilliant Nigerian chef, gave me his mother Shirley's okro soup recipe as a possible compromise:

---

[15] Femi Kúsá, 'Natural Remedies for Sound Body and Mind', *The Nation*, 14 January 2010.

crabs and lobster are cooked in the stock. Chopped onions are added to the stock towards the end of cooking it. The crabmeat and lobster meat are removed from their shells and put in a bowl. Blended Scotch bonnet peppers, Ketchup, tabasco and Worcestershire sauce are added to the meat. The okro is cut up and plainly steamed. The shellfish sauce and cooked okro are accompanied with steamed rice, pasta Aglio e Olio or a Greek salad

Like Mitter's Bengali description, the wording is beautiful. It appeals to the mind (the determined and vigilant centre of hostility toward the okro vegetable) but the average Nigerian would see it, admire it, and conclude it very hoity-toity for a bowl of Nigerian okro. Not real; just some kind of pretension or make-believe okro soup.

If I was going to attempt restaurant-quality okro soup, every detail would need particular attention. I would need organically grown okro. The soil matters as the very first incontrovertible requirement. The okro must not travel far from the farm to the market. It should be no bigger than an inch in length, with cactus-like needles and petite linear leaves at the base. You shouldn't be able to handle the okro without getting needles in your fingers. They must be so fresh that you feel the crack under the weight of the knife when you cut them.

That fresh feeling also translates into the quickness of cutting through each okro. In Nigeria, cutting fresh food into large pieces is done against the hand as opposed to using a chopping board and there is some sense of pride invested in this style of cutting. If you were going to chop okro into the masticated food pieces that produce the heavy-draw version of okro that I described earlier, you would start by cutting each okro against your hand. Even if one cannot comfortably handle the fresh okro, one would persevere because only wimps cut okro against boards!

The emphasis on freshness is because I believe that no one who is given fresh okro to eat can resist them. The crispness of plump pearl-coloured seeds and contrasting clover-green flesh cannot possibly offend anyone. Best of all is if the okro have fuchsia stalks.

Okro Soup

450g small, fresh, prickly okro, each cut into 6-8 large pieces

200g bawa peppers or sweet green peppers. (Bawa are large red peppers between sweet and Tatase)

50g Leeks

1 or 2 very hot Scotch bonnets, if you like

300g fresh prawns (weighed in their shells)

1½ cups palm oil

Lightly smoked catfish

A few pieces of smoked fish ground in a dry mill to accentuate the flavour of the soup

A handful of dawadawa

Ground Cameroonian pepper and good sea salt

1 cup water

The palm oil is poured into an unglazed earthenware pot and heated very slightly. The heat under the pot is kept low at all times. The peppers and leeks are ground in a blender with a few drops of water and poured into the palm oil. The dawadawa and ground smoked fish are added to the ground peppers and oil. The pot is covered and the blend allowed to cook. Water is added to rehydrate the soup, especially because unglazed earthenware pots absorb moisture. The cooking of the peppers and leeks should take about 20 minutes. The smoked catfish is placed carefully in the soup when the flavours of peppers and oil are well fused and cooked. Stirring is kept to a minimum to retain the integrity of the fish. The okro goes in with a sprinkling of ground Cameroonian pepper. The heat is turned down completely and the soup covered, so that the okro steams and retains its greenness and some crunch. Once the okro is cooked (about 8 minutes if the hob fire is kept low), the prawns are added and allowed to cook for a further 5 minutes. The seasoning is adjusted. Another sparing sprinkling of Cameroonian peppers will make the face of the soup very attractive.

White bowls are warmed to serve the okro with a small hill of gari or steamed ripe plantains.

There remains the possibility that the average Nigerian will look into my pot, fold his face like an unironed napkin and proclaim it 'too fresh', but the combined aroma of palm oil, smoked fish and cooking peppers will uphold the integrity of the soup. The ground smoked fish will give quick and powerful umami and depth of flavour. The blended peppers will embellish the mucilaginousness, making it multidimensional, enjoyable for the palate yet retaining its binding quality. The draw will be elegant: light enough for the uninitiated, mucilaginous enough for the lover of mucilage. It will be green enough for the colonic irrigator, pretty enough for the fine diner.

At the very least, it will be an authentic conversational piece at the global dining table.

Longthroat Memoirs

The slow holiday weeks belonging to July, August and September were spent in Oke-Ado, Ibadan at my paternal grandparents' house. The back of the house faced the clamorous Ìjebú bypass, but with such a wide setback from it, that the sounds generated all the way from Molete roundabout made up a delicious playlist. As a child, if you had asked me what the theme music to my life was I would probably have answered Chief Ebenezer Obey's Evergreen Songs playing on the wind: mute, loud, mute and loud again. It was because of the positioning of the house and a nightclub pouring out early evening highlife and wistfulness from somewhere. You got the hors d'oeuvres of swift spats, excerpts of conversation, engines revving cantankerously, the straying redolence of soup, sometimes even Rex Lawson's trumpet, loud, mute and loud again.

I spent most of the daytime going between the back and front balcony. The front balcony had the best seats in an open-air theatre a million times more compelling than people moving around in a soulless electronic box. Rarely did anything out of the extraordinary happen during these months, but the street had a rhythmic slow-motion-picture feel to it.

Food hawkers passed with basins balanced on their heads, each one's call projected powerfully into the long bars of stillness, cleverly fashioned to the food on sale. The balancing of the weight was done with so much impossible grace that you watched the necks of the hawkers as they passed, wondering if they would not snap in two. So dazzled were we by the hawkers' calls that we kept vigil over the balcony for their passing, then went about the house imitating them until we were told off for shouting.

'Fine bread!' the bread vendor called out. In the Queen's English, 'fine' means 'superior'. In Oke-Ado, Ibadan, it meant the exact same thing plus a commendation for the loaf's beautiful complexion. It made you think of the face of the bread. It instructed you that bread, in fact, had a face. The word on the street for proclaiming the bread tasty was 'sweet'.

'Yeeeeep!' That long exclamation was the call of the meat vendor, whose meat was far from fresh after he had carried it in brown paper through so many streets. For many years I wondered what it meant, until one day I realised that the answer was there. It was simple: the call remained everlastingly in your mind, and so proved its competence. That same meat vendor walked through my mind calling out 'Yeeeeep' whether I liked it or not, never mind what yeeeeep meant.

'Moyínmoyínelépo' was the cry for moin-moin cooked with palm oil. The vocal exaggeration of the 'moyínmoyín' straightaway evoked, in vivid images and textural appeal, the turmeric colour of palm oil mixed with milled beans, a distant suggestion of onion and the close, ticklish aroma of hot pepper wrapped and cooked in the rain-on-grass smell of thaumatococcus leaves.

'Mele mu, mele mu!' was the orange seller's call. If you bought an orange, you were given the extra treat of watching the dexterous peeling of the skin with a delicate knife. In a matter of minutes, you would be handed a beautiful sphere with perfectly spaced green rind stripes left on the orange for no other reason than to embellish it. If you took a closer look, you would notice that the knife had been a Blue Band margarine tin in its former life.

'Òòògì bàbàà!' was for sorghum ògì but the melodrama in the call would have suited opera. The call of 'Eko-tútù!' promised that the white maize patty would be a refreshing counterbalance to the peppery efo ŕirò waiting in the house for it. You called back 'Eleko ò!' to stop the hawker from going past your front door. She would request 'E so mí' (Help me put down my basin) after offering her greetings. It was that word, 'tutù' (cool) in 'eko-tútù': it was powerful enough to momentarily send the sun behind clouds.

Even if you had the self-control of a saint, or the snobbery of an aristocrat, and never bought food from street hawkers, the day would surely come when you succumbed as a result of curiosity, boredom or sheer defeat to endless invitations to put something in your mouth. There was a special college where the hawkers all enrolled to learn to project sound into the rooms in your stomach, in loud vibrations through every corner in your house. In time the call got inside your head and would wake you from the depths of sleep.

My grandmother sold trunks in Dùgbe market in the path of these street food hawkers (every route was their route) and she couldn't resist them. On an average day, she bought roasted groundnuts to snack on, and she might buy some guguru (roasted corn) to go with the groundnuts. She bought five oranges to quench her thirst. She bought eko-tutu to take home at the end of the day, and servings of husked white maize boiled till exceptionally soft, eaten with freshly broken pieces of coconut.

There was always something gracefully standoffish about street hawkers. If you did not hail them, they did not stop or linger. They walked at a measured pace. They kept their expressions as pedestrian as their mode of transport. They sold what you requested and then asked, as if they were in charge, that you help them put the basket that weighed as much as a mountain back on their heads. On quiet rural residential streets – "Before the time of the South-Asian man and his tribe" who made a fortune by helping us all sell our souls to intrusive, knocking, grinding, generators, a time when even the hum of NEPA was audible – the preparation, smell, sale and consumption of street food was the reassurance of life happening.

Even if you hadn't greeted your neighbour in days (which didn't happen at that time) you would get notice of supper being prepared. Over time you learnt who owned what ensign. You mentally put all the ingredients in the pot and knew that, because supper was being cooked as usual, all was well. Even when hawkers were thin on the ground and one successfully went about one's mental business, some woman – and only Nigerian women do it in this way – would bring her pot out of the cupboard with such a loud clang it would immediately set everyone's salivary glands into overdrive.

Then came that poc-poc-poc sound of pestle and mortar from the house on the right, where Mama something or other had started to pound yam. She might be a terrible cook and there might be lumps in the pounded yam the size of a child's head, but in your imagination, standing on the balcony, it would be perfectly made. The yam would be supple, succulent. It would pucker its lips and kiss that pestle with fervour until its bottom came off the wood of the mortar.

In Lagos, I lived in an apartment. The smell of my own cooking has me slightly alarmed. I'm anxious to restrain it indoors, like a mischievous child. The pounding of yam might not be impossible but it is almost taboo. My mortar and pestle have become decorative. They pose at the entrance to the kitchen and people admire them when they come round. A hawker would never dare raise her voice in this neighbourhood. Someone would send the security guard to give her a stern warning. The generators are as garrulous as ever. There is no more nuance of sound, no mute, loud, mute. It's loud or it's dead or it's the kokomaster. DSTV subscriptions have been paid for three months. And as for that necessary sense of community, and all those other wonderful neighbourly virtues, we are scheduled to discuss them at the next residents' association meeting. God willing!

be so bold and expressive proves you are not repressed. And one is not allowed to be a sexually repressed writer.

The lack of sexual repression is now an essential part of a writer's curriculum vitae. If I was not asked, I would have said nothing at all. I would not have carried my trouble to this area. I escaped other vocations because I have a problem with authority and I hate being told what to do. Now I'm a writer and I have a list. I must be feminist. I must beat up Pentecostal Christians, hate the Nigerian government, support homosexuals in defining themselves in sexual terms of reference, and lambast the homophobic. I thought I had cleverly snubbed the word 'African' but I was probably naïve in thinking that I could escape those yawning holes of African wars, those withering African children with rheumy eyes that are drinking pools for flies. The newish epithet is that *Africa is in*. I certainly wasn't consciously signing up for the cynicism that presents a whole continent as a commodity. Yes, I want to win a prize, and the polarising prose might win me an international one, which I'll pretend not to want if I get it.

But here I am being presented with another writing cliché and we are back where we started. I won't give myself up that easily though. I was brought up Pentecostal, even if I don't go to church. I don't hate the Nigerian government. I'm moving to Togo, near my supply of coconut oil, to show my indifference. And I'm a woman. A homosexual man shouldn't expect sympathy from me because I have thirty years' experience of being thought of as a sexual object and a baby-making machine. For twenty-eight of those thirty years, the be all and end all of my life was meant to be marriage. This gives me way more justification to whine about unfairness. When I meet people, I don't want to know if they are homosexual.

I don't want to care. I want to know what they eat for dinner and breakfast. I'm squeamish about the minutest details of their sexuality, and I don't expect them not to be squeamish about the details of mine.

Binyavanga Wainaina, by the way, is a force of nature. He waves his hands about, pulls back his eyelids until his eyeballs threaten to fall out of their sockets, and purses his lips and says, 'Me, I think' more times than is necessary for a man sure of his brilliant opinions. And he is excruciatingly brilliant, like a tree of ideas. He takes many cigarette breaks, but I think they are really breaks for me, because he gives me a splitting headache with the force and presentation of his ideas. He drags my brain all over the place, and I am a slow thinker. His introductory lecture on writing was about the romance novel, and how Nigeria needs successful ones yesterday.

Romance, of course, is not old-fashioned Love. No one wants to read about that. He says the world wants men thrusting women (or men or alien creatures) against hard walls, if you please, wants bruising kisses, shredded lingerie, pages of prose that make you sweat, and gasp and secrete. In other words Nigerian *Fifty Shades of Grey*, or tame Mills and Boon, or steamy Mills and Boon with men in white cotton shirts on the covers. You know those ones, where men's shirts are always torn to show ripped chests and six-packs, and women are always swooning and dangling as if their busty, wispy figures are all cartilage inside. The whole lecture confused me more and more as it progressed. In case I forgot to say it, I am one of the few sexually repressed Nigerian writers. The only Nigerian writer who I know, to date, to have admitted it.

If we want an example closer to home, Binyavanga said, we need an amplified, more assertive Myne Whitman. That might work, might sell, might be the way that the next Nigerian writer takes the world by soft-porn storm. More definition! More opinionated Nigerian sexuality! Better branding! I am being a little melodramatic, but this expresses how scandalised I was that Binyavanga should search for a niche with which the Nigerian could invade the world with neologisms, and suggest it should be soft porn. We were the perfect candidates for it, he said. The door had been held wide open by Chimamanda Ngozi Adichie, Helen Oyèyemí, Binyavanga himself, etc. Africa is in! Where are the fresh stories? What are you waiting for?

I fidgeted anxiously for the punchline until he started to nudge in the direction of *Fifty Shades of Grey*. Then I was furious with him for wasting such luminous traction on romance, on sex. My workshop class had already been primed to perfection. They'd left me well behind. So what if it had already been discovered that I was the class prude? And the worst kind of prude, with three children that I must have thrown up via oesophagus.

We were a group of women and men in a closed off, air-conditioned room with sheer cream curtains dancing flirtatiously in the cooled air at the sliding glass entrance, and maroon coloured drapes banning all lookouts. One of us was a Ghanaian sex blogger for heaven's sake, with a name that sounds like it belongs on a stage: Nana Sekyiamah. She had a sticker of an erect penis and two scrotal sacs on her Mac. There was Chika Oduah: petite, gorgeous long dreads, mellifluous American accent, already causing some salivation across the table. Her introductory piece was an orgiastic, trance-like narrative about a woman in a poetry nightclub having some kind of hazy spiritual/sexual experience. Everyone loved it. I had to be honest and admit, in critiquing her piece that I couldn't for the life of me understand what was happening.

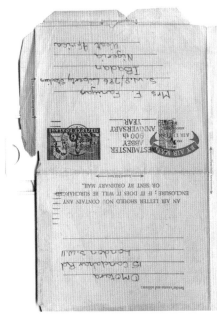

E o ri iwe Aburo
yin laipe o.   15 Candahar Rd
              London s.w.11
              27.1.66.

Mama mi,

Mo dupe gba fun
iwe yin ti ari ninu ose yi
ati odo mrs Fashoro. A ri
wipe o ti pe ti e ti ko
iwe wa. O si bebe na
wipe on ko mo ile riu,
on ba post re si wa.

Oluwa alanu yio ma
ranyin lowo o. O fi zorro
die juse ninu eyiti e fu
range o ni eyiti oku, se
ni on gbe by ship. Bi mo
ba ni kin ma sure, yio
ti gbo ju nkan ti e le ka
ninu iwe lo. Oluwa
Alanu yio seki Oni esan
rere o. Ao ma ri yin ba.
Bi ki igbin yen ti de
lo nse mi afi bi enipe
ko je igbin ri lo se nwon

Wa je Oluwa alanu yio
wai apo yin o. Oluwa
nikan ni ole ba gbogbo
wa gbe bukata wa, ko
se fi enu so. Laigbara
Oluwa ra, Oju ko ni ti
wa o. Se alafia ni awon
oko mi wa gbogbo? Ki
eba mi ki won o.

Ha!! Mo dupe lowo
Olorun fun rogbodiyan
ti o be ni Nigeria nipa
awon oselu ti ko de ado
awon enia wa. Orisirisi
awon enia patakipataki ni
a ti gbo pe nwon ti pa.
O kan mi ko bale rara
afi igbati ari iwe lodo
brother Isaac lana ni a
to le jeun wo inu.
Opelope brother Awomolo

ni nwon koko fi wa ni
okan bale ni Friday 21.1.66
ti ari Cable grame ti nwon
send wa si wa gba.
Oluwa alanu a ran won
lowo. Ijaya na po to je
wipe o di aisan si mi lara
Gbogbo awon ti nwon pa
Bi Akinjola, Sadauna, Tawa
ati awon opolopo ti nwon
ko mo oruko won ti nwon
ni nwon ti pa ni nwon show
lori television lu yi. Adupe
lowo Olorun ti eleyi ko
je pim ti wa o. O se
wa lamu pupo fun awon
ti nwon ti pa ati bi won
ti se pa won, ko se maso
rara. Ki Olorun lowo seki
ilu Nigeria toro o. Ki eba
mi ki awon iyami ati awon
brother ra dada o.
                Emi ti yin
                Bisi Omotara

Letter from Bísí Omotárá, dated January 1966

Ogbono soup cooked with nsala spices - Uda, uziza, smoked crayfish, palm oil, hot peppers, chicken, lamb. Fresh king prawns added in just before the end of cooking.

A bowl of pitanga cherries, a gift from Nene Akan, my neighbour in Sacramento Estate, Calabar. You pick a pitanga cherry and you feel that you are holding a red jewel in your hand. They make beautiful jam with Himalayan crystal salt and coconut sugar and some slices of fresh pineapple.

TOP:The idea of a pot of soup starts with water, chillies, a yellow habanero, some uda pods in a local earthenware pot.

BOTTOM: A few of the essential aromatics for a pot of soup: grains of paradise, fragrant yellow habaneros, smoked catfish, parts of a stockfish head, Ukazi/Afang leaf & country onions.

TOP: The Aridan fruit (Tetrapleura tetraptera), a dark-brown oleaginous pod with a sweetish aroma of the Afia Efere (White) soup.

LOWER LEFT: The Uda pod with its menthol note and strong pungent aroma gives the Nsala soup its balanced piquancy.

LOWER RIGHT: Stockpot with hot peppers, stockfish and nkonko (shelled grey turban-shaped periwinkles).

Magnificently aromatic, hot-aniseedy Calabash nutmeg.

The red complexion of Nigerian soups comes from palm oil – the extracted vegetable oil from the pulp of the palm fruit.

A bag of tomatoes dusty from its journey from the North of Nigeria.

Ogbono soup - the quality of drawing
defines the animation of the soup.

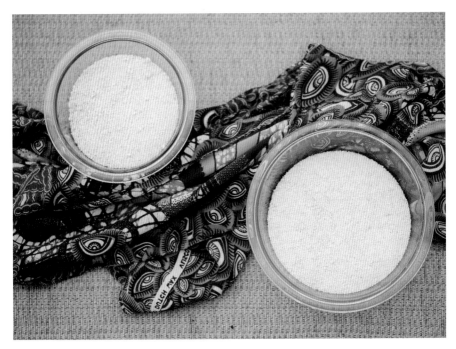

Yellow gari, colour courtesy of palm-oil added during processing. White gari the Yorùbá preference, sour and thirsty.

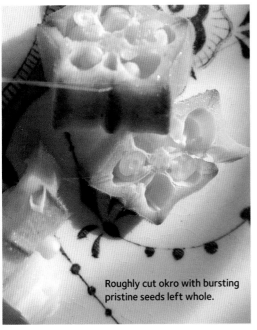

Roughly cut okro with bursting pristine seeds left whole.

The 'Swallow' market in Mushin, Lagos. Air-dried tubers of yams to be milled into Elubo flour.

Beneath the informal bureau de change in Bogobiri, Calabar is a mudu on top of a basin of yellow corn, millet and red jeero (sorghum).

TOP: As a child I was taught how to carry crates of eggs. You dipped the crate slightly so it formed a valley for the safety of the eggs. I'm standing in front of my grandfather's store of chicken feed. The facial expression is shouting: "These eggs are getting heavier!"
BOTTOM: Recipe from Barbara Page-Phillips' collection.

1 Kikife

Ingredints;
6 medium size unripe plantains
4 tomatoes, sliced
6 medium size pepper
2 onions, (chopped)
4 medium sized snails, (pre-cooked)
bunches
4 servingspoonful crayfish (ground)
5 servingspoonsful palm oil.

salt
kaun (native salt)
seasoning
2½ litres water.
.wash, peel and cut the plantains into small pieces
.Boil in a saucepan with a small chunk of kaun for 15 to twenty minutes
or until plantain is soft
.Add the sliced tomatoes, onions, pepper and crayfish, salt and seasoning
and allow to simmer for five minutes.
Remove fish(to prevent it from breaking, and add palm oil..stir thoroughly
.Servr immediately.
                                    Recipe by wilson Bodisea
                              owei. (Ijaw, rivers state

2 Yorkshire Curd Tart
I prepared 20cm (8 in) tart shell
225g (8 oz) curd cheese
50g (2 oz) castor sugar
finely grated rind of 1 lemon
2 tablespoons currants
15 g (1/2 oz, melted butter
grated nutmeg
3 eggs
Prepare the tart shell(basic recipe) and chill. Measure the curd cheese
into a medium mixing bowl, add the sugar and beat until soft and creamy.
Stir in the grated lemon rind, currants, melted butter and a grating of
nutmeg.
Heat the oven to 200 C or gas no 6. Separate the eggs, cracking the whites
into a second bowl and starring the Yolks into the cheese (curd) mixture
whites. Beat the egg whites to stiff peaks and fold them
into the cheese mixture using a metal spoon. Spoon the mixture into the
tart shell and spread level.
Set in the heated oven and bake for 10 minutes. Reduce the oven heat to
160C or gas no 4 and serve warm or at room temperature

3 Cream Cheese Tartlets
-provides a base for autumn fruits or a mixture of nuts.
sifted icing sugar is the best way to decorate
1 recipe 7.5cm (3 in) tartlets
225g (8 oz) cream cheese
75g (3 oz) castor sugar
finely grated rind of lemon 1
3-4 tablespoons double cream
225g (8oz) ripe fruit such as black berries or seedless green grapes,'or
6 ripe plums, or 100 g (4 oz) toasted pine nuts or walnuts pieces, or a
mixture of both.
Prepare 6&7.5 cm (3 in) tart shells and chill. Heat the oven to 190C or gas
no 5. Set the tart shells in the heated oven and bake until pastry is
golden; about 12- 15 minutes Let baked tarts cool 1 minute, then remove
from the tins and leave to cool. Turn the cream cheese into a medium

The men, especially Abdulaziz Ahmed Abdulaziz, had already written one or two enthusiastic odes to flying buttons, bursting bosoms and other fleshy parts. Chinagorom Martin already acknowledged in worship our main facilitator, Chimamanda Ngozi Adichie, who I code named 'Ambrosia'. The thing was already dangling in the air like a cobweb waiting for someone's head to catch it.

My brain only kicked into full gear at one point in Binyavanga's lecture: when he said something about Ama Ata Aidoo and snails. Something about a snail tree. What a picture. What a sprint my mind took: a tree cloaked, dripping with snails, in a country where people consider snails a delicacy. Or better still, a tree of snails in a country where people despise snails. Yemisí arrives in this country with some friends and we do our best to keep a straight face about the whole thing ... Now this is a worthy cause. This was the novel idea that the world was waiting for. The tree must be transported to an empty field in Nigeria where surrounding bareness highlights it. And we must visit it reverentially and talk about it. *Come and worship.*

But wait a minute Binyavanga: snails don't live or grow on trees, nor does Ama Ata Aidoo write of a tree of snails. I think Binyavanga's imagination was in overdrive. Hunger will facilitate this. I'm clinging to the other side: suggestiveness, innuendos boiling under tame language. Suggestiveness, for me, has always been more potent than the clichés, than describing trains rushing through tunnels. Snails are a worthy cause.

When the bridegroom comes to ask for the bride's hand, he comes with his people – his friends, aunties, sisters – and a pious script on a scroll. At my wedding there was a yellow and blue scroll backed with aso-òkè. You can order one from a lady in Victoria Island. You'll choose your colours and a basket, box or some other receptacle, if you like, for carrying the scroll to the bride. A formal introduction from the groom's family. The words on the scroll will be the same for millions of women, and it was the same for me:

Our son told us of a beautiful flower growing in your garden. We've come to ask your permission to pluck it.

You are a flower, and they've come to ask to pluck you, and like all flowers separated from the tree, you will wither and die. I had to steal Binyavanga's snail tree, as eye-catching as a flame of the forest, with black velvet labia minor for flowers, turban-shaped curlicue lips, dripping mucilage pistils …

I left the class at the end of that day and went to see my friend Adérewà. She wanted me to pick her up from home and take her somewhere we could talk. She wore these earrings that I have always wanted, ones that look like old cathedral windows.

Come and Worship

'My body's changed Yemisí, and all the rules don't work any more. I'm on a fast … abstaining.'

'From what? Did they call a general fast in church and you want to take advantage of it to lose some weight?'

'I'm serious. I'm abstaining from sex.'

'You can't do that. Have you consulted your husband about this fast?'

'He's got other options. I don't need to ask him.'

'That doesn't sound right. You can't just up and abstain from having sex when you are married and then say he's got other options. You always knew he had other options. You should have done this sexual fast before getting married.'

Adérewà exhales. 'I've been married twenty years Yemisí. You are not making any sense.'

'I'm certainly making more sense than you are right now.'

Ade looks at her hands … 'Things are different. I feel like … I'm dying.'

'Are you ill?'

'Tch! No! Look, the reason why I'm talking to you is because I don't have to say everything. Don't make me use words I don't have to. I've already used up my quota today, shouting at everybody. You understand exactly what I'm saying. We've been having this conversation for twenty years. I'm 45 years old and I've spent all my life applying my sexuality to other people's … I've never had the opportunity to define the holy of holies.'

'Holy of holies?'

'My heart is in my body and it doesn't like or agree with what is happening.' Ade's voice trembles. 'Anyway,' she says sniffing and looking away, 'I've made up my mind; all my erogenous zones have been transferred to my mouth.'

'Just like that? And what are they going to do when they get there?'

'Eat.'

'And?'

'And eat.'

'And you expect that that will work? You mean you will eat to curb your sexual appetite abi?'

'I've done it for a year and I'm fine.'

'A year! I don't believe you. No peeking, no cheating, no desperate masturbation?'

'A year and a half. Nothing. It's cleared my head. Sex is a hard taskmaster and he never allows me to come to work as myself.'

'You are insane. You'll convince yourself of anything. OK, tell me, what do you feed your transliterated erogenous zones?'

'Ice for tension ...' Adé rubs her thumb against her palm as if there is something she's written there and she's erasing the words. 'Hard ice for passion, soft for pain. I crush the ice between my teeth. They crash against my nerves, burn a hole in my tongue. They set off all my pain receptors, and then I'm fine.'

'Please!' I roll my eyes. 'And for just wanting to be held?'

'Chocolate.' She stretches up, leans forward.

'For the desire for deep penetration?'

She goes quiet, searching my face. 'You don't believe I don't want to be penetrated.' She stresses the word. 'OK.' She smiles wanly. 'I'll play along. For penetration, steamed overripe plantains, suspended high over the steam so that not one drop of water touches them. You know they cook and the plantain skins blacken and loosen and shrink back, the plantains themselves slip out from the tops, bottoms, their colour burns not like bright yellow but like the honest to God complexion of sexual arousal.'

'This is my point Ade. No one as filthy minded as you can abstain from sex for a year and a half. You are compensating with something and it isn't soft ice or hard ice.'

'In the mornings I drink one cup of espresso and then one cup of decaf. Once I've had the real stuff I don't mind.' She laughs then goes quiet, sad again. 'Did I ever tell you that I had an abortion when I was eighteen?'

I shake my head quietly in response, imploding. If I react, she'll stop talking.

'If you had the money,' Adé says, 'you would go into a proper hospital. You won't go anywhere dirty and demon-infested. I didn't. The doctor was probably a deacon in his church. Everything about him was clean and calm. He was balding and had good skin. He was not tall and his voice was quiet.'

I say nothing.

'He gave me an injection and I swooned. I wasn't under though. I was in-between somewhere and I was singing a song. I could hear myself singing but I couldn't stop myself. I was standing in a dark room full of bubbles. One of the bubbles was floating upwards, climbing up somewhere. I can't say into the air because we were in a dark room, water not air, or maybe it was air ... and I reached out my hand to burst the bubble. It turned on me and I had never experienced that kind of rage. I heard it loud and clear.

'You have no right to do this, no right at all, it said. But it was not a voice; it was a bowl of feelings that formed audible thoughts. I felt as if I had destroyed a universe, not a bubble, and I could feel that bubble becoming nothing in the dark. I can't explain the rage and the ... grief. It was like going back to my own beginnings in a place that I couldn't recognise, and before I had the opportunity to become, I was nothing, a bubble expunged in the dark. Do you understand what I am saying?'

I shake my head. 'No,' I say looking down at my hands.

'I came out from under the anaesthetic and I was screaming, and someone was shushing me and holding my hands down.'

'Horrible.' I finally say.

'I wasn't able to sleep in the dark after that.'

'So what did you do?'

Ade laughs. 'I went to Bible school.'

'Tell me again about your erogenous zones in your mouth,' I say, trying to escape the gloom.

She laughs louder. 'Now who's got the filthy mind?'

'No I'm serious. I've got a class of salacious colleagues waiting for a story on sex.'

'What … don't they know you threw up your children?'

'I tell you, I don't know what to write. I'm the wrong person to expect any titillation from and now your depressing, horrible story …'

'OK … hot showers …'

'Are you drinking your bath water now?' We both laugh.

'I mean prima facie hot showers … hot. The kind that beats you up.'

'Please tell me what's for dinner, while your poor husband glares at you from across the table.'

'Yam pottage with lots of pepper and soft plantains buried inside like mines. The yams must be hairy; efuru that break up into floury mash-mush that slides against the palm oil. Slivers of half-cooked onions that crunch and melt at the same time. No meat, only softness and oiliness. You know how those yams keep heat inside and when you put a piece in your mouth, the steam percolates out like steam from a kettle, carrying the essence of hot pepper?'

'Stupid woman!'

'You asked.'

'Instead of pounding yam like a good wife, you are cooking yourself pots of yam pottage. But seriously though, why did you never tell me this before? I'm probably your oldest friend.'

'You are. But there are some honest-to-God secrets that are between you and your creator. You know what happens when you tell people these kinds of things: they give you a painkiller. They want you to feel better quickly. Now-now. They feel contaminated. Sometimes they are angry with you. You've ruined something. You're doing it right now: trying to make me laugh because you feel I shouldn't regard myself as having killed someone. But I've joined the scoffers, couldn't bear their happiness and I left them again for my grief.

'Do you know what happened when I got to Bible school? I think it was a two-week, fast-track Bible course or something like that. Maybe it was a month, I can't really remember, but that Sam Adéyemí man, he'd taken a lot of our classes, and I think there must have been one class that hit a nerve. I honestly don't know what prompted me to walk up to him during the lunch break. He was coming down the corridor and I came the other way. I stood there and told him I couldn't sleep in the dark. He looked long and hard at me and said, "Have you ever had an abortion?"'

'Oh my God, what did you say?'

'I said no.'

'What did he say then?'

'I have no idea. I was doing my best to hold myself upright, to keep my expression intact.'

'You said no.'

'I said no. And then it became like I was being followed by a ghost. I couldn't get away from it. I would meet people and they would bring it up out of the depths without knowing anything about me. Every time I went to the hospital and complained about a headache, they would ask me, "Have you ever had an abortion?"'

'Guilt probably.'

'Don't do that …'

'I'm sorry. I didn't mean to.'

'… I had this boyfriend whose mother was really intense, you know. Very standoffish. Always dressed up and propped up. She would be in the room but her spirit wasn't there. He told me that she and her mother never got along and it was a long-standing thing, from birth. I wondered how that was possible, until he said that the problem between them was that she had heard her mother talking about her while she was in the womb. She'd heard her say she didn't want her.'

'I'm not going to get any sleep tonight,' I say, holding my head in my hands.

'Would you believe I scoffed? The same person who had battled an air bubble and come up screaming and singing; I scoffed. All my life Yemisí, I've conformed my sexuality to other people's convictions. In university, they said you wouldn't fit in if you were a virgin, what's the big deal? So I became not a virgin. My mother told me that I had to have children, so I did. I was told I couldn't have children outside marriage even though I could steal food and eat if I was hungry, so I had an abortion.

'Then I got married and my body was officially signed and sealed, no longer mine. Now my sisters tell me I have to cook for my husband even though he isn't hungry. He eats out all the time and wants to eat at home as well to make sure I don't also eat out. I tell him I don't want to eat at all, I don't have an appetite and he shouldn't worry about my stomach on my behalf. He gets angry and says I must eat because he says so. But then I'm at the end of my obedience and I want to know what he's going to do about it ... I can't really remember the number of meals I've cooked for myself.'

'Oh oh!'

'The only opinion I can trust is my own.'

'I understand that bit. I was thinking that as I was coming here. How uncanny. Everyone wants rights to something so private. Everyone wants you to use your sexuality to prove and buffer their own opinions. They want you to donate it to their cause. They want to legislate it. It's worse as a writer, believe it or not, because writers are always pretending to be politically correct. They want everyone to buy their books so they have to love all the rationales that sell books.

'I can't say that gay rights get on my last nerve because I'm going to be branded as homophobic, but you meet someone and you want to be invested in something other than their sexuality. You are more interested in their brilliant mind or the book they've written or their creativity or their political ideas. All they want to talk about is sex. It's the foot they are putting forward all the time. It's frustrating. If you don't want to talk sex with them, if you are not interested then you are the one with the problem. And they always insist that "it wasn't us who brought up the conversation about sex in the first place. We don't have a choice but to talk about it."'

Ade nods. 'When I say that I'm tired of doing what people say ... If I tell people that I've read that mothers and the babies in their womb have the same dream at the same time, they'll cut me off or try and neutralise my own experience because they are uncomfortable. They'll say you can't really prove it. For goodness' sake, I've had people who've tried to make me disconnect my vagina from my womb, disconnect it from my mind, disconnect it from my heart, disconnect it from my intuition and my dreams. They don't want to talk about babies but they talk about sex. I don't understand how to do that. I don't want to be a man. I don't want to fight for equal rights to have sex like a man. And now with the benefit of hindsight and pain, giving birth to a child is plain amazing.' Adé smiles for the first time in many long, drawn-out minutes.

'And I want to own the reality that babies happen through my vagina. I mean at 45, should I be having this conversation, hiding away from my own house, and should I be getting angry as I say the words?' She points at me. 'You are so invested in my husband's rights; well I'll tell you that men respect hunger more than the ability to eat, especially now that hunger is so rarefied. They'll canonise you if you don't sleep with them. They instinctively give the highest accolades to the woman who got away. They can't help themselves. I can't pretend that I don't yearn for that canonisation over the ability to eat another meal.'

'Wow!'

'Yes, wow. Holy of holies.'

'I don't know what to say.'

Ade laughs. 'I've burnt hot holes in your eardrums abi? Did I tell you about my colleague who rode a bus to work and heard the bus conductor calling this woman a slut?

'No,' I say, beginning to laugh already. 'What did she do, slap him?'

'No. She agreed with him. She said, yes I'm a slut, but so is your mother, because if she wasn't a slut you wouldn't be here.'

'Oh oh, and then what happened?'

'He went dead quiet as if manna had descended from heaven.'

'Are you serious? I thought you were going to say *all hell broke loose.*'

'You don't understand do you? They weren't speaking English. I just translated it for your understanding. What he said was, "You sleep with men" and she replied, "Yes, so does your mother. That's how you got here."'

We both laugh, until my stomach feels like it is turning itself upside down. 'What an idiotic old woman you've become.'

'Yes, I know,' she says. 'I never got very far being smart.'

The next day in the workshop class, before Binyavanga arrives to discuss our anthology, we gather around Nana's laptop, her erect penis in our faces. She is a natural leader, and has a paced, confident way of expressing her views. She embraces other people. I think I remember her saying she has trained policemen in Ghana. I sit in my chair, away from the discussion, and listen in. She speaks and often turns in my direction to include me. I'm drawing a tree for Adérewà because I can't get what she said last night out of my mind. I didn't sleep. It's not a very good tree. The long, curved pistils are almost touching the ground. They dance around the tree trunk and look like ribbons hanging from a tree. I stop to look over it as the discussion progresses. I feel like Antoine de Saint-Exupéry's aviator, who has to explain to adults that there is an elephant in the boa constrictor. The drawing is too elementary even for a child's imagination. I write 'The Snail Tree' on top of the page, but it doesn't help the drawing. I scrunch up the paper and the sound draws everyone's attention.

'Are we all agreeing that it's sex?' Nana says looking at me.

'Yes,' I say quietly. 'Sex and food.'

Nana waits for more words and when I say nothing, she says, 'If you can make it work, why not.'

I tear out another page from my notebook. I write at the top, 'The Snail Tree'. I recall the detonation that went off in my head when Binyavanga said 'snails', 'tree'. Under the heading I write:

I have saved the best words for you, Adérewà, and for you, Yeshua, who gave me the secrets and the treasures of hunger.

Blessed are they who are hungry for they will be satisfied.

Fainting at the Sight of an Egg

I love the congeniality of eggs, how quintessentially composed they are, the way they snuggle into the cupped hand. The way the eye is compelled around the ovalness, the different coffee-and-milk-complexions, recycled-manila-envelope pores, the fragility. Yet it feels slightly pretentious to be a Nigerian and muse about eggs.

Nigerians are supposedly too no-nonsense for that, too seasoned. I think about the disdain for sell-by, use-before and best-before dates. How we might drolly concede their significance when heads of lettuces left in the fridge turn to black mush, or green peppers melt into slime. Or perhaps when we open a can of chickpeas on which some industrious Nigerian in Aba-Owerri has replaced the blue-stencil 2008 with 2012, and find some furry creature on top and a quarter of a tin of something that resembles chickpeas underneath.

But as far as the egg in the average Nigerian fridge is concerned ... I mean in that fridge powered by something so wilful, so malevolent, so animated it cannot be accurately termed electricity. The fridge itself is a pampered, lukewarm cupboard, connected to a stabiliser that vigilantly cuts off the 'electricity' when it senses anything resembling a threat of explosion of compressor gas and mutilated electrical wires. The egg sitting in that fridge is so perfectly composed, so convincingly aloof and seemingly above all manner of reactions to its melodramatic environment, so cool when we are not, that we are doubly reassured that all we believed about those òyìnbós, those global northerners and their hang-up about dates (sell by, use by, or use before) is true. I have never seen a sell-by date on an egg in Nigeria. And maybe I never will.

Our point of view on the matter is that if the egg has salmonella, it is too bad for the egg! Tout le monde knows it is like that other Creutzfeldt-Jakob disease rumour: if the cow is mad, once it's cooked 'well-well' it will be cured.

I think of that British health minister whose career ended over eggs in 1988, when she prematurely declared that most eggs in Britain had salmonella bacteria. Think of how impossible it would be for an elevated Nigerian public official to become public enemy number one or the Antichrist because he said something about an egg or because egg prices fell dramatically. What's an egg price anyway? Imagine trying to convince the average Nigerian that such a phenomenon might occur in Nigeria.

My maternal grandfather bred farmhouse chickens. He introduced me to guinea fowl, duck and turkey eggs; all as food, not as objects of contemplation. As a child I was taught how to carry an egg and how to move protesting chickens gently aside. When we were on holiday in Ososàmì, Ìbàdàn, my siblings and I had to collect chicken eggs as one of our chores. My younger sister, Morótì, has a scar near her eye that looks like the Igbo scarifications given to sickly children for protection. It is nothing so dramatic. We are not Igbo. It was only a furious chicken flying up in the air one day and pecking her for touching her eggs.

I know, to an acute degree, what my perfect chicken egg is like. Its shell must be brown paper. The yolk inside must have the energetic, luminous complexion of yellow maize. In size, it must be average. It can be small. When it is broken into hot oil, it must spread no further than three to four inches. The yolk must spread not at all but must drop with the weight and firmness of a spoon of àkàrà in new oil. I mean that it must fall into the pan and not budge.

And the egg must smell like an egg. This is not stating the obvious. In 2003 I lived in Houston, Texas for five months and in that time I did not encounter one fried egg that smelled like a fried egg, like that lavish, heady, tangy aroma of grease and creaminess not only sighing your name but calling for onions, green peppers, roasted mushrooms, sausages ... It was bizarre. It was the clincher, believe it or not, for whether or not I could live in Houston.

My nostalgia extends to crates for eggs. It seemed like my grandparents had thousands of them. Not the plastic ones, but the old dim grey cardboard ones that smelled of closed trunks and sawdust. They were always stacked up in the corner when not in use; enough of them to build a house to live in.

Once, on Twitter, with the uttering of six words, the famous food writer Ruth Reichl broke down my carefully built defences. All she had to say was 'soft custard of slowly scrambled eggs' and I teared up. Longing burrowed from my stomach to my heart. After some unjust metabolic illness several years ago, my body refuses to quietly digest eggs. After I eat them, I can recognise where all my nerves start and end. They converse loudly, and this goes on for days, even in my sleep. It might be bearable if they are speaking words, but my nerves speak painful electrical currents firing across my head and my arms.

So no eggs for me, no matter how excruciatingly I love and long for them. And there is nothing like a boiled egg: a freshly laid chicken egg boiled for seven or so minutes, still runny, yellow, white, precarious, beautiful to look at.

Yes, I am musing about half-cooked eggs even though I am very Nigerian. A more appropriate dish would be egg with sardines. Not 'sardine omelette', not a wobbly, wet formation considered close to an aberration in our cooking. If you offer a typical Nigerian steak tartare his face would not be able to contain the affront. Cooked 'well-well' is the desired degree of cooking for most, if not all foods. So what we like to say when we want to have a laugh at the expense of those global northerners who love to eat tinned beans and raw meat is that if only they would cook the beef and eggs 'well-well', there would be none of the hysterics about mad animals, and use-by dates.

Nigerian egg with sardines is a confidently aromatic, savoury pancake. Not dry. Not wet like a French omelette, but fully formed and fully cooked, served with formidable wedges of boiled yam or thick slices of buttered white bread. Not crusty bread (leave that to those skinny francophone boys in tight wax-print shirts) but that sweet, soft, pale bread affectionately called 'Agége bread'.

I can never cook eggs with sardines as well as nostalgia can. Two tablespoons of coconut oil, or King's groundnut oil in a frying pan. One tin of Titus sardines; the original thingamabob with the curly headed bust of someone (surely Titus) on a maroon and sepia tin. There are many tins of sardines that are red and sepia without the true head of Titus. Six eggs. A few thin slices of onion. Maybe one tomato, half a green pepper, and one yellow, scented-not-hot Scotch bonnet.

The Scotch bonnet is chopped extremely fine and tamed (the first lone ingredient) in the hot oil for a minute. The oil will have the powerful fragrance of hot pepper, which will linger tantalisingly well past the end of cooking. The tomato is chopped roughly and added to the frying Scotch bonnet with the onion slices and green peppers, and stirred until the onions are translucent. Drops of water are periodically added to the mixture to stop it from drying out. The sardines are broken up into large pieces with a fork and added to the beaten eggs with a good pinch of salt and a splash of water. The heat is turned down completely, and the beaten eggs and sardines are added to the mixture of tomatoes, onions and peppers in the pan.

As the eggs cook, the edges are lifted carefully, the pan tilted, and the uncooked eggs directed under the cooked parts to form a thick crust. The heat is turned up. Crisping at the edges is not a crime. It might even add a sophisticated point of view to the aroma of the food, especially if the oil is coconut. But one must manage that without overcooking the eggs.

I suppose there is something about not being able to have eggs that compels another, more acute level of obsession: staring at them, obsessing about shades of khaki, reading egg recipes that taste fabulous in my head, and collecting egg stories.

Stories like the one about Obásanjo and some students from Ìlarò Polytechnic who went on an excursion to Ota Farms, the ex-president's retirement home and extensive poultry farm. Obásanjo is discreetly informed that the students have stolen some of his eggs and that the eggs are hidden in their bags. The field trip ends and he bids the students farewell as a weary old man, with soft smiles and slow words of wisdom.

He goes in and calls the main gate. He instructs them that there is no need to search the students' bags as they exit, but the security men must give each and every bag an enthusiastic dusting down.

There are so many stories about Obásanjo that one must doubt them all, and one must believe them all. The one about him studying theology at the National Open University of Nigeria in particular should be taken with a pinch of salt. But eggs vindictively scrambled inside the students' bags sounds so much like him, so true to character. I can imagine him sitting reading his newspapers the next morning, enjoying the thought of egg, glasses, notebook and leather wallet sandwiches, the powerful, organic smell of raw eggs hounding the owners of the bags for weeks to come. I can see him sitting and chuckling, drinking his Lipton tea overwhelmed with milk and sugar, his viagra pill patiently waiting on the saucer, moving the train of his thoughts swiftly on to the next agenda of the day.

My favourite egg story, however, is about fainting at the sight of an innocuous egg. It may seem an absurd idea at first, but that is exactly what makes the story my favourite.

I have a friend who, as a child, had to go and live with his grandparents after his parents' marriage broke down. His father was a proud man who did not believe men should say they are sorry. His mother had another suitor. The matter had gone well past the attempts to pretend all was well, and live together like flatmates for the sake of the children. My friend's grandmother was an extraordinary woman. She was willing to embrace other people's children and care for them, but she was famous for her uncompromising views about everything, especially disciplinary issues. She was a hardback manual diligently compiled over sixty years. Many relatives sent their daughters to live with her because they wanted them to be like straight lines. They wanted them to have an unequivocal induction into life by a no-nonsense matriarch with the means and the heart to feed and care for children not her own, but like her own. These girls had to learn to keep a home, farm competently and take care of children. Their parents believed that, at home, the girls were too comfortable to take instructions to heart. They had to be thrown into the deep end at my friend's grandparents' house.

The grandmother apparently saw through everything – doors, walls, closed lips – and she read minds and bodies too. She could tell by the angle of a woman's bottom whether she 'was fornicating' or 'contemplating fornication'.

If you were on your way out of her room and your head caught a cobweb, you would be grounded and made to sit with her the whole day. It was clear that if you were allowed out, something bad and irrevocable was going to happen.

There was an impromptu test for virginity administered to all the girls and young women in the house. On the relevant morning, they would be made to wait outside the testing room, not in a formal queue but an informal positioning of reluctant, apprehensive bodies sitting, standing, leaning, fainting from fear.

The apprehension was not unreasonable. In those days mothers told their daughters all manner of stories to try to get them to abstain from sex. From the minute a baby girl was born, she was inundated with stories, with nuance, and taught, to head-of-a-pin precision, 'the manual'. In those days teenage girls gave a wide berth to those delicate-looking old women who sat outside their homes from dawn till dusk.

Those women were like my friend's grandmother: they saw and sensed everything. As you were passing, a hand would suddenly reach for you with a strength you could never ascribe to old bones, and as quick as anything, you would feel the other hand cupping your crotch. The weight of the pudenda in the old woman's hand would immediately convey to her if you had just been with a man.

What mother had the energy to chase these frivolous little girls around? You started your work from birth to ensure your bones didn't break handling young girls. You told them that if you kiss a boy you immediately become pregnant. If a man sees you naked, you become pregnant. If you see a naked man, if you are fondled, you become pregnant. With twins. Some girls had become pregnant just by having a man brush against them on a busy street. It was dangerously contagious, this pregnancy business.

It was not that this was a naïve world in which all the girls one encountered were virgins; it was more like a world not yet force-fed sex, definitely not versed in every minute detail of the sexual encounter. Tins of cigarettes, toilet-soap and bottles of Venus de Milo body cream were not yet sold with sex.

On hot days, elderly women might be seen selling their wares bare-breasted in the marketplace. There were women who put their babies on their backs and passed elongated breasts under their arms to suckle their babies. Breasts on many women were functional appendages, like long flexible flasks toughened far beyond the handling for pleasure. They were sturdy comforters. The words 'oloyan pandoro' – breasts like rowing paddles – were a jovial description of elongated breasts proudly abandoned to the whims of age and gravity and the careless breastfeeding of toddlers with teeth.

By the time a young woman had spent long hours on the farm, fried a vat of gari, taken turns to cook meals from scratch and cared for the younger children in the household, sex was possible, desirable, hormonally pertinent, but not a life-threatening condition that needed seeing to. Sexual energy was gainfully employed ... and in that unique matriarch's house, there was the fear of the egg.

To be sure there were girls who knew everything and had done everything, but they dared not live in my friend's grandmother's house because they would never pass the impromptu test with the egg. Many of the girls who lived in there would not be 100 per cent certain if sex was viral or if pregnancy was contagious; not until their wedding night. So they waited in that line with great apprehension. It was about that boy who sneezed on you in school and the possibility that you were three months gone. It was about the quick fondling behind the walls of yams strung together with lengths of grass. The matriarch might catch a whiff of green. It was also about the invasiveness of the investigation. The test was a deterrent. It was a warning. The grandmother didn't need it to tell who was a virgin and who was not.

It was like that surreptitious sign you got when you were out with your parents visiting their friends and you were asked if you would like something to eat. Yes, you would! Indeed you would love something to eat. The smell from the kitchen is making your stomach growl and you've lost your senses thinking of what exactly is cooking and if you will be offered any and if and if ... and everything in your body language is already saying yes until your eyes meet your mother's and there is a flash, an expression so very subtle that no one but you sees it. It is meant for you alone and it is a firm warning that you must not even think of accepting the offer of food. You must not move a muscle that suggests you are accepting the offer. You must not even entertain a hangdog look of appeal. The answer is superimposed on your senses like the sureness of electromagnetic waves before telephone wires. It is not the fear of God. It is the fear of the matriarch.

The grandmother's instrument of investigation was a small free-range egg. You would have to lie back, hitch up your dress, close your eyes for goodness' sake, and instinctively clench. You hoped for the best with what little you knew of your body or of rudimentary biology or the phenomenon of contagious pregnancy. Whether you liked it or not, whether you were willing or not. Whether or not you were clever enough to think of the ambivalence of values. Whether you thought it was unfair that the boys in the house could do what they liked and fondle whomever, or wondered why pregnancy seemed to be the punishment for sex.

'Cluck cluck!'

If you could reverse-hatch that egg, your life was not going to be worth living. The excuse that your hymen 'broke during physical and health education' was never going to fly with this omniscient grandmother. All hell would break loose if the egg passed from the grandmother's hand into that dark part of your anatomy you knew so little about. Before the week ran out your parents would come to get you even if they were coming from Kotangora.

It never happened though. Not in all the years my friend lived with his grandmother did a girl fail the egg test. The fear of that egg was overwhelming. And you never looked at an egg the same way ever again. It wasn't possible. The egg was such a ubiquitous object that you were reminded constantly of contagious pregnancies. You reached for warm eggs laid by chickens and you thought of the mysterious regions that produced eggs. Of what it is like for a chicken to pass an egg and whether it is the effort that makes them so irate.

You would not hold it and be consoled by its khaki blandness. You would not tear up at the sight of eggs. You would not love Ruth Reichl because of one line that had both custard and eggs in it. Even when the wedding night comes and goes and you have permission to fondle and be fondled, the sense of shame will be ingrained. You will wonder about the shape of things; the discrepancy between that which is oval and that which is long and tube-like. You would think of the wages of sin. By then of course you will understand that there is nothing like a Bluetooth pregnancy and you will feel both ashamed at your own foolishness and angry that you allowed yourself that degree of ingenuousness. When you are bearing your children you will wonder if this is a good or bad thing. You will wonder if perhaps that is why chickens are so foolish and confused ... too much coming and going, too little understanding of the reasons why. You will sleep and imagine yourself turning into a large chicken but you won't tell anyone because of the shame.

Sweet Stolen Waters

One February we were inundated with lime-green plantains ripening to unblemished yellow. They were the sort of plantains you can't buy in the market, the kind Lagosians only see in their dreams. Never, ever in real life. They are luscious and thick and the yellow colour of ripeness burns holes in the retinas. Frying them is sacrilegious; they must be steamed in their skins. When they are removed from their skins they look too good to eat, like beautiful golden rods. Their texture is soft, spreading slightly on the tongue. They're sweet with hints of treacle, hot all the way into the depths of the stomach, every atom delicious in every ramification.

I sat in my kitchen brooding over the fact that they had come: some as a present from a friend from Port Harcourt; some purchased on the expressway on a journey from Ikom, up north in Cross River State. It was a shame to have perfection in such abundance. They would ripen quicker than we could eat them, running from perfection to old age in a matter of days. They wouldn't taste the same once they were stored in the refrigerator. I had to give many of them away, knowing that I might not run into more of them for the rest of the year. I brooded because I'm a worrier, my glass often half empty. Instead of enjoying the sight and arrival of the beautiful plantains, I was annoyed at the expediency of giving even one of them away.

It had been a peculiar beginning to the year. Two weeks into the middle of January, I drove through state housing streets in Calabar and found heaps of fresh white maize for sale. *In January!* Fresh maize is supposed to be harvested in late April or in May, but at that time the previous year you could barely find one decent cob of maize in Calabar. And when you sent to the village, they told you the chickens had eaten them all. It was their diplomatic way of confirming that it was a bad year and they planned to keep what was harvested for themselves.

I bought some of the January maize and the smell of them wafting from the boot of the car almost caused a small accident as I rushed home to steam them with pellets of sea salt. In my mind, I still conjure up the bursting of sweet tender kernels, strands of silk wedged between my teeth, and the intoxication of hot, salty, maize-fragranced water sucked from the cob. My family sat round the pot of maize in the evening and made quick, noisy work of it. We didn't dwell too long on the abnormality or illegality of finding fresh maize in January. The sweetness of stolen waters helped put all our consciences to bed.

The week before, we'd had an April storm, the sort that carries roofs and topples old plantain trees. It was gorgeous but uncomfortable, the way postcards with pictures of hawking children are. They might be romantic, beautiful, but you know that it is a naïve, sad representation of the truth. The imagery is gorgeous; the destruction is heartbreaking.

When it rained again the next week I found myself asking, bewildered, if it really was the dry season. January felt more like harvest than August, the true harvest time, had. The nectarous, fat-noduled carrots begging to be juiced that normally arrived in November had only come in January. The tomatoes felt out of place at the beginning of the New Year. They had no tartness, but were so sweet that a pot of delicious stew could be made as simply as a shrug of the shoulders.

I wondered what the farmers were thinking. There was a time when you could count on the weather being predictable: dry season, wet season, August break, dry season, harmattan. Now, it rains when it likes. The sun blazes when it likes. Harmattan stays till January, February, even March. It's cold in July and the paediatric ward is overwhelmed with appointments for ailing children. The previous year presented a few alarming, dust-cloaked days that the Nigerian meteorological agency informed us were days of acid rain. They felt just like dusty harmattan days.

In 2010 the agency warned farmers not to be deceived into planting crops early because of irregular rains, but to clear their land in preparation for planting and wait for the normal scheduled planting season. If the farmers had listened, we wouldn't have had fresh maize in January. Nigerian farming is, after all, a balance of rules and belief. Yes, you would normally plant maize in March – that's a rule based on science – but when you are planting maize, you must do so in absolute silence because maize have ears and it is rumoured that they respond to negative remarks. They are sometimes offended by farmers' idle chatter. That's custom. Most Nigerian farmers don't question what they know on the inside. They just abide by it, and when you ask why, the answer is that their fathers and fathers' fathers, planted maize in sacred silence and it yields a bountiful harvest.

While the world is dialoguing about climate change, global warming, freak storms, changes in precipitation and rainfall patterns and how they affect food production, I feel a little bit like a child marvelling at the colours on the back of a snake without worrying that it is deadly. The delight I feel at eating these foods out of season is 80 per cent *because* they are out of season. I have to force myself to think about what is really happening.

Thomas C. Schelling, the Nobel Prize-winning economist, warns that developing countries – i.e. us – don't have the capacity to adapt to climate change. We don't have scientific assistance to agriculture. Unlike the West, our income is not climate-resistant and we have not prepared ourselves to respond to climate shifts with appropriate changes in crops and cultivation techniques. Instincts alone will certainly not do. I really wonder what Nigerian farmers are thinking.

Forgotten Seasoning Secrets

Everyone, without exception, owns sketchy memories of a grandmother who hand-shelled her egúsí (seeds of the bittermelon gourd) before toasting them, milling them by hand and adding them to soup. In the context of challenging careers, days of endless traffic jams, stressed children and husbands, pedestrian meals prepared by the cook-steward, and the consoling obsequiousness of instant noodles, these memories are evocative remnants folded deep in the consciousness of the urban Nigerian wife, mother, and young, upwardly mobile female in pencil skirt and heels. These memories have no contemporary relevance. They are at stringent odds with French manicures, asking way too much of the average Nigerian with a long wearying working day.

I intentionally filed away the process of hand-shelling egúsí for over thirty years. Once, when I was a child, my mother brought home a large, fragile bamboo basket of unshelled egúsí, and I vividly remember my irritation, my mind turning over how on earth she could have lost her way in the market and come back with such a large basket of futility. Why would anyone buy unshelled egúsí when they could effortlessly buy the shelled?

Fast-forward thirty years to my reintroduction to honest, lovingly handled and shelled, meticulously clean beige seeds rightfully sold for an arm and leg at the market and rushed home to dry roast in a pan on the hob. The pan moves back and forth until the smell of toasting seeds fills the air. The sounds, like popcorn opening up into white petals, initially catch me off guard and then tantalisingly stir my senses. The seeds brown, grow rotund bellies, exhale nuttiness and jump out of the pan. The question then becomes how I could have cooked for so long and remained so naïve of this simple yet charming process.

Michael Mukolu, a friend of the family, filled in the cultural blanks for me. He drew a picture in words of women instinctively shelling egúsí as easily as breathing, hands skilfully accompanying the conversation. They did it during the day or sat outside in the cooling night air, minds winding down before bed. Shelling baskets of egúsí was no chore if you knew how, and you'd been brought up with the process woven into the fabric of your day. If you had two women sitting and shelling egúsí and a guest entered the house, she would join them seamlessly without drawing attention to doing so. In the context of rural living, without the antisocial intrusion of televisions, shelling egúsí was conversational aid, communal grease, industriousness and therapy all deliciously wound together. If my mother had painted this picture all those years back instead of telling me to 'Shell them because I said so!' perhaps I would not be such a cultural idiot.

In addition to cultural savvy is the million years of difference in taste between machine-shelled and hand-shelled egúsí. I am not sure if there is even a scientific explanation for this, but might not the industrial machine used for shelling be taking off parts that hand-shelling keeps intact? This sounds so unscientific I am ashamed to say it, yet the hand-shelled seeds are nuttier in aroma and taste, with a layer of enhanced flavour on top of the familiar egúsí flavour. Toasting adds yet another layer. Machine-shelled egúsí categorically won't rise and pop like the hand-shelled.

The other day I was toasting egúsí in preparation for cooking a pot of soup, and I distractedly put a few seeds in my mouth. I was compelled to turn off the fire under the soup and sit down to a snack of toasted seeds. My five-year-old son came in, had a few seeds, and wrestled the bowl out of my hands. It took three attempts before we got past shovelling down the seeds to making the soup. I marvelled that in all those years of wondering what to give my children as healthy snacks, nutritious, toasted egúsí never crossed my mind.

If one puts perfumed dawadawa in a pot with nutty palm oil, toasted ground egúsí and ground crayfish, the result is a dramatic enhancement of flavour. One could even go ahead, if not impaired by a French manicure, and grind the seeds and crayfish in a mortar instead of the dry mill of a blender, adding yet another dimension of flavour. It was the anticipation of this amalgamation of flavours that made our grandmothers bear the effort of cooking the pot of egúsí soup in the longwinded, detailed manner inclusive of toasting of seeds and grinding in mortars. I can imagine that they would, justifiably, turn their noses up at our relatively insipid contemporary versions.

A Beautiful Girl Named Ogbono

Ogbono soup is the classic 'draw' soup. It requires both technique and light-handedness to create the perfect degree of draw. In another world, the word 'draw' would be an instruction, and the person to whom it was said might obligingly get out a piece of paper and a pencil and draw a bowl of soup. In our world, 'draw' is defined as the animation of the soup. The quality of 'drawing' has nothing to do with making pictorial representations of any kind but refers to that thing that connects two kissers moving apart to catch their breath: organic strings pulling in two directions. It means 'mucilaginous': the structural elasticity that creates the shape of a climbing whirlpool in a pot on the fire. Structure not texture: a kind of upside-down soufflé-type fabric with stretch. Both okro and ogbono soups are mucilaginous. They are both 'draw' soups but their textures are dissimilar.

I have all kinds of romantic notions about ogbono that have no grounding in long-standing cooking methodologies and sometimes not even in reality. These ideas are constantly colliding with the margins of technique. Perhaps if I had cooked ogbono all my life the familiarity would have curbed my irreverence, my flights of imagination, my constant need to tweak. I personally don't consider this restlessness a bad starting point for a relationship with a pot of soup. The purist might. I know a particular Efik food purist who takes it all very personally. My first attempt at ogbono was only a few years ago, and I tweaked it to the point where my mother and a friend who were in the background calling out instructions threw their hands up in despair and declared that what I was cooking was no longer ogbono soup. I think the last straw was the thin slices of onion I put in.

The name 'ogbono' niggles. It is inelegant, like trying to talk with a mouth full of hot yam. Even 'àpon', the Yorùbá word for ogbono, sounds equally malignant. Ogbono is a beautiful girl named without considering how the blend of letters that make up her name sounds. No matter how time-honoured the name, if it tumbles around the tongue and lips, it somehow takes away from the girl's beauty doesn't it?

The best ogbono soup I've ever eaten is from twenty years ago. Although my mother had instructed me not to ask for seconds when eating outside our home (in fact, I was instructed not to accept offers of food at all if she were not present), I took full, excited advantage of her absence and asked for thirds. I was promptly put in my place with that sort of bruising facial expression that said I must be very badly brought up indeed. I didn't care! The soup was that good, well worth the attempt and rebuff.

In my mind's eye, I can bring up the soup in the vivid colour of diluted palm oil: not moody dark brown or red, but stunning turmeric. The soup was lightly viscose, velvety, embellished with luscious, fresh giant prawns. As if to prove how skilled the 'Benin aunty' who made the soup was, I have tried uncountable times but never been able to replicate the attractiveness, the perfect degree of draw, the flawless timing allotted to the prawns at the end of cooking so that their pink, taut flesh detonated between my teeth. I have not even been able to replicate that exact shade of hunger-inducing turmeric. I suspect that my memory keeps raising the bar on cooking this soup to the point where I could never cook it as well as I remember it. Or it might be that I could never, ever cook it as skilfully as it was cooked that day because Benin women have a reputation for cooking the best ogbono soup in all of Nigeria. The best in the world, really, since ogbono is a Nigerian soup.

I often hear people talk about ogbono soup with reverence, longing, and unmistakable notes of addiction in their voice. To this soup alone have I heard sermons on the necessity of getting the draw just right. The draw cannot be half-hearted in any way; it has to be fully committed, to the degree of 'well-well'. To this soup alone are there reams of nostalgia on 'returning home to the village', whether at Christmas or for an impromptu visit, where one of the obligatory rites of the visit will be ogbono soup cooked with stockfish in a native pot by an elderly matriarch.

Ogbono soup does have something about it. Pinpointing the thing is so elusive that people have ended up in the arms of cliché trying to define it. Ogbono is often referred to as the King of Soups, but that title feels lazy. It sounds like an accolade that a man with a limited imagination resorts to in describing an unusual woman: he can't eloquently express what makes her fascinating so he summarises that she is a queen.

Ogbono, in any case, cannot be the King of Soups because it is too self-effacing. There are soups that are made up of expensive ingredients, take hours to put together, and declare their own glory more confidently. A child can rustle up ogbono with someone standing by calling out instructions, maybe helping with the liquidity. But the palate, no matter how naïve, knows ogbono soup cooked by an old hand. All of its qualities – its mouthfeel, the unique aroma, the temperament of the soup when it is cooked right, the way it moves in the pot when it has been handled perfectly – is in the skill of cooking. This is, I think, the reason for going back home to eat ogbono. There is no beginner's luck in cooking the soup skilfully. In that way, ogbono becomes the quintessential representation of the Nigerian craving for draw, for mucilage. The likelihood of eating the genuine article, the kind that makes the eater want to marry the first woman he kisses, is all down to technique. Yet this is the technique that I am often at loggerheads with.

Bush mango seeds, the condiment used to create the ogbono draw, are themselves fascinating. Ground up, they provide the draw in the soup. The seeds are a subsistence living for many women in villages in Cross River State. The bush mango looks nothing like the mangoes one is used to seeing – the kidney-shaped ones that dip in their bellies. Bush mangoes are dull green, round and small; the size and shape of undeveloped oranges, but with a sweet smell that makes you want to devour them. Some people eat bush mangoes, but they are mainly considered elephant dessert. It takes an inordinate amount of energy and time to crack open the mangoes, retrieve the seeds, dry them and sell them to market traders.

The cost of bush mango seeds in Calabar is kept low by the seeds coming across the water on trawlers from Bamenda in Cameroon. They are stacked high in old rice sacks on the boats, warily making the three-day journey on rough waters. One is forced to wonder at the divine intervention that keeps the boat and seeds from ending up at the bottom of the Atlantic.

I have imagined the dimensions of an old world where they were a form of currency. Their weight is right, as is their click-clack sound on the kitchen's granite surface and the taupe to tan colours of the worn-edged, lozenge-shaped seeds. All these agree with the integrity of my imagined currency, but there is a paradox in the fact that ogbono seeds feel like old-world coins in your hand. In large quantities, in the bigger picture, they represent hundreds of thousands of naira; a kind of dancing, elusive wealth. For the midddleman from Cameroon smuggling ogbono seeds, dried Cameroonian peppers, and white-fermented honey from the Cameroonian highlands into Calabar, the sale of ogbono seeds contributes substantially to the earnings from smuggling" But for the women on farms knocking open mangoes with stones, cracking open the seeds, and sunning them over days of erratic sunshine, the eventual sale of those seeds will never, ever be the making of a fortune.

I've heard people say that the old ogbono seeds, the ones that have dried leisurely, are the best for soup because they give the ideal draw. I've heard other people claim it is the newer seeds that are best, that the old seeds have a strong aroma and give a thickness to the draw that makes it smelly and heavy. Both sides are often just favouring the kind of soup they've been brought up eating. The arguments abound on the lightness or heaviness of the draw; on whether the soup in its most authentic form is dry or wet. Dry means that all the meat that goes into the soup is smoked or air-dried: bushmeat, stockfish, dry-smoked fish. Wet means the way I like it: with fresh prawns and lightly smoked catfish, both meats added in at the very end.

In my opinion, the dryness and wetness also determines the effort put in the stock. If the soup is dry, then there is no need to go through the effort of preparing good stock because the meat will carry the necessary flavour. If the soup is wet, then the stock has to be good because the flavour of the soup depends on it. The prawns and catfish that I put in at the end fulfil the need to have some kind of meat in the soup. They are really there to represent themselves.

The dried seeds have a lifetime of about five months outside the refrigerator. Presumably the best seeds are never on the vendor's table when you go to buy ogbono in the market. You have to ask the vendor for the superior stuff and ten out of ten times she will reach behind her for another bag secured with twine, dip the cup into it and sell you that instead. I wonder if this truly means that, if you don't ask, you'll get the substandard seeds, or if it is all just a play on your intelligence. A tin cup of ogbono seeds, falsely heaped with the help of the vendor's cupped palm on top of the lip of the cup, costs N500. (One wonders at the drama of forming a heap on top of the cup. Why not get a bigger cup?) The seeds are passed through an old-fashioned mill that needs winding with a lever.

The grinding of the ogbono releases a sweetish smell begging for pepper soup spices. I lay the blame for the irrepressible need to tweak at the feet of the sweet perfume of ground ogbono. I want to enhance that smell, turn it up to the fullest volume. It pleads for cinnamon and grated root ginger at the very least.

But you won't find many people tweaking ogbono. The most basic way in which to cook it is to put some ground seeds at the bottom of a pot with a few drops of palm oil, enough to turn the colour of the seeds from beige to mince-in-tomato. The ogbono is fried until it has drunk up all the oil, and stirred until the granules are unctuous and even. Then plain water or stock is gradually measured into the pot until the granules dissolve evenly and swell up into a smooth, whirling, swelling, collapsing soup. The soup is allowed to boil evenly and well. Some people require that a quantity of the soup burns into a skin of flavour at the bottom of the pot. The soup is seasoned, and the meat or fish is added. Chopped pumpkin leaves (ugwu) are tossed in last, and it is ready.

The minimalism of that description might give the wrong impression, but it's the simplicity of the soup that allows it to showcase the quality of the ingredients and the skill of the cook. The soup is best cooked with first-rate palm oil produced before the month of March, after the very first heavy rains. The clusters of palm fruit are not harvested until these rains have descended. The winds that accompany the first rains are usually the most powerful, the most destructive of the season. They characteristically pull down old plantain trees and electricity poles, and take off roofs as effortlessly as blowing off a woman's head-tie. The villagers in Boki, where my oil comes from, wait for this rain and wind, for the way it vacuums chaff and dust out of the palm kernel clusters. It's a lot like using a vacuum cleaner to get an eyelash out of your eye: a rude overstatement. After the first rains the palm fruits are brought down. The oil hand-pressed from them is blood red, not bright red. When held up to the light, the head is as clear as watered down red wine. The bottom has no more than two inches of bright orange sediment. This sediment is shaken into the rest of the oil before it is dispensed for cooking or eating. The oil never coagulates at room temperature, its water content is the minimum for oils throughout the year, and it has a deep, fresh scent.

For me the less meat and fish in a pot of ogbono soup, the better, but I will say something about the addition of smoked crayfish: that condiment that is as ubiquitous in the kitchen as salt, and as esteemed as the Metropolitan of the Cross River State Presbyterian Church. You can't talk negatively about it. If you do, the room will go quiet and everyone will look at you as if you cursed loudly in church. The typical Cross Riverian woman cooking ogbono will put in ground crayfish, but for me smoked catfish ground to fine bits of thread do very efficiently what ground crayfish does for the Cross Riverian, and more subtly. The aroma of smoked crayfish is a big bully; at the end of cooking, all the olfactory qualities of the soup are defined by smoked crayfish.

For heat in ogbono soup, I use both dried/ground and fresh Cameroonian peppers. There is logic to this: fresh Cameroonian peppers are extremely aromatic and their confidence lasts through the long simmering of stock, but at the end of the cooking the heat mellows slightly and the aroma remains strong. The mellowing creates a comfortable degree of heat: tempered, yet adding to the other flavours in the soup. The combination of the leftover aroma with oily smoked catfish is an irresistible backdrop for the other flavours in the soup. Cameroonian peppers are grown in fertile soil dark as chocolate in Santa Mbei, Akum and Pinyin, and in Cameroon's breadbasket, Bamenda. These peppers are special; their smell, flavour and powerful travelling heat are unique, incomparable to habaneros from anywhere else in the world.

My stock is the real heart of controversy because it is the medium of rebellion. Many Nigerians don't cook with cinnamon but I believe the sweetness of the bark complements and enhances the sweetness of ground ogbono seeds. Cinnamon is strong yet gentlemanly; a team player. It never forces its identity on the food. Over long periods of cooking, it blends and yields, enhancing the finished product. But no matter how many times I've tried to recommend cinnamon as a natural complement to ogbono, I get the fiercest resistance from Nigerian cooks, so I have stopped talking about it. When my guests come over and I give them ogbono soup with cinnamon in it, they can't eat enough of it, nor can they decipher, without a hint, that there is a 'foreigner' in the soup.

Cooking ogbono soup with spices is not an entirely foreign idea. My friend from Benue State cooks her ogbono with ginger when she doesn't cook it with shredded ugwu. She might not agree with my degree of tweaking, yet we agree that part of the skilful cooking of ogbono has to do with what is playing in the background. My stock sometimes has ginger in it, sometimes onions, sometimes cumin seeds, often turmeric and cayenne. Stock is always relevant in my cooking because most of my food is slow-cooked and I love layering flavours, but as I pointed out earlier, many people will cook ogbono without all the fanfare of slow-cooked stock.

Sometimes when I need a strong pepper-soup-like brew as the base for the ogbono soup, I do the following:

3 uda pods (selim peppers)
1 teaspoon uziza pepper (cubeb peppercorns) (a complement to the ginger root)
½ teaspoon freshly ground bush pepper
4 teaspoons whole dawadawa (the black split pea is very attractive on the face of the soup)
¼ teaspoon fermented ogiri (fermented castor oil seeds)

1 inch ginger root
2 teaspoons dried ground Cameroonian peppers
½ teaspoon cinnamon
Sweet salt
6-8 cups of water

I use a local earthenware pot, so at least a cup of water will be lost in cooking. In the pot, combine the water, a quarter of a white cod (stockfish) head, some smoked catfish head bones, four heaped teaspoons of smoked catfish belly ground in a dry mill, and the spices and condiments. Allow it to boil, then simmer for at least an hour and a half. One and a half cooking spoons of palm oil are added thirty minutes into the simmering of the stock, but it can be put in at the beginning of cooking. The bones are fished out of the stock when it is ready for the ground ogbono. For a stronger impression of selim peppers, refresh the uda over a small flame, then grind it up and add it to the pot at the beginning of cooking. The heat is turned up because the boiling stock is needed to constitute the ground ogbono.

I don't like my ogbono to draw 'well-well'. I use two level teaspoons of ground ogbono seeds for one pot of soup. Place the ground seeds in a bowl that allows for brisk whisking with a fork, and spoon boiling stock directly over it. The stock needs to be added carefully and it needs to be boiling hot otherwise the constituted ogbono will have lumps in it. With each addition of stock and whisking, the structure of the ogbono and stock should yield more and more until it is a cloud of golden mucilage. The elasticity of the mixture should be such that it merges easily with the rest of the stock when it is deposited in the pot. I pour the ogbono into one corner of the stockpot and allow the stock to embrace it in its own time. The heat is again turned down, the pot covered.

I realise that one of the requirements for cooking ogbono is never to close the pot with a lid. This technicality is meant to keep the mucilage at the right thickness, but I don't want my mucilage thick. I want a more delicately structured soup. I *always* want a more delicately structured soup.

Ogbono soup must be allowed to come fully to the boil and do so for a few minutes; otherwise it will cause a stomach ache. Peeled, deveined prawns are added five minutes before the end of cooking. Ugwu is put in last of all, the instant before the soup is taken off the fire and covered.

In my opinion, structurally perfect ogbono soup swirls up in the pot when it is boiling yet the cooking spoon breaks up the mucilage with ease. The draw is not so dramatic that you have to wave the spoon around to cut up the strings of mucilage. It isn't so thick that the morsel of gari can't carry the soup to the mouth without leaving lines of soup everywhere and making a mess on the plate. Most people disagree with me on this. For them, the mess is the surest sign of a structurally accurate ogbono soup.

When this soup is skilfully cooked, there is a synergism of structure, texture and aroma. There is smoothness in the movement and feel of the soup. There is an underlying sweetness to the savouriness. The texture should always be velvety on the tongue and in the mouth. The appeal of ogbono, I think, is ultimately this mouthfeel and the undercurrent of sweetness in the soup's aroma. It's mucilage cooked to the pinnacle of comfort food. Briskly cooked prawns complement the soup perfectly because their texture offers a yielding,

Henshaw Town Beach Market

Esuk: An Efik word for a waterfront location where there is commercial trading activity involving men, boats, ships, fishing, timber/wood logs ... all sorts of exchanges going on.

Ivor Ekpe

Henshaw Town Beach Market or Marina Market, known as the 'esuk' in Old Calabar, Calabar-South Local Government Area, is the reason you would find me on the marina on a sweltering Sunday morning. I had lived in Calabar for five years before I realised the profound span of history that the Calabar Marina represents, but that isn't entirely my fault. Consider the Lagos Marina, Broad Street, Balógun Street, UBA House at one end, Cowry Bridge at the other, lanes of roaring traffic in-between. The First Bank (the first branch in Lagos), Stallion Bank, Union Bank, NAL building (now Sterling Bank). Oníkàn Stadium, Muson Centre, The Old Governor General's House, NITEL, Cathedral Church of Christ, the General Post Office, the NPA building, the Ministry of Transport, the General Hospital. The Bank of Industry Building that used to be the Ministry of Defence, PHCN that used to be NEPA (but Sàngó the god of thunder has not left the building), Mamman Kontagora House ... And how on earth can I forget Mr Biggs!

Everything - culture, art, architecture, narcissism, new money, old money, history, pinstripe suits, area boys, fast food, slow food - absolutely everything that Lagos is about is on the marina. It might be stating the obvious, but there is no other hub of commerce quite like that stretch of real estate. Imagine going there in 220 years and finding rubble, a few old buildings still standing, fishermen casting lines into the water, drinking warm beer and talking about the village at Christmas. Imagine finding nothing there but Oke-arin market. Then imagine the majority of the residents of Lagos State being sure that the Lagos Marina was never more than a humble waterfront and the site of the Oke-arin market. It sounds impossible and ridiculous and tragic but that is what has happened here on the marina in Calabar.

Cadbury chocolate has lived for two hundred years. They make it look so easy.

I am standing on hallowed ground, on the banks of the Atlantic where one of the most vibrant marinas and international seaports once stood. This was the first Nigerian capital city, once the seat of government of the Niger Coast, Southern and Oil Rivers protectorates, with a successful merchant colony that traded in 'red gold' (palm oil) and Igbo slaves (30 per cent of the 2.5 million slaves shipped off the west coast were processed through the slave ports in Duke Town). Calabar's waters were one of the hottest trading zones on the West Coast of Africa and in the world. In the Bradt travel guide on Nigeria, Lizzie Williams mentions how World War II might have made the Calabar Marina even more illustrious because palm oil was used as industrial oil for military machines.[16]

There was a time when the fish wharf on the waterfront was as busy as Billingsgate fish market, and every mother,

---

[16] Lizzie Williams, *Nigeria: The Bradt Travel Guide*, 3rd Edition (Bucks: Bradt Travel Guides, 2012).

grandmother and wife worth her salt took a walk down to the esuk to buy fish for the day's meal. By 5 a.m., the trawlers and canoes would be depositing their catch at the wharf and the efficient wife would be on her way down the hill in the crisp, foggy weather to buy fresh crayfish and half a pound of nkonko. I can hear the rolling of palm oil drums on the quay on their way to the ships, sailors telling smutty stories, logging boats dragging timber across the waterfront ...

But all I am seeing and hearing are ghosts. One of the most significant ports on the West African coast has got up and disappeared into thin air. It is a Wednesday morning and it is perfectly quiet. The stretch that you can walk briskly in perhaps forty-five minutes starts from Ansa-Ewa, past Hawkins Street, a.k.a 'depot', where you can eat a plate of hot rice and dog-meat stew for breakfast if you like. The cemetery is also there, past the Brotherhood of the Cross and Star headquarters. Then comes the sloping descent to the waterfront, where the market is garrulous on Thursdays and Sundays, and nods in and out of sleep on other days. The okrika (second-hand clothing) market is the biggest event on a Thursday, not fish. It animates the Beach Market to a degree of what the marina might have been like. On a Thursday, the money exchanging hands over second-hand clothing smuggled on trawlers through Cameroon is mind-boggling.

Towering abandoned ships are anchored at the edge of the water. On the frontage of office buildings with the strong smell of old glory on them are the names CFAO, Elder Dempster Agencies, First Bank plc (the second branch that opened in Nigeria), UPC Nigeria, UAC and their subsidiary hotel, G.B. Ollivant, John Holt plc, Harbour Import/Export ... They were all proudly housed here; and you can still feel the presumptuous assumption that the world would never change, that in a thousand years from the time those buildings were put there, you would still find a clerk at Elder Dempster issuing Bills of Lading.

I can only imagine what a weekday in this place was like in 1895. A woman like me would not be strolling along here at 11 a.m. trying to buy crayfish! The Atlantic Ocean is just there. To think that it has watched things unravel for hundreds of years and it's just there. The same. This water is not water with which one can be on a first name basis. It is dark, secretive, moody. It gets turbulent and quarrelsome. When the tide comes in, it is like the tantrum of a child who won't be appeased. The people who one sees on it were born on it, have lived on it for lifetimes, yet you will hear of fishermen, sinewy and strong, drowning on a clear, beautiful day.

Flying boats (not real flying boats, but seasoned camwood boats with engines, named 'flying boats' because the engines make them move considerably faster than canoes), yachts and large ships give the impression that the water is deep from the very point where it meets land. Farther down is the boat park. People sit on benches, watching the water as if mesmerised by it, waiting for a flying boat to take them to Oron, Creek Town, the Marina Park, Tinapa or Le Meridien at Uyo. There is a considerably more gentrified quay further down, its entrance guarded by a wrought iron mammywata, where you can take a luxurious yacht to the same places with white leather seats and D'banj playing on the radio. I suppose these things are a necessity for the tourists. But before that quay is the Volvo Market Cooperative with the fishwives sitting outside, aloof, deep in conversation.

When you've stood long enough trying to get their attention while the conversation continues as if you're not there, you'll get the idea and simply say what you want. One of them is wearing a Rolling Stones t-shirt for goodness' sake. Their cooperative building only has one wall, like a stage prop. Behind it water laps against what is left of the concrete flooring. In the evening, when the tide comes in, seawater overwhelms the concrete floor. In a few years' time, the whole house will be gone.

Once, I went in there and found a baby alligator bound as tightly as a catfish on its way to be smoked. The alligator was waiting to be picked up by some Chinese men. Its stillness was so intense, its unflinching wide eyes so unsettling. It could have been five times its size, and free in the swamps. The women were quite sure that it was going to be eaten.

Instead of the wharf, this cooperative is what we have now for fresh fish: one or two women on the beach at the market, nothing like that large, buzzing warehouse and the urgent enterprise it represented. Never presume that the fish is going to be cheap because it is caught behind the house. Fish is not cheap in Calabar. Fishwives often turn eloquent in expressing this fact. An elderly fishwife once looked me in the eye and said, 'Fish is cocaine!' Her comparison is not flawed: negotiations for catfish may start at twelve thousand naira, a figure not too far from a hundred dollars.

Parts of Marina Road brighten and dim, some parts close, sinister and quiet, while others struggle in secretive patches of enterprise. It would be a mistake to walk this road at the wrong time of the day.

Hotels? The only aspiring one is Nsisak Seaside, on your way out of Marina Road, after the hairpin turn onto Eyo Edem.

It's an affront to the word 'hotel'. An incongruous sign on the frontage of the top floor reads 'fully air-conditioned'.

A man shouts 'Udo!' like he has a mouth full of okro soup, and you can hear it all the way to the top of the road. On the opposite side of Marina Road, half-concrete, half-mud houses are built into the sides of a hill. On top of the hill is the famous Duke Town, infamous for its slave history. The houses are homes, shops and small bukas, which I suppose are still there because of the patronage of the construction workers on the other side of the road.

Ivor Ekpe, an Efik friend, had to define 'esuk' for me and I was glad I did not try to myself. It is like mentioning the name of a country. It means 'wharf' and 'port'. It means 'to drop' or 'offload'. It means 'beach' or 'beach-head' or 'leave' or 'leave behind'. It draws a picture of the past, of hundreds of years of interacting with the marina and the Atlantic Ocean. Living on it and off it. If you've lived long enough, you'll have seen slaves and palm oil and British ships and shipping clerks. Mimusop and camwood being dragged along the water, onunu trees, gliding yachts, fresh fish, Cameroonian gendarmes, smugglers ... all in that word.

I have to admit to a newfound respect for the Efik language and for the esuk. There is a novel argument that Tinapa was not, in fact, named after a fish of the same name but came from the Efik's unique pronunciation of the word tilapia. The marina is infinitely more than a rough-and-ready market on the beach. Henshaw Beach Town Market! I think I like 'esuk' better.

Ekoki Like Gold

I have given up ever successfully speaking the Efik language, but because I'm a glutton, every syllable of every word concerning food falls on my ears like the sound of a running stream. One Efik food that I am passionate about is ekoki, made from fresh maize. The Igbo and Anioma call their version of ekoki 'ukpo oka'. The Efik's full name for it is 'ekoki ibikpot'. There seems to be no way of getting round onomatopoeic consonants in whatever Nigerian language you are discussing steamed, blended maize.

It also seems that no matter how many times it was explained to me why ekoki is disregarded, my mind could never embrace the explanation. Everyone I asked in Calabar about ekoki said it was their grandmother's old-fashioned, old-world food, or it was market food that no one bothered to make at home because you could buy it cheaply. At that time it cost N2; currency that no one remembers spending on anything that had real value. Someone said his hatred of steamed ekoki was underscored by the fact that his grandmother put efirin (bush-basil) in it. I met ekoki in my thirties without the footnotes of disregard, so I cannot get enough of that warm, velvety, grainy, peppery, palm-oil unctuousness of perfectly steamed prawns snug in the middle of an ekoki dumpling.

For me, ekoki will always be one of the queens of delicacies. I love steamed foods and I love to make my ekoki with the fresh maize that you can only buy between the months of March and May. For those three months, women who petty-trade in fruit throughout the year turn their altars of trade over to glowing basins of coal with roasting grids. The first rains bring with them beautiful evenings with fog, cool nights and the aroma of fresh maize roasting over open fires. Ekoki becomes a necessity.

The season passes too quickly, so I compensate by making a freezer stock of ekoki wraps. An Efik friend assures me that you can cook ekoki with any maize at all, even if it's not particularly fresh. Making ekoki with fresh maize is probably considered extravagant when you can boil the maize briskly and eat it. I understand what she means, drinking salty maize water through the porousness of the boiled cob. My mind is made up though: the aroma of fresh-maize ekoki cannot be replicated with older maize.

At the beginning of one season, I was given seven cobs of white maize. It felt reassuring to peel layers and layers of leaves, and detach the heads of silk to reveal the unique shape of each ear. I had not done this since I was a child, when I considered it a chore. Now, it was pure joy to have my senses awakened by the smell of fresh, bursting kernels oozing milk

I painstakingly pried out each kernel, much to the annoyance of members of my household who passed by and observed what they considered wasted diligence. Someone suggested that I use a knife, another that I use an old-fashioned grater, which is what women who sell ekoki in the market use. I self-righteously declined. The first would only retrieve half of the kernel, the other too much of the cob. I did not want to waste the maize, nor did I want the grittiness of too much cob. Sore thumbs and the passage of time were a small price to pay.

I blended my kernels with water, garlic, ginger, salt, leeks, onion and fresh pepper. I found that no matter how long I blended the maize, the consistency remained grainy. The blended maize was so fresh it looked and smelled like milk. I must note that I used parts of the cob, near the head where it was youngest. When you boil fresh maize, that part of the cob is delicious anyway. To the maize, I added blended smoked fish and a generous amount of palm oil. It was the first time in my life that I had seen palm oil that resembled red wine. Like the maize, it was a gift from Ogoja, presented in a recycled Ragolis water bottle. Unlike the palm oil I was used to, the top of the oil was transparent; the very first grade of oil, which the Yorùbá reverentially call 'ogere'. City dwellers like myself may never encounter this grade of oil in their lifetimes.

In Lagos, the Thaumatococcus daniellii leaves (ewe-eran) for wrapping the ekoki are sold to us with the greatest condescension in the market. The market women make you buy both the small and large leaves as a package. You are not allowed to pick and choose the leaves you want. In Calabar, the leaves are as broad as you like, and for N50, you get enough to roof a gazebo.

I gently divide my ekoki among folded leaves, add deveined fresh prawns, and steam the wraps for about forty-five minutes in a steamer. In the first five minutes of cooking, the smell of steaming leaves completely ravages the house.

Perfectly cooked ekoki bounces when tapped with the fingers. It retains its grainy maize texture. The smoked fish gives it maximum flavour without fishiness. The prawns, protected from direct heat yet perfectly steamed, add personality.

Ekoki Ibikpot

450g fresh corn, shucked, kernels removed from the cob (hard work!)

6-7 cups water or coconut water

1 inch ginger root

2 medium-sized leeks

2 green Scotch bonnets. Red or yellow can also be used

1 (be brave) cup first-grade palm oil

1 teaspoon hot ground Cameroonian peppers

2 small cloves garlic

A few sprigs of efirin (optional)

450g prawns

Smoked catfish

You need two leaves per ekoki wrap, one slightly bigger than the other. Break about two and a half inches off the back of the petiole on each leaf. Make sure not to tear the leaf or remove the whole petiole because you will have a leaky cone. The cone is folded and the bottom bent backwards to create a leak-proof container.

The kernels are removed from the cob and washed. I blend them at home in my blender, but I know some people so finicky they need the industrial-type mill used in the market to make corn pap.

The blending needs some form of liquid to help it along. I use coconut water because I like the idea of it, but I have to be honest and say I haven't tasted much difference. The smell of cooking, however, is dramatically enhanced.

I hand-grate my ginger and garlic because I don't want to risk whole bits in my blend, but the leeks, efirin and green Scotch bonnets go in with the water or coconut water. You'll know when you have the right consistency because you'll want to just lick it all up. It'll be milky and frumpy and frothy, wrapping itself around the spoon like a blanket, but still grainy. The cup of palm oil is stirred in, as well as the Cameroonian pepper, salt, grated ginger and garlic.

Fill the cones like this: first a portion of blended corn, then a washed and deveined prawn, another portion of blended corn, a piece of smoked fish and a last portion of corn. Twist the heads of the cone carefully and fold them back to meet the folded bottoms. Gently place them in the bottom of a steamer.

Place some leaves on top of the wraps before putting the lid on the steamer. I suggest steaming over medium to low heat. My steamer has very little space between the perforated plate and the pot it sits in, so I can't go too far from my cooking. Steaming takes about one and a half excruciating aroma-filling-the-whole-house hours at moderate heat.

It is best to leave the wraps alone as much as possible so you don't risk spillage. The recipe makes about twelve medium-sized dumplings. I typically eat three in one sitting.

To Cook or Not to Cook

I learnt how to cook during the Biafran War while at home in a village with no electricity, no running water and no gas cookers. Making Gari meant harvesting, peeling, grating, drying and frying the cassava and that applied to yam, corn and palm oil …

Amma Ogan, my editor at *234NEXT*

When women tell me they hate to cook, I don't scoff, I understand. If you cook day in and day out, you're probably not sweating glamorously over the hob, like Nigella Lawson or the Hemsley sisters with their buttery skin. Your nails probably aren't French manicured. You probably smell a little of food all the time, instead of Chanel N°5. You're most likely a little overweight, with a few commemorative tyres around the midsection.

Strangers make unfair inferences about you. If you're cooking all the time, then by simple deduction, you can't also be interested in a serious career. Neither are you particularly interesting, because you're cloistered in a kitchen with an aerial view of pot lids. You can't be the type of elevated homemaker who gets an allowance that takes cognisance of spa visits. You have to be the worst sort of housewife, the lowest rung of doormathood, waddling about the house in a bou-bou; a functional androgynous robot. It's better to be drop-dead gorgeous and successful at your career in human resources than renowned in the backwater of your kitchen and home.

Better the accolades of one's peers than the demanding, unacknowledged integrity of home-cooked meals.

There is nothing easy or fun about the cooking Ms Ogan describes. There is in fact something tragic about women cooking under these same conditions, thirty years later, in peacetime, with time-saving equipment available yet unaffordable to them. It's back-breaking, relentless, posturally inconvenient, thankless work. It's charcoal smoke in the eyes and calloused, burnt hands. It's a chain to the allegorical sink (and what some women wouldn't give for a glorious sink).

Even now, there are those women who arrange a precarious kitchen by the side of the road first thing in the morning. They pack it up at the end of the day and take it home. They do it every day for six days a week. They only take Sundays off, and on Sundays they cook for their husbands and children. They are roadside food sellers. No electricity, no running water, no gas cookers, but by 6 a.m., people will be shuffling their bottoms along wooden benches around the cooking pot set on firewood for a quick bowl of rice and stew, or a plate of beans with fried pepper stew; breakfast on the hoof. No thought is given to the processes before and after the eating of the food, such as the fact that these women still have to supervise their families' meals. The portfolio for cooking is instinctively given to women, and women often receive it like a calling. I once heard a seventy-year-old Nigerian woman admonishing her husband, stretching the words so tight they stepped out of her mouth with their enforcing militia: *That is not your department.*

She was referring to her kitchen in response to some innocuous questions from him about the arrangement of his meals.

I remember the pressure of answering the call of owning ones kitchen – the first steps of learning how to do a moin-moin wrap as a child. I was the first daughter so this pressure was tenfold. No Yorùbá girl worth her dawadawa dared progress into adulthood without knowing how to secure a moin-moin. It had to be wrapped and placed perfectly so that it didn't leak into the steamer. The pressure was absurd but the threat was tangible. If you couldn't wrap a moin-moin, you were in danger of becoming an incompetent woman and wife, an embarrassment to the house in which you were raised, perhaps even ineligible for marriage. So I was admonished.

This was probably too much cultural anxiety for a ten-year-old. The typical Yorùbá kitchen had no walls in the sense that aunties, older cousins, grandmothers – every female who was more than six months older than you – felt it was their duty to pass on their ideas of what it meant to be a woman in terms of cooking in that room. There were many culinary tests of womanhood: if you could handle a pot on the hob without mitts; if you could cut up fresh peppers without incurring burns or complaining of being on fire; if you could skilfully cut up yams and plantains against your palms without using a chopping board; if you could drop akara into hot oil so that it formed perfect cushions. A lot of these tests had to do with ignoring discomfort or pain. At university abroad, I caught a flatmate looking at me as if I was crazy when I had my hand inside a pot of boiling water, about to take out a hard-boiled egg.

When my maternal grandmother came to spend time with us, she was always particular about me and my abilities in the kitchen. Perhaps she believed that if you got the first daughter right, the others fell in place behind her. When I was preparing to make an omelette for myself, she came into the kitchen and insisted I ask my brother whether he would like one as well. One day I asked her why it was never the other way round: why was my brother never told to enquire whether I would like to eat something? She said it was because one day I would get married and have children so I'd better start getting used to cooking for more than one.

The socialisation worked beautifully, not because I agreed with it or didn't question it, but because I believed her, and I believed I had no choice in the matter. I found myself in my thirties, with children, standing in the kitchen waiting for everyone to eat before I ate, eating chicken neck, chicken back, chicken feet and leftovers and thinking nothing of it. Not particularly resenting it. It was securely ingrained by then. I'll still do it without complaining.

On the other hand, I know many women who give their children Indomie noodles when their N60,000-a-month cook-steward takes his day off. They order pizzas and Chinese takeaway for lunch and dinner. They work long hours in an office and come home exhausted. The myth of men's unfailing sexual devotion to frumpy women who can cook well has died. That was the final frontier, the last justification for the socialisation of the girl who wouldn't carry the calling with grace: that men only want women who can cook well. There is also the exquisiteness of defiance. 'Won't cook' and 'won't pay for not cooking' wears like cashmere. Never mind that the willingness to cook has become particularly pertinent and fashionable again, because mothers are being urged back into the kitchen to cook for their families, to care more than anyone else whether what goes into a three-year-old's mouth will give him a good foundation for the remaining sixty-seven years, if it will affect his cognitive skills or his neurological development, whether or not he will have cancer by the time he is ten because he came into the world with a delicate colon and was never able to fully pass out toxins from his system. No guesses as to why mothers are not responding to all the wholesome prompts with enthusiasm.

In 2010, I wrote an article titled 'To Cook or Not' for *234NEXT*. Amma Ogan, who edited the article, took out an anecdote I wrote about my mother-in-law coming round to stay with us. My husband and I were going out to dinner and she made a face and looked away when we asked if she would come along. As we drove out of the compound, I asked my husband why she had reacted in that way and he said traditionally, women who go with their husbands to restaurants are considered significantly worse than women who allow their husbands to go to restaurants to eat. By my mother-in-law's culture and standards, such women were no better than prostitutes. That was the precise word; no negotiation on its usage. It was a little bit more complicated than that. In my mother-in-law's world – which was not an extinct world but a concurrently running one happening in a rural place, with more committed ties to the values of the past – you would rarely see men take their wives to 'a kind of place' where you could get a bowl of pepper soup and a shot of locally brewed gin. It would be the good-time girl who was being fed for the work she would do after the meal. Being given a few drinks for courage, if she needed it. The man would return home at the end of his date with the girl and still find his meal at the head of the table, kept warm in his flask or with the swallow folded into many wrappers to keep it hot. He would eat it, or just touch it to show allegiance to the head of the department.

The crossroads of the two worlds is that persistent belief that good women cook for their husbands. Eating out is not for the purposes of being fed and nurtured; it is a form of entertainment that you follow up with real food at home. My required response to whether I would like to accompany my husband to the restaurant was a firm, 'No'. My sprucing myself up and jumping into the car was the wrong response.

A friend once called me a housewife over the phone. It was one word in a jovial conversation that put the lights out without warning. I heard nothing in the word but contempt. I heard nothing after the word, and all I wanted to do was get off the phone. We had been scheduling a visit to the house, but after dropping the call I sent him a message that I was suddenly incredibly busy and could not host him.

Housewife!

I ruminated for months over the conversation, over the most keenly felt insult I had been served in the last year. My mental thesaurus kept agreeing with me that it was the word 'housewife'. Yes it was that word. My paternal grandmother's international passport had 'housewife' in the column where it asked for profession, but she was anything but the contemporary disparaged person. At a point in her career, she designed and made clothes for Julie Coker, the television broadcaster and beauty queen, but she was also housewife to an employee of FAO in Rome and a thrower of high-powered tea parties, where she never, ever passed up an opportunity to show her collection of silver teaspoons brought back from every country of the world her husband had travelled to. She wanted you to be sure that she was a housewife and that she cooked or supervised each meal that T.S.B. Aríbisálà ate. Her Singer sewing machine in a glossy laminate box was prominently placed in the living room so that you understood every detail of her sophistication. Her sense of fashion was so intuitive I still wear clothes and jewellery from her wardrobe even though she's been dead twenty years.

However, in contemporary terms a housewife is a drudge with no ambition. That's not the dictionary definition, yet that's what it means when it is uttered by my friends in this new world we inhabit. No one in their right mind would admit, in a public place, to being a housewife, not when people sneer at homemakers. For my friend to call me that, when his wife was a successful banker who cooked as a hobby, was a definite put-down, even if it was one he wasn't consciously invested in. I wanted to tell him that I probably worked longer, harder hours at home than his wife did at work but that was beside the point. The work was not the issue, nor was his hard-working wife. It was the *kabod*, the accompanying glory of what I did and what I was that he had tried to taint with his ignorance. I worked at home. I had a small business, I wrote a blog, I cooked for my husband and children, but I was no housewife. No small-minded drudge with no choice or ambition. There was no context left in the contemporary world that did not embrace and express disparagement in the use of the word. It was a reference to leisure, laziness and a PhD in television soap operas. Regardless of the word's definition, that was what it meant and, worst of all, this man was supposed to be my friend, i.e. a comrade of choice. He could never convince me that he did not know the ambit of the word. I was so angry and disgusted I wasn't going to dignify the put-down with my defensiveness. He just wasn't going to get much more of this 'housewife's' time.

When I'm in the UK, I dream of Margaret Thatcher, the grocer's daughter, prime minister of the United Kingdom of Great Britain and Northern Ireland, ruling over lords and commons during the day, and then going home in the evening to cook and wash dishes. It is rumoured that men forgave her tight-lipped, overbearing rule of them in the workplace, granted her just that extra degree of awe and the presumption of dignified super-competence, and considered her a 'real' woman because she went home at the end of the day and stood over that kitchen sink. I hear they were powerfully reassured that, no matter how elevated she was, she inadvertently landed in her place, her crown on her head, her apron tied at the back of her dress with a pretty bow. It is important to give credence to all the things that helped keep that crown balanced: a sink, running water, a hob, electricity, cool weather, processed convenience that you can buy in the supermarket.

Margaret Thatcher could never, ever have been Nigerian. Never could be prime minister now. Could not even be that perpetually heavy-lidded sonata-playing Diezani Alison-Madueke, minister of petroleum resources, washing dishes. The elevation is the rationale for not being seen anywhere near dirty dishes. One's importance would immediately be irretrievably damaged by the attention to such menial details.

I find it particularly interesting that Thatcher's era has passed, even in the United Kingdom, and people would rather watch others cook on BBC Lifestyle and the Food Network and proceed from there to eat in a restaurant, than cook for themselves. After all, the appurtenances of the crowned drudge are now even more refined, more fine-tuned, more affordable. And there's the beautiful Nigella Lawson whose bosom gleams over the landscape of cooking; an irresistible contemporary role model.

The antiquarian, hallowed department of home science is being deserted by women all over the world and taken over by manicured men with trendy haircuts and indigo Crocs. Men rushing in and turning the kitchen into a celebrity stage worth millions and millions of pounds. Why cook when we can watch them cook on television? And there is just something engaging about watching a man cook. Why cook when their expertise and luminosity makes one feel inferior? In my opinion, not only have men gloriously taken over cooking in the media, I also think they often do it better, much better, more creatively, with ostentatious flair. Maybe it's just a thing in my brain – dregs of delight that a man is the drudge 'for real' and he is doing it on television. And I'm watching from a place where older women turn up their noses at younger women not cooking. A man chose this as a career in a world that has 'inequitably' agreed to give men accolades for cooking. They've turned home-cooking into a pastoral term, the plodding itinerary into competitive sport. Many of them grow sinewy in the kitchen, not fat. Their sweat is eau de cologne. They come out of the kitchen and people applaud in awe. The ironies overwhelm me.

The glory of men in the kitchen is only peripherally celebrated by Nigerian men, if it is celebrated at all. After my husband came home several times to find my son watching BBC Lifestyle with me he said, 'We'll have words if that boy comes to me in fifteen years' time, and tells me he wants to be a cook!'

I'm with those who would like a little appreciation for how hard it is to put a pot on a fire and produce something edible and creative every day without any glory in sight. It really doesn't have to be the round of applause that a man gets when he enters the kitchen. I believe in the integrity of home-cooked meals. I really enjoy my daydreams of Maggie Thatcher. Sometimes when Rachmaninoff is not playing on my iPod, I won't cook. I agree that the kitchen department is not democratic. Each to his own. To each woman her single-minded own.

Okro Soup and the Demonic Encyclopaedia of Dreams

What does a demon look like? You should know, so that if you meet it in the vicinity of your food, you know to avoid both the demon and the plate of food, if you want to. I'm in danger of being glib about something we take obstinately to heart. And when I say 'we', I mean hard-right Pentecostal Nigerians speaking a lingo that other Nigerians at first considered oddball but have now ideologically assimilated. Everyone now says and understands:

It is well.

In Jesus's name.

By God's grace.

Stay blessed.

We mean well and we are adapting to where we have found ourselves, yet there is a real obstacle in attempting to explain what the average Nigerian Christian means when he uses the words 'demonic', 'deliverance' or 'backslidden'. As the words become more tolerated, as they become fatter spirits, so they become more intractable. What does demonic mean when the word is attached to okro soup? What does it mean when it is attached to anything at all? You would not be able to engage the association and say to yourself *that makes sense* even if it is comfortable to say those things. If the fish in the okro soup called your name, you would have every reason to stand up and excuse yourself from eating the soup. Or if the okro soup melted your stainless steel spoon. But melting stainless spoons and talking fish are unsophisticated in the environs of demonic soup. It's not even grown-up enough for Africa Magic entertainment.

Suspend what you know to be coherent and legitimately diabolical and taste these for starters:

- Tinky-Winky from the Teletubbies is demonic.
- All the Teletubbies, plus all the host of *In the Night Garden* – Makka Pakka, Upsy Daisy, Tombliboo Ooo, Tombliboo Eee – are demonic. The Tittifers are especially demonic.
- The short dress that the woman across the street is wearing, the one that's riding up her bottom and showing off her cleavage, is demonic. It's a demonic dress.
- Eating okro soup in your dreams is demonic.

I can hear how the sentence ricochets in the mind, and taste how revolutionary it is in the mouth. The words are English but they are not. I feel proud to be a Nigerian in this sense. We can acquire and own an idea, a thing or a word and invade its body like a spirit, thereby changing its face, moving the facial muscles and creating a new personality. Someone confronts the face and asks, 'Who are you again?' And it answers, 'The same person. The very same.' But it is not. We have possessed it.

'Eating okro soup in your dreams is demonic' is a competent statement as long as it remains at home. On its way out of the country, it will have problems at immigration. The easiest way the sentence can be disambiguated, if it needs to be, is to postscript it in pidgin English with the words, 'Na winch dem wan give you'.

And by this grammatical contrivance, it is as clear as day that dreaming of eating okro soup points to a coven of witches somewhere, with your Blackberry pin, attempting to recruit you by manipulating your spirit. It means subliminal initiation into ideology through food. In wakefulness we fight so many things, but if it is fed us in sleep, there is no resistance. It is faster than organic assimilation, than hanging around in an environment and gradually, minute by minute, getting used to an idea.

I admit that okro has turned up in my dreams a couple of times, and on at least one occasion it had snails in it. Snails in okro soup is significantly more demonic than ordinary okro soup with beef or chicken. As can be imagined, the okro soup in my dream was cooked to perfection. I suppose the more subjectively enticing the dream-soup, the surer the bait, the more effective it is as a tool of initiation. The soup in my dream was a compromise between the okro soup I was taught to cook as a child and the okro soup I married into. The okro I grew up eating was a light-hearted affair. It was fresh. It had a side-dish feel to its simple preparation: grate, pot, water, salt, kaun (kaun can stand for potash or for that hitting of the pot we do to signify the end of cooking) and it was done.

The okro I married into is a market trip, a song and dance, an assortment of green leaf, special fish, beef, ntong leaf, ugwu, palm oil and snails. This soup has the episodic feeling of a dream. It has the attention to detail, the layering of language and symbols, and it fits the stereotype of the kind of soup that is used for bewitchment. The soup fits like the shoe fits … an area, an idea, a kind of woman, context, details. All of these in turn fit the stereotype. The coven is amongst us in daytime even if it mostly opens for business at night. The cooking of the soup fits the form of the owners of the coven. And who are the most sophisticated Nigerian witches? Who are the real-time owners of the coven?

The owners of the more detailed soup of course. The owners of the song and dance and nkonko and luscious snails. *You catch on nicely.* The riverine witch, the Calabar witch or winch. There's a joke my sister cracks with her bottom lip unwittingly sticking out and a notable underlying inferiority complex: *Do you know what happens if a Calabar woman wants your husband? You package him up nicely and ask her if she wants anything else to go with him.*

It is a joke, for all intents and purposes, but her body language says so much more. You laugh when you hear the joke but it hangs like a comma in the mind and you wonder. It is a sophisticated joke even if it sounds like a bland stereotype. It has layers and years of invested virtuosity, like a good pot of soup. For those scoffing, I have a true-life anecdote that has to do with naming my food blog. My first choice of name was 'Calabar Winch'.

I was already celebrating my own cleverness, my elevation above the superstition and small-mindedness of people who feared real-life witches. And anyway, the word was 'winch' not 'witch'. I was merely harnessing the kaleidoscope of representation that the word 'winch' offered, harnessing the humour attached to it. After all, the dictionary definition of 'winch' is a lever that throws gliders into the sky. Nigerians instinctively laugh when you say 'winch' because we are laughing at ourselves, at our mispronunciation of an English word, and because one can presume that the replacement of 'it' for 'in' is a mutual agreement among us all that we aren't going to take this witch business so seriously.

I found out soon enough that this agreement was not watertight when I told friends I was going to call my blog 'Calabar Winch'. It was like watching the expressions of people who were seeing a plane fall out of the sky. I should have taken to heart the fact that the mispronunciation is only a joke to the Nigerian who knows it is a mispronunciation. Many, many Nigerians, say winch when they mean witch, and it is often only the elite who discern the difference in sound and laugh at it.

I persevered based on the fact that I was talking to those who thought themselves the elite, and this wasn't about real witchcraft, black witchcraft. It was about bewitchment with food. Why was it okay to joke that a woman was a winch because she had put something in a man's food in order to get him to fall in love with her? People laughed; that definitely tickled. This woman in the joke who you put your husband in a box for and tied him up with nice ribbons to make a good presentation, the one where there was some okro soup in the joke served with some sensual ego massage, some scented candles and special dishes to serve the soup and swallow...

You laughed at it, yet accommodated the ambivalence of the facts of the story. You could play with it in your mind and admit that that kind of witchcraft was perhaps only representative of primeval patterns. Woman cooks for man because man has been programmed to feel vague, warm feelings for women who cook for him, especially women who know how to add theatre to kitchen drudgery, know how to convey the coquettish message that the time spent in the kitchen is proportionate to the worth of the man. *Here I am cooking ekpang nku kwo for you for twelve hours my lord and master.* Man begins to feel some deep stirrings that may or may not be recognised as being firmly attached to the effects of good food on the stomach and brain. Man begins to be ever so slightly intoxicated by the strong insinuations of worth conveyed by the movement of the woman in the kitchen: sweating, pounding yam, whistling strains of Pentecostal choruses, all in the effort to produce one pot of soup and one mound of pounded yam just for him. And in his intoxication, he starts to imagine that she is not just a woman, but one with superpowers.

A woman who can cook exceptionally well evokes cultural fear and admiration because of the power she represents. She has the ability to cook so skilfully and instinctually that the primeval nuts and bolts fall in place in the minds, bodies and spirits of all those who eat her food, both women and men. Her cooking brings love potions to mind. It may be believed that her spirit was given a gift before it was sent to her body: *God asked her to hold out her hands and he spat in them. The hands become spoons and the woman was born into our world as 'Olowo síbí'.* Literally translated, 'olowo síbí' is 'spoons for hands', meaning someone endowed with the supernatural ability to cook. The Yorùbá go one up to call a woman who can destabilise a man's senses with food 'Sokoyokoto'.

Why can't we embrace the facts of this scenario and laugh openly about the witchcraft ascribed to it? Ambivalence is part of our cultural terrain, so why can't humour embrace that it may or may not be real witchcraft? Why can't I borrow the nervous humour for the title of a blog? The response I got was that witchcraft would never be a wholehearted joke in Nigeria. It could perhaps be one in Glastonbury, where people wear ridiculous black outfits and play at being witches, but never, ever in Nigeria. Especially not when, for about six months in 2012, yellow banners belonging to a Pentecostal church in Calabar were stretched across trees all over the city, boldly advertising a long-running church programme titled *My Father, my father, that witch must die!* The people driving past the banners were not reading the word 'witch'; they were seeing and saying 'winch'.

I'm a stubborn woman. I went on to give the name Calabar Winch to a contact in Abuja who makes a handsome living registering company names at the Corporate Affairs Commission. A couple of weeks went by, then six weeks, then two months. Eventually I got a response saying I had to go to Calabar Municipality office and request the use of the name Calabar Winch. I demanded to know why, already irritated by the two months of silence from the Corporate Affairs Commission.

Firstly, they replied, I could not use the name Calabar without requesting the permission of Calabar Municipality. Secondly, the CAC wasn't sure where I was going with the whole winch matter. What was I selling? What was the nature of my business? What was Calabar Winch Ltd going to be trading in? Why, for goodness' sake, the choice of the words 'Calabar' and 'Winch'? Last, but not least, I was informally advised to reconsider the choice of the name as there are in fact people who are practicing Calabar winches and a clash with them would not be pleasant unless I was one of them, in which case I should just say so.

I asked my contact if this was serious. Very, very serious he responded. And he drew my attention to the last informal suggestion again. Imagine my letter falling into the hands of a born-again Christian staff member of the Calabar Municipality, he said. I would have to go to her and justify my insistence on calling myself a winch. I would be the talk of the town for at least the next two decades (Calabar is a tiny town). It was especially pertinent given that my husband was a civil servant. Not only would I have to deal with the backlash of admitting to witchcraft, my dear, Christian, civil servant hubby would also suffer the effects of having a professed, unrepentant, proud winch who declared it at Calabar Municipality for a wife. The very kind that yellow banners had been stretched all across Calabar for. And the banners were no joke. They were real battle lines.

At this point, I gave in. Not because I was afraid of being believed a witch – a real witch – but because I didn't have the time and energy to fight. Calabar, after all, was the same town in which I had taken my son to a hospital after his head had met the edge of a table. I got to the hospital and instead of being treated like an emergency case, the nurses grilled me for details of which church I went to. They insisted I fill in the details of my church on the registration form.

Was I really married? The nurses and the matron didn't like my grey, blood-stained hoodie and, to make matters worse, it was old and beloved. Nor did they like my jeans, my youthfulness, or my hips and flat bottom, which did not look like they had pushed out children. They didn't like my natural hair, with beads, hanging down to my shoulders, or my white gold wedding rings that no properly married Nigerian woman would accept as ensigns of ownership by a worthy man. None of these things fitted the description of the typical Calabar married woman. And while we stood ironing out these details, my son's head bled and the fury rose in my stomach until I could have spewed fire and burnt down the whole hospital. My husband had to leave work to come and rescue the situation. He walked into the room in a white Friday babanriga and the air cooled like he had descended out of the clouds sans wings.

And thus Calabar Winch was discarded for *Longthroat Memoirs*. The CAC still came back asking why I was registering a blog and if I was also going to sell foodstuffs like peppers and onions. Tell them whatever they need to hear, I told my contact. Tell them whatever they need to hear to just register it; I'm bored and disgusted with the whole thing.

Then I settled down and asked the opinions of a pastor and a few others on the relevance of dreaming of food, of eating in dreams, of the whole enterprise being ominous, especially with regard to mucilaginous foods.

The pastor surprised me by suggesting that if you dream of food, you might simply have been hungry before going to bed. A friend declared, uncompromisingly, that it was a sure sign that you had been spiritually initiated by a witch. Like the Pentecostal church's goal of converting non-Christians to Christianity, the witch's goal was to convert the uninitiated to witchcraft. Obviously there must be some tarred runway for the witch's broomstick, some existing foothold, some dark space welcoming the initiation. Nobody is truly initiated without their consent. When you ate okro soup with snails in your dreams, it signified that you had a foot in the door at the very least.

One person was not quite sure what the spiritual significance was, but was certain that something just wasn't right about eating in dreams. Someone wanted to know if I had personally eaten food in my sleep. I wasn't going to give that information away freely, after the informal advice from the CAC in Abuja.

If I had been able to stop myself from eating in my dreams, that showed spiritual strength. If I ate willingly, weakness.

Jollof rice and plantains were not as effective as tools of bewitchment because the mucilage was missing. The *draw* was absent. And the draw was significant, if not crucial. I wondered if the swallow and soup did not appeal to a deeper level of the Nigerian's subconscious because swallow and soup is 'awa' food and jollof rice is imported, adopted fare, even if our spirit had already changed the appearance of its face. The bottom line was that if you dreamt of okro soup or snails, you were, without any doubt, a candidate for a 'deliverance' service, which means going to a pastor or pastors to be prayed for and to have the effects of the witch's initiation reversed.

Were these people serious? Deadly so! Everyone but the pastor was reluctant to give details of their own okro soup dreams. You can imagine the condescension with which I was regarded when I suggested that okro soup and snail dreams might be our collective way of dealing with the reality of eating foods that are mucilaginous, perhaps visually uncomfortable, and giving ourselves license to enjoy those foods. How else can one navigate the psychosis of regarding cooked snails as a delicacy in wakefulness and then rejecting it in ones dreams as a tool of the devil? Of eating with relish while awake and with dread while asleep?

As I noted at the beginning of this essay, many things that Nigerians or Nigerian Christians consider demonic or demonically inspired are not coherently so. Tinky-Winky the Teletubby carries a red lady's handbag, has a man's voice and sometimes agrees to wear a tutu and dance. In Nigeria, he or she is the most reviled and demonic of all the demonic Teletubbies. In light of all the contradictions and incoherencies,

I am all for committing to an encyclopaedia of demonic food. A hardback one, diligently updated as more information on the matter comes to light. I suggest the following entries:

- All ice cream and chocolate cakes, by virtue of sublimity, graded for inherent evil from sublime through sublimer to sublimest.
- Brie and fufu, by virtue of alluring softness and colour deception, taking note that Satan disguises himself in white as an angel of light.
- Ofada stew, for fast, strong cords of irresistible temptation. The footnotes must stringently warn that eating these stews in life or sleep will make you fat and eventually kill you, spirit, soul and body. *Patapata.*
- Stewed Bible tripe, because of the vanity of comparing the word of God to something so dirty, disgusting and, in the final analysis, so delicious.
- Isi ewu, for the visual and tactile evil experienced when you put your hand in a bowl, intentionally reaching for eyeballs and tongue brazenly tossed with chopped vegetables.
- Apples, for their hard work and diligence in the representation of the willy-nillyness of evil from the beginning of time.

Oseani Mellowing, Bursting, Deepening, Merging

I don't believe in love at first sight but the home-cooked red curry my South Asian housemates introduced me to at university was love at first inhalation. From the first proposition of dry roasted cumin, coriander, cardamom, cinnamon bark, cloves, fenugreek and fennel seeds, the fashioning of incense for meat and potatoes, the curry became such an obsession that when I began to attempt to make it at home, I refused to use pre-packaged spice mixes. If I carefully weighed and dry roasted my own spices I could walk into the house and catch the delicious undertones of mellowing, bursting, deepening, merging fragrances. I could detect the variations in scent when the spices blended, when they were all cooked up in coconut milk, or when they were placed on the tongue, and perceive the different measures in the spice mix. I think the curry will endure till the end of time because aroma consciousness in food has to be the foundation of food-finesse. A bowl of soup sashaying towards you can get full marks even before it is placed on the table, purely because of the headiness of its aromatics.

In Nigeria, Cross Riverians might be the culinary heavyweights, but I think the Niger Delta has the most sophisticated aromatics, with their nsala (peppersoup) and oseani. I will eternally be grateful to the visual artist, Victor Ehikhamenor, who drew a riveting mental image for me. All I had asked was why the Esan and the Anioma don't cook with the uyayak, the tetrapleura tetraptera pod. You could not cook a pot of white soup or abak (banga) without half a pod placed in the soup. If you wanted a vigorous olfactory sweetening of the soup, you held the pod above the fire first and roasted it for a few minutes. Victor explained that widows use the uyayak to mourn their husbands. It is placed in a burner and set on fire. The levitating smoke is a flag of mourning. No guessing why the Esan and Anioma don't want it near their food. The other thing about the tetrapleura tetraptera pod is that it isn't a team player. You either allow it to take over the soup or you don't use it at all. The Anioma lose nothing by discarding it in favour of a wider variety of spices when cooking the nsala.

When I cook couscous, I toast the grains in a hot pan first, paramountly for aromatics and colour. I know many people who are content to simply pour hot water on the grains and this is the beginning and end of their cooking. In my opinion it is a wasted opportunity. Roasting the grains before soaking them enhances the depth of aroma and nuttiness instead of just presenting them bland and fair-faced. The same applies to quinoa: the result is a beautiful bronzing of the grains and a deeper complexity to the flavours; the bitterness is mellowed, the aroma enhanced.

Even in its simplicity, the Anioma's unassuming oseani soup showcases the geographic dedication to aroma fashioning, to virtuosity in soup aromatics. The ruse is that the soup happens very quickly. Michael Mukolu, who introduced me to oseani, nicknamed it the three-minute soup. At the end I learnt that the three minutes is the cooking time and does not include the hour probably spent in preparation. Or the time spent arguing about whether the egúsí in the soup is the egúsí we are all familiar with, or whether it is another genus of egúsí. This long, tangential argument remained inconclusive even after many minutes of 'no, it's bigger', 'yes, its edges are not as hard as the common egúsí', and 'no, it's not as flat'.

Such finicky discussions of egúsí are not unusual. A husband of a friend once took me to the market and spent many minutes trying to show me the difference between hand-shelled and machine-shelled egúsí. I stood in the sun, rubbing my fingers over both types and gave up in frustration.

For the oseani, the egúsí is roasted in a hot pan without any oil, until the popping begins and the nutty aroma starts to assault the senses. The brown swollen-bellied seeds are transferred to an nkpirite – a flat-faced, wooden hand mortar. (A note to the urban dwellers: an authentic nkpirite *will not* be found in Lagos. You must send to Ubulu Uku, Asaba or Ogwashi Uku.) The seeds are ground in the mortar until they become a smooth, oily paste; smoother than any blender can achieve. White crayfish is added and meticulously ground in, then dawadawa or ògìrì, and finally, dried ground pepper. Everything is processed until completely blended and punctiliously smooth. In the background, pounded yam or gari is prepared. All the elements of the meal must be ready at the same time because the soup must be eaten hot at the end of the three minutes.

Boiling water is kept on the fire for finishing up the soup. Once the pestle and mortar work is finished, the paste is put in a dish and the boiling water is stirred in. The consistency of the soup is a personal matter, and the amount of water added will determine whether it is a thick or thin soup. Once the water is mixed into the paste, the soup is ready. The seasoning is adjusted and it is eaten *immediately* with the gari or pounded yam. The soup must not be left sitting around, and it tastes significantly different if it is reheated. So, like the sacrament, every drop of it is eaten right away.

Like the egúsí, the ògìrì was another bone of contention. Technically, ògìrì and dawadawa are two different fermented seasonings. Ògìrì is fermented sesame or egúsí seeds and dawadawa is fermented locust beans, also called irú. We finally agreed that traditionally it would be ògìrì isi (moist fermented egúsí) used in the oseani and not locust beans.

Another version of oseani is made from nsala spices (the word 'nsala' reminds me of 'masala'). The spices are ground up with the crayfish, ògìrì and dried pepper. This version needs some of the pounded yam added to the hot water to give the soup the body lacking due to the absence of ground egúsí. The result looks a little like the Efik afia efere (white soup sweetened with uyayak). A third variation uses fresh pepper vine leaf. Cross Riverians call this leaf 'hot leaf'. The leathery vine leaf is processed in the same manner, with added seasoning, and eaten straightaway from the nkpirite turned serving dish.

My excitement over this soup and its variations has to do with more than the enhancement of flavours through dry-frying at the beginning or with that skilful releasing of oils and flavour achieved with pestle and mortar. Here is a soup without oil or meat, with big, satisfying notes from the egúsí and crayfish, and savouriness from the ògìrì and dawadawa. It's nutritious, not only because of its ingredients, but because it has only been exposed to heat for the shortest time. The briskness of cooking applied to the nsala oseani makes me want to open the doors to all the rooms of the house to let the aroma waft through and experience what I call olfactory eating – the kind of eating that begins before the food comes anywhere near the mouth. The processing of the spices satisfies hunger before the food is served. The palate and all the senses are stirred and intoxicated. It might be the rationale behind cooks declaring they can't eat much of their own cooking: they are already full from inhaling aromatics.

Institution of Stew

My opinion is that stew was never meant to be a monogamous relationship or a form of religion. If it were, there wouldn't be so many potential ingredients. But in the time and place that I grew up, people were certain about what the mouthfeel of a stew was. The Yorùbá are self-conscious about having one of the least imaginative cuisines in Nigeria and are as finicky about their stews as they are about headtie trends. Only a Yorùbá stew cannot be like a gele; it isn't really allowed to be trendy. It is a conservative offering connecting nostalgia and hunger; the daily rehashing of a comfortable idea. It is the overriding say-so of stew-the-way-my-mother-cooks-it, the way her mother cooked it, ad nauseam. It offers the psychological comfort of eating what we are used to eating, what we have eaten for fifty years, and what we shall probably eat on our last day on earth.

In every Yorùbá home, in the middle of every afternoon, there is a stew pot resting on the hob with the lid slightly askew. The oil is tantalisingly settled an inch deep on top of cooked peppers. The cooling skin of oil and pepper is creased around meat like lazy gelatine. The pieces of meat are coquettish protrusions under a soft blanket.

The jokes about Yorùbá people and their stews, about the habitual, come-rain-or-shine pot of omi-obe, are threadbare.

Omi-obe literally translates as 'stew water'. It means exactly that: the body of the stew minus meat or fish. It is unquestionably derogatory when it comes out of my Igbo friends' mouths. 'What's for lunch?' they ask provocatively. 'Omi-obe?' Meaning, what else could possibly be for lunch! For the Yorùbá person it is omi-obe with everything.

Stew ingredients had to be carried to the market for grinding, an exacting, passed-thrice-through-the-mill invasion masticating every 'child in the witch's belly' (i.e. the pepper seeds) and every membrane, pore and atom of every tomato, pepper and onion. The grinding machine was a barking, clanging, convulsing, categorically blue or green mill that also ground corn, millet and sorghum, as well as beans for moin-moin. We called it 'ero' and sometimes 'ero ògì' because most of the time it was used to grind off batches of fermented corn for making ògì (corn pap). However, in most markets where you found this melodramatic machine, there would be one or two women grinding peppers between a cylindrical stone and a large slab made from the same stone, using biceps and triceps, the small of the back and the firm back-and-forth motion of wrist joints. You would find queues for their services as well.

My family, like most Yorùbá families, was extremely particular about our omnipresent red puddle in a pot, so easily applied to anything from steamed rice, àmàlà and ewédú to croissants. If there was stew then there was food, and the conclusion was so clean that your brain could turn away from the necessity of food preparation to other things. This is no insignificant detail in a culture where people drop round without invitation and expect to be fed, at the very least, a bowl of white rice and stew. In a neighbourhood with many Yorùbá families, a mill on a bench, attached to a small generator on the side of the street, is a lucrative living for its operator.

The grindstone was a controversial issue at our house. It got the same God-forbid reaction as dòdò Ìkirè – those balls of mashed pepper and ripe plantains that you could only buy from the sides of the expressway of the small town of Ìkire when travelling between Ife and Ìbàdàn. My father would not eat them if he were starving to death and there was nothing else to eat. He could not bear the thought of strange hands handling his food, or of beads of sweat falling into his food.

For the same reasons, he would not eat suya, or groundnuts that had been deshelled by hand, tossed up in the air, and mouth-blown to separate the skins from the nuts. He would not be caught dead in a buka eating a plate of àmàlà. We ate machine-pounded yam on Saturdays because he could not, would not eat yam that someone who was not my mother had inevitably sweated into in the process of pounding it with a mortar and pestle. It wasn't as if he didn't already have issues with my mother's sweat gracing the food.

So a grindstone was an offence to every sensibility and sensitivity, every working of my father's imagination. He loathed the necessary tactility in the handling of food, the inevitability of bodily fluids escaping from the handler and entering his food from talking while pounding or grinding. The thought of people hanging around, yapping away in that demonstrative Yorùbá manner that causes spit to fly, scratching their heads, or worse, their groins: my father could not handle it. This fussiness was no respecter of persons. You can imagine how overpowering my father finds the idea of a celebrity chef on television: someone who is paid to be voluble and cook at the same time. So even though we were particular about the stew ingredients being ground fine, the melodramatic mill was considered, by a wide, untraversable margin, to be the least of many evils.

For my mother's part, she had impenitently rejected the grindstone. Women like her left such stones in villages and small towns and sometimes even big cities, and swore never to look back. Having two degrees gave my mother the firm justification to decide this, to turn up her nose and declare herself too worldly to grind peppers with a stone. It was an abuse on the hands, wrists and self-esteem that education had the sacrosanct right to rescue you from.

My parents hadn't left just any city behind. They courted in the sophisticated, intellectually and culturally proud city of Ìbàdàn, age-mates with the first university in Nigeria in Ìbàdàn, living close to the 40,000-seater Liberty football stadium, once home to the renowned Shooting Stars SC. They had been teenagers in the seductively intoxicating Adégòkè Adélabú years and become adults against the backdrop of Nigeria's cocoa-boom and Ìbàdàn's self-assured economic dominance of the south-west and the whole of the western region of Nigeria. In those days, no one left Ìbàdàn for Lagos and equated it to moving up in the world. Leaving that grindstone behind gave more integrity to the aspiration of upward mobility. The path of their courtship can be mapped along a short walk between Ososàmì and the Ìjebú bypass at Òkè-Àdó.

My mother graduated from Ahmadu Bello University and was married by the time she was 22. She had her two and a half degrees, a toddler, and a Volkswagen Beetle bought with her first salary. Her wigs were tall and her wrappers tied above her knees. Her wedges were precarious, her sunglasses were horn-rimmed. She had worked hard and run fast in the opposite direction of the grindstone and all the things it stood for. The fashion sense and finickiness were at odds with each other: no matter how sophisticated the hills and valleys of Ìbàdàn, or how fashionable the Yorùbá woman with a university degree, the fundamentals of the Yorùbá stew would not change and the taste of a stew ground by hand with cold, hard stone could not be compromised. It could not be replicated by a machine yet it was an ideal that my parents, Yorùbá relatives, and all those who snubbed the grindstone and harassed every piece of mechanical equipment they met into grinding peppers and tomatoes, perfectly refused to discard. No one thought of using all the intellectual snobbery suspended over the south-west to create a machine that kept its cool like a stone when crushing the soul of a pepper seed so that the heat and smell of moving machine parts did not alter the aromatics of the stew ingredients or the overall character of the pulp.

One of my mother's first cousins who came to live with us could not endure a stew that had not been attended to by an anal-retentive mill operator. She was like that princess who could feel a pea through twenty mattresses. A few years ago, I watched in amazement as she, now mistress of her own home, berated her help: 'Kò kúno! Kò kúno!' Which meant the stew was not texturally perfect. Which meant another trip to the market for the overwhelmed help.

Meanwhile, blenders expired, and are still expiring all over the south-west of Nigeria, endeavouring to do the job of pulping skin and seeds and water to the required mouthfeel. I cannot count the number of electric blenders I personally saw my mother destroy in the attempt to make them grind peppers to the specification of texturally perfect Yorùbá stew. You would hear the blender going for a stretch of about thirty minutes and then you would smell burning wires and you would know, without doubt, that the poor blender had, in great bitterness of spirit and thorough exhaustion, given up the ghost. And even after giving its life, it still had not got the job done. There would be no reverent folding of wires and putting away of the blender. No fitting burial. There would be angry, disgusted kissing of teeth. The blended peppers, tomatoes and onions would be transferred to a plastic container and sent off to the market, to the Pentecostal mill.

From as early as ten years of age, I was considered capable of going to the market to grind peppers on my own. I didn't have to decide the ratio of tomatoes to peppers to onions. My mother did that. All I had to do was take two containers, one with water, the other with the stew ingredients, which my mother had measured out. I was to hand them over to the mill operator. I had to demand, in my most authoritative ten-year-old voice, that he give his machine a rinse so that someone else's ground beans did not become part of our stew or so that the stew did not acquire the aroma of fermented corn kernels, or was not made ultra hot by the peppers that some other customer had put through the mill before mine. The operator also had to rinse the wooden stick he used to push the peppers and tomatoes into the belly of the machine. He would agree to do all this but with the facial expression of someone smelling something bad. Then I was to demand that the blend be put through the mill once again. Three times in total, no matter how many people were waiting in the queue and no matter how irritable and close to exasperation the mill operator became on account of my insisting. Lastly, on no account was I to allow him to put any of his own water into the machine to rinse the rest of my blend out. The whole experience was as traumatic as performing on stage. When I got home the blend went into one big pot to be simmered to death.

'Ìgbawo ló máa jiná?'

The question of when this blend was considered 'cooked' was always met with the answer, 'When it is cooked. Full stop!' You tasted it, and then *you knew*. That was the measure of time.

And that made perfect sense in the context of different species of tomatoes, which we had not bothered to distinguish and which market women had not bothered to distinguish for us. Even though we were finicky, we bought whatever tomatoes we found in the market as long as they were fresh. So today they would be sweet, tomorrow tart and next week as bland as water. You had to adjust the other stew ingredients to accommodate the ambiguity of tomatoes. The treachery of Scotch bonnets was worse. They all looked the same, and you had to use your sense of smell and touch to guess how hot they were, and how many you needed.

On many occasions we got it wrong, and the stew was either too hot or too mild and you had to repair it with tomato puree from a tin to cool it down, or ground dried peppers to hot it up, or water to thin it out. The blend was then divided among white plastic bowls, cooled, covered and deposited at the bottom of the deep freezer. Every morning, without fail, a plastic container of frozen, boiled blend came out of the freezer because my father had to have a fresh pot of stew every day. The recipe was the same. Three cooking spoons of groundnut oil were heated. The blend went in and cooked for another stretch until there was no more tartness in its taste and the heat of the peppers was muted and harmonious. Then the stock was added with the Maggi and the boiled beef. The seasoning was adjusted and the stew was done.

I threw this recipe out the moment I left home for university. I embraced the blender and its runner-up competence. All the finickiness about perfectly ground peppers was unrealistic in the context of an unfamiliar university town where I had to go and find a mill in the market, scrutinise the hygiene of the mill operator, and do research on where his water was coming from. The recipe needed to be thrown out if only for the sake of the unnecessary drama of the whole thing. My struggle with the idea of Yorùbá stew came to rest in peace at the feet of my son's sensitivity to tomatoes. Before that, it worked in my favour that I married out of the institution of stew, so there was no husband compelling me to cook it for the sake of nostalgia.

So I began to question the entire endeavour.

Why did I have to cook with tomatoes or onions?

Why red Scotch bonnets and not yellow?

Why not anything I want, really?

Why a smooth stew and not a lumpy one?

Why not roasted stew instead of one cooked on the hob?

And thus, by virtue and reason of such questioning and rebelling, the doors of the institution of stew were never formally declared open in my house.

Recently, my friend Damaris Onwuma gave me a grindstone that her mother took to Lagos for her from Benue State. Another friend brought it all the way from Lagos to Calabar for me by bus. The package came with some oyster shells that I was meant to sharpen the stones with. You put the shells between the two stones, ground them fine and thereby sharpened the stones. It is not because I suddenly gained religion and wanted to go back to texturally finicky Yorùbá stews that the grindstone is now sitting in my kitchen. It is because it has recently dawned on me that only a grindstone can extract certain aromatics from fresh peppers. The corollary is that only a grindstone can retain certain aromatics in fresh peppers. Only a grindstone can pulverise roasted groundnuts and peppers with the willpower needed to create pepper kola: that moreish groundnut paste served to guests with fresh garden eggs. The Yorùbá have a point. The inertia in creating a machine that can do the stone's work might be resignation to the fact that no such machine can, in fact, be created.

And perhaps Lagos has been good to the Yorùbá stew because it has, out of necessity, straightened some of the kinks of Yorùbá finickiness. It's given the stew the opportunity to exist as stew even if imperfectly made in a blender. The Yorùbá woman in Lagos has to live the fast-paced life. She has to drop children off at school, do long transits from home to work and back, go through the motions of replicating interesting meals for the husband who is much like the *Ancient and Modern Hymnal* because he wants a gorgeous wife who fell out of the middle of a glossy magazine, but pounds yam too!

Women have had to make peace with the blender. At least in Lagos, one hears expressions like 'obe imoyo' for the chopped-with-a-knife or pounded-with-a-mortar-and-pestle stew. 'Designer stew' is the fried-to-death version analogous to a cardiac arrest. Don't get me wrong; it is deliciously oily and dark in the face, the intense maroon complexion of deep-frying. The beef in it is fried so resolutely, you can take it apart thread by thread. The peppers seem almost non-existent under a brazen pool of oil, but it is stew nevertheless. The most fashion-conscious translation has to be ofada stew: peppers cooked with fermented dawadawa and palm oil, served with locally grown short-grain rice in thaumatococcus (moin-moin) leaves. Even the snootiest of party guests will discreetly massage the sleeve of the server carrying a tray of ofada stew and rice.

Stew my way is made with sweet green peppers, tatase or bawa peppers (larger than sweet red peppers, sweeter than hot), yellow and red Scotch bonnets, and leeks. There is no technical detail to the recipe. It is, in fact, not a recipe. It is a no-fail pleaser that allows the most satisfying self-expression. Tomatoes are out for the reasons mentioned before. Those suffering from arthritis will find that, because of the absence of tomatoes, they can eat this stew without paying for it in days of pain. It is noteworthy that the Yorùbá 'obe ata' has been in existence since antiquity so there is, in fact, nothing novel about cooking stew without tomatoes. The equipment, however, is important. One needs a glass oven dish and an unglazed earthenware pot, preferably one that does the daily job of stew-simmering. A year-old one is ideal because of the inadvertent slow seasoning of the pot that has taken place over that time.

Other ingredients are palm oil, coconut oil, and unground dried dawadawa (this can be excluded, but the combination of palm oil and dawadawa is so appealing). Use the meat of your choice and good salt. Add beef stock only if cooking beef stew. Most of my stews are made with smoked fish and need no stock on this account. Dried Cameroonian peppers can be kept handy in case the heat of the stew needs adjusting.

All my peppers and leeks are washed meticulously, especially the leeks, to ensure there is no soil between the lengths of leek skin. All the ingredients are kept whole, not cut up at all. The peppers are deseeded, except for the Scotch bonnets. All the ingredients are given their own floor space in the glass dish for the reason that if there is too much crowding or one ingredient is put on top of the other, the desired charring of the peppers and leeks will be compromised. Better to spill over into another dish than put the ingredients one on top of the other. When the ingredients have been arranged, a sprinkling of salt and a sparing drizzle of coconut oil is applied, preferably rubbed all over the peppers and leeks.

The roasting is done at low heat, the ingredients covered and tucked in with some foil, ovenproof paper or any other appropriate wrap. This removes the necessity of adding water to the ingredients. The peppers and leeks will steam, collapse, and release water that will come up in the base of the dish, and then it'll be time to roast them uncovered. The uncovered roasting should be continued until all the peppers and leeks are equally charred golden and brown (not black). The stock from the ingredients – the water from the vegetables released in the first minutes of roasting, and then absorbed back again – completely negates the need for any kind of stock cubes or even beef stock. This respectful mode of cooking releases the innate deliciousness of every pepper and leek. The peppers and leeks are cooled and blended with water, depending on how thick or thin one wants the stew. I declare this the answer to the finickiness of the Yorùbá. The peppers are cooked down to the inside of each seed left in the Scotch bonnets, so that when they are blended, they yield willingly and the stew is so smooth it glides over the palate.

The blend is transferred to the unglazed earthenware pot with a slick of palm oil. The pot is kept closed, the heat kept low. The stew is smooth, so it splatters ferociously. The seasoning is adjusted, the beef, fish or chicken is added, and the next few minutes are ceremonial. The stew is ready.

Lost in Translation

My Chilean friend Carolina Melendez and I once traded airplane food stories. Hers was egúsí soup on the last leg of her trip from Kuala Lumpur to Lagos. She used the word 'pungent' in describing her first impression of the soup and I tried to do a quick estimation of the number of times I have heard the words 'egúsí' and 'pungent' in the same mouthful of air. she said egúsí soup looked and smelled like some kind of egg dish gone bad, and it was a very bad smell.

The interesting thing was that everyone else seemed to be eating theirs. She meant the Nigerians. She didn't want to be the whiner in economy class. Doesn't everyone hate an economy-class whiner even if she has a legitimate complaint? So unfamiliar was the terrain on her plate that she could only manage a ravenous eating of the serving of beef in the soup, leaving behind all of the unhappy, crummy, textured eggs.

My story was of heading to London for the first time at 16. My airplane meal was supposedly three courses: a salad that, to my Nigerian sensibilities, was really only incidental to the main meal, which was familiar but insufficient to feed a toddler. There was a dessert course of cheese with three diminutive crackers; nothing like what I expected a sweet course to be. It should, at the very least, have been *sweet*. I ate the main course wishing it was larger, nibbled on the biscuits and the rubbery triangles of cheddar, rifled through the salad for anything resembling meat, and wondered – still ravenous – why, over the Atlantic, the British had to live up to their reputation of being as tight as Japanese handbrakes. Why not persevere till we landed in Heathrow?

No sooner were my bags unpacked at my aunt's house than I had to get the issue of the meal on the plane off my chest. She laughed and explained that the British don't eat like us. Nigerians would be happy to eat one course at the most sophisticated of dinners, and that course would only need to be served in generous portions or include a variety of dishes. The quality, variety and size of the meat portions would most accurately indicate the importance of the occasion, not the number of courses. If one served five courses of salad without meat or fish to the average Nigerian at a dinner party, he would not be impressed by the variety of vegetables. He would be urgently looking about for the meat and the rice, the fried rice, the jollof rice.

In order to be satisfied with my airplane meal, my aunt said sympathetically, I was required to eat all of the bitter cos in the salad, all of the main meal and all of the cheese and biscuits, as well as the five or so perspiring grapes.

It was an important precursor to the many disappointments with food I encountered in cosmopolitan London, Wolverhampton and Cardiff. The lasagne was too cheesy and milky, making me exceedingly gassy. There was a strong suspicion that I was lactose intolerant. My father had warned me that many southern Nigerians are.

The delicious-looking potato bake smelled divine – the aroma of the tomatoes spread on the potatoes prickled in the nostrils, and set off some undignified watering of the mouth – but the whole thing tasted overwhelmingly of tart, barely cooked tomatoes that, in Nigerian lingo, 'slapped you'. It was completely pepperless to boot, and the potatoes had not browned in the whole enterprise. They were just-cooked potatoes, with no edge, no crunch, no golden colouring, confounding my Nigerian palate. The pesto was murky and alien, with a brawny taste of fresh grass. The greenness of the smell was familiar, like a milder form of the smell of bitter leaf, or afang leaf maybe. It looked like cooked afang but there was no comforting palm-oil liquor on its face. It had pine nuts, which I had never heard of, and cheese. Cheese! Anything that uncomfortable-looking surely had to be eaten either with discretion, for medicinal reasons or be a laboriously acquired taste.

The doner kebab was nothing like suya, and if you wrung it you got a bucket full of grease. It didn't come with the smell and decoration of newsprint, or the groundnut, pepper and ginger to sprinkle on top. There were no crunchy red onion slices, no juicy fresh tomato chunks. The roasted chicken flesh came off still-bloody bones like toilet paper. The chicken was as bland as toilet paper too. The steak and kidney pie was as phlegmatic as a NIPOST clerk. It could never in a million years hold a match to the ubiquitous shortcrust pastry meat pie that you bought from Munchies in Lagos. Even the Jamaican patties stood outside my visual comfort zone with their bright turmeric colour. Everything except Yorkshire pudding was overrated, inappropriately bland and in need of a dash of Tabasco sauce, which I carried about in my bag. I discreetly laced a few chocolate mousses with Tabasco sauce out of desperation for crawling, walking, burning heat on my tongue. My disappointment was deepened by the fact that I had spent so many years staring at Jeni Wright's *All Colour Cookery Book*. Lasagne and steak and kidney pie had looked unarguably delicious on the pages of that book.

The parties I was invited to in my early university days were the worst affairs of all. I prepared earnestly for them by wearing my good jeans and eating nothing the whole day in stomach-rumbling expectation of rice and chicken. Or rice and fried beef at the very least. The people who advised me that parties in England were always dress-down affairs omitted some rather crucial information about the food at British university parties. After all, no self-respecting Nigerian party could take off without the presence or imminent arrival of jollof rice and chicken. One could actually count on the fact that there would be two kinds of rice – jollof and fried rice. Nigerian fried rice, mind, with tiny, meticulously cut cubes of meat, chicken, shrimp and green peas, not Chinese fried rice with egg. If a Nigerian could not provide rice and meat, then they would not call a party and get their guests' hopes up. I could never sufficiently conceal my disgust at the cold, salty quiches that were the preserve of these UK university parties, the romaine greens and raw baby tomatoes, the cheese balls and hideous orange Doritos that attacked your throat, the cheap fizzy wine frugally measured out in Styrofoam cups. The raw tomatoes were delicious but that didn't matter. The point was that you never, ever presumed a Nigerian wanted to eat raw tomatoes at a party or that their appetite would go to rest on a few raw tomatoes, smile and accept that it had been fed.

I was so annoyed with one particular host for inviting me to dinner on a cold day and feeding me quiche that I found myself sinking into what I must admit was an unreasonable degree of despair. The tears trickled as I rode the tube home. The people on the tube must have wondered if someone had died. Not only was I still hungry, I felt completely misunderstood and exhausted. If you invited a Nigerian to a meal, the smallest obligation you had to fulfil was to make sure that that meal was piping hot. No matter the day or the weather, the food must be hot. My host hadn't taken the time to discover what I liked, hadn't bothered to ask me. She fed me what she liked and then required that I compliment the food because the British require that people eat and compliment the meal incessantly at the same time. The company was too small to wield the bottle of Tabasco sauce without getting caught. I kept up a good front for hours but in the light of recurring dinner party disappointments, that quiche was the absolute last straw that broke the camel's back.

After spending three years studying an undergraduate degree in Wolverhampton and eighteen months on a master's degree in Wales, I did learn to love Gruyère cheese quiches. I could even keep down some blue Stilton if there was something to counteract the saltiness, like an apple. I bought mutton neck and small, brittle-boned chickens from local halal meat shops. I discovered the health food fringes embellished with creative treats: delicious, seeded handmade bread, goat's milk butter and home-made jams. I made stew from sweet red peppers, canned tomatoes, onions and Scotch bonnets. I never made friends with baked beans, never joyfully ate a teaspoon of the stuff. I binged on freshly baked Yorkshire pudding. I resolved that if I had been fed Yorkshire puddings and water on my first flight out to the United Kingdom, I would have been blissfully happy, and thought better of the British.

My best friends in Wolverhampton were a doomed South Asian couple. The man was a reluctantly devout Muslim who wasn't allowed to marry the woman, a fragile Hindu named Hemel, after Hemel Hempstead in Hertfordshire. The Muslim mother sent palak paneer to her son on weekends, and the Hindu mother sent potato and mushy pea samosas and lamb curries.

No one ever said to me, 'Right Yemisí, tell me all about Nigerian food.' Angelos, boyfriend to a Greek postgraduate housemate in Wales, came up to me one day while I was cooking and asked if I was cooking tiger or lion. He didn't wait for an answer. He grinned and told a long anecdote about an old housemate who cooked Nigerian food all the time and how the food and the house 'smelled like shit'. I spent a week with a family in Poole who cracked endless jokes about 'African chickens' being like vulture meat, and 'swallow' and 'draw soup' being like starch and glue. This family had lived as missionaries in Uganda and believed that they were experts on all things 'African'.

There was the inscrutable conclusion that the food I ate at home in Nigeria was 'African'. It was 'jungle fare'. It was something you ran out to the bush for. It was cantankerous and makeshift. It jumped off the plate and fought you for the spoon. The anecdotes for the week I spent with the family in Poole were nightly affairs, told with sniggers over dinners that felt rationed and miserly. If one could have Yorkshire puddings and roast, why on earth would one want Nigerian food? So you didn't need to ask Yemisí about Nigerian cuisine. She was living the life in Britain eating British food.

I must admit to having been caught completely unawares by this, so much so that it was difficult to begin to defend myself. I imagined that if people lived in cosmopolitan cities and collided with Tanzanians and Thais and Koreans and Ghanaians on a daily basis, if they embraced lamb curries, lasagnes, dim sum and Jamaican patties, they shouldn't enthusiastically jump to conclusions that have 'jungle fare', 'African chickens', tigers and lions in them.

I waited for someone to respectfully enquire about my food, the sort of enquiry that would draw out epistles to Nigerian food, but in five years of going back and forth between Nigeria and the United Kingdom, no one ever did. Not even the South Asian housemates who were so generous with their palak paneer. There are over twenty years between Carolina Melendez's and my plane-food story. Supposedly, airlines have since made a genuine effort to try to understand their clients' local cuisines, not presume that one size fits all. But the misunderstandings about Nigerian food remain.

Yes, our food is mainly a combination of soups and what probably comes across as stodge. We have not bothered much with dressing it up to global fine-dining standards. Our soups are some of the best-kept secrets in the world. While the rest of the world has gone on and on about their cuisines, we have remained mute, with our mouths full of food. We love our food but we've not tried to win the world over with it. This might be a combination of being a little smug and feeling there is nothing to prove while feeling slightly intimidated by other peoples shouting so loudly about their food.

The egúsí soup on the plane could indeed have done with a makeover. It didn't need to overwhelm the cabin with the smell of dawadawa. It might have needed a bit of PR to tailor it to the context. But to be fair, when people talk about food being smelly, sometimes all they mean is that it is unfamiliar. After all, this same Carolina Melendez who said egúsí soup was smelly was once caught trying to smuggle a durian fruit on a taxi in Malaysia. The taxi driver's nose caught a whiff of what has been described as 'a smell from hell'. She and her fiancé were asked to disembark the taxi with their precious durian. They could have fared worse; it is illegal to carry a durian fruit in a taxi in Malaysia. Perhaps the egúsí needed a manual saying it was made from melon seeds, not eggs and that it had fermented locust beans in it. Perhaps the airline that went through all the propaganda effort of turning dull crackers, cheap cheese and four or five grapes into dessert should have called an expert to interpret egúsí soup for high altitudes.

Afang Soup and Hairy Legs

It took my husband a decade to tell me that he had a thing for hairy women. Saying it at any time was going to be a major gaffe. He liked women who had curly sprouts in their cleavage, or dark spots on their chins from where they had made the naïve decision to shave with a razor before they realised it resulted in coarser, longer, more resilient hairs. Women who had committed to shaving daily, sporting razor burns like a man. It's wiser to take each individual hair out with a pair of tweezers, except of course one is soon overwhelmed and bored with that commitment. These facts tend to be discovered too late in the sensitive feminine relationship with coarse hairs. My husband wasn't that specific about how much hair and where, but if you are from Cross River State and you say 'hairy women', when the average woman there is already fighting a losing battle with facial hair, then you must mean a comprehensive hirsuteness.

And perhaps he didn't say 'hairy women' but rather women with a little more body hair. 'Flocculent' like a pretty rambutan. Or 'barbigerous', like a velvet wrapper with a generous pile. Because, of course, the words 'hairy woman' collide with the image of a desirable, sexy, warm creature who you have stored in the closet for ten years and are trying to describe to your wife. Living in a dark closet for such an extended period of time would make any creature significantly hairier. If you come from Calabar it makes sense to have a thing for a woman with a beard. The women there eventually give up on pulling out hairs. The forbearance is apparent in the upended chin rugs, brushed-fuzz legs, moustaches defying thickly layered make-up, and the unmistakable, peppery aroma of hair, warm skin and humid heat.

I was once standing in the Arik Air queue for the Calabar flight at Abuja's Nnamdi Azikiwe Airport behind one of those congenitally fashionable young women. Her skirt was appropriately short and she was wearing sheer stockings. She was looking for her suitcase. The men at the check-in counter were losing their minds helping her to look for her suitcase. She moved them on strings with every brisk convulsion of her bottom, every swish of false hair, every whimper about her lost luggage. And was that a moustache? Hairs peeping from behind deep cleavage? One or two wayward strands reaching from her chin? The fashion consciousness that mandates full hair extensions over glorious real hair, wearing nylon stockings in 34°C heat, and tottering on beautiful shoes so precarious they should have been kept for the short walk from the car to a crisp restaurant table, has omitted a mandate on stray hairs. It made sense that she was on her way to Calabar in Cross River State: there she was a showstopper, full stop.

Here is possibly the image my husband had kept secret for a decade. It isn't pedestrian for me. I grew up in Lagos, and I am not Cross Riverian. The same way I cannot summon any genuine wistfulness for boyish men with no facial hair, chest hair, or strong, hairy arms, is the same way I cannot be open-minded about hairy women moving out of the realms of Calabar into international glossy magazines.

It was a friend who first suggested that Cross Riverian hirsuteness had to do with eating afang soup. It couldn't be the weather, not when bordering Cameroon is more elevated, has more wintry Christmases and is therefore more deserving of hirsute females whose bodies have adapted to the need to keep warm. There must be hairy women in Cameroon, but they don't have the renown or the statistical strength of those from Cross River State. It could be natural selection, a dominant trait passed down from one ancestor who wasn't too hot on gender disparity and liked women with coarse facial and chest hairs. It could be about the heightened sexuality of Cross Riverians: the more hairs, the more apocrine glands, the more pheromones, the more attraction between members of the opposite sex, the more motivation to produce females who have more apocrine glands ... Again, natural selection.

It is significant that Cameroon sends most of its rainforest afang leaf across the water to Nigeria. Afang soup is not popular with French-speaking Cameroonians so their afang gets sent to English-speaking Cameroon, which eats afang soup but would rather eat a little of it and exchange the majority for the stronger Nigerian naira.

The oval leaves on a bunch of cut-up afang stalks will wave diplomatically at you as if they are not the same plant recently unwound after years of looping around a host tree. It climbs stealthily, one slow step over the other, stealing food, water and nutrients, all the time pretending to only embrace the tree. Someone with a good eye will point out a spectacular tree in the forest of Akpabuyo on the fringes of Calabar. It will be covered with bridges of afang, fat and glossy, with all the virtues of the host tree. But if you push the tree with one little finger, it will fall over like a stage prop.

There was a wiry orphan called Dickson Bob, named for his father Dickson Paulinus God-Dey Bob, who was unusually adept at harvesting afang in the Okuni-Ikom Union. He was originally from Anang, Akwa Ibom and lived in the care of his mother's people in Okuni, Northern Cross River after his parents died. In her youth, his mother was renowned for climbing trees for afang. They called her Ifumi and she was the chairperson of Iwa-Rock. She climbed better, faster, than her male contemporaries, so it seemed natural that her son should do it as effortlessly as if it were a genetic imprint.

It wasn't unjust that Dickson Bob's aunty sent him into the darkness of the forests to harvest afang after school. She had ten children of her own and they all worked after school and farmed in the mornings before school. Dickson Bob spent many afternoons unravelling roads and bridges and monkey ladders of afang. He cut them up, bound them in neat bunches, and stood at the edge of the forest, offering them for sale to passersby. Whatever he made went to his aunty, who paid his school fees and bought meat, clothes and toiletries with some of the money. She saved the rest for when he would need a dose of chloroquine for malaria.

In this piddling way, many children have paid their own way through secondary school and university. These stories sound fantastical, almost patronising, until you sit in on an Okuni union meeting in the town hall at 9 a.m. and watch the bush in the distance come to life with moving towers of afang. Dickson Bob was part of Sally-Rock, whose chairman was a thirty-year-old man called Funky, who was so good at climbing that he was a part of Sally-Rock by pure merit. Many of the Sally-Rock harvesters are from Akwa Ibom, like Dickson-Bob's father.

If you want to see a Cross Riverian's hairs bristle, remind them that they have eaten almost all their own afang and are now eating Cameroonian afang. Deeply offended, they will retort that they are doing no such thing. They are eating afang trained around bamboo stalks in their backyards or cultivated afang, if they have no other option in the world. And, by the way, you are being nonsensical: no one could have unwound the totality of afang in the forests of Cross River State. And if you must know, English-speaking Cameroon is Nigeria. Sally-Rock, the Nkani arrangement of the Okuni-Ikom Union, can spend a whole week in the forest, cover the Okuni town square with afang and not have harvested a bowl of the afang in Cross River's forests. The purist will pout and tell you how he will never touch a cultivated afang leaf because his grandfather and great grandfather were cooked a fresh pot of afang soup by a loving spouse every day. Real afang. Forest afang, thank you very much.

By and by you will learn that it is true that the forest afang has, over the years, become endangered in Cross River State. The proof is in the trawlers weighed down with afang coming across the Etung River, from villages at the foot of mountains in Ubenekang in Mamfe, Cameroon. Ikang, Ekang, Ubenekang, Ekoi, and the Calabar River were all one region before a line was drawn on a map in the hands of General Gowon and Ahmadou Ahidjo of Cameroun in Yaounde in 1971. They say they sat in a room somewhere with this map, trying to chart where Nigeria ended and Cameroon began, and ended up defining the point somewhere in the middle of the Cross and Calabar rivers, granting most of the area to Cameroon.

The afang from Cameroon is unloaded into large trucks at smugglers' coves in Ikom on the Cross River State side. A few tips are paid to marine police who stumble on the process, a few more in small change to checkpoints on the roads from Ikom to Calabar.

The smallest bunch of afang sells in the market for N250. There are women whose sole profession is standing in Marian Market cutting afang leaves into strips more perfect than juliennes. They stand to cut, because the leaves are so fibrous you can't do it sitting down. The women do this from 8:30 a.m., when the market opens, to 5 p.m. when it closes. Their knives are sharper than butchers' knives, sharp enough to cut a finger clean off. There is always a sharpening file nearby, and a piece of wood to balance the rolled up afang leaves while cutting. The leaves are rolled into balls as tight as a fist, then sliced through as if one were making strands of hair.

A woman will charge N100 for her cutting. From there most people will take their cut afang to a man in the market with a small mill on a table. He'll painstakingly pass the fibrous strips through the mill, winding an ancient lever around and around to grind the leaves, the other hand pushing the afang deep into the belly of the mill, until it comes out at the other end with the consistency of green pesto. You'll pay him another N100, and wonder why someone would charge so little for so much straining and sweating. Only after this longwinded journey is the afang ready for cooking, but don't leave the market before buying a dried cod head from Mumsie's smoked-fish stall. Buy the one with the ugliest, most sour expression. Ask Mumsie to cut its grimace into manageable pieces with a saw. This is the foundation of the afang soup: the foremost ingredient in the patient stock simmering for an hour and a half in an earthenware pot with uziza seeds (cubeb peppercorns). The bedrock of flavour. This head has sailed all the way from Norway, from under the turned up noses of those silly Europeans who don't understand the first thing about flavour. Give thanks for it and for their snobbery towards many things wonderfully pungent and malodorous and ugly.

The long list of ingredients for a family pot of afang soup gets the point of its hedonistic superiority across.

Afang Soup

6 cups freshly, finely julienned afang leaves

6 bunches dainty-leafed waterleaf (The waterleaf must be very young and small to give more flavour and release less water into the soup. They are plucked from their stems, the lilac flowers and stems discarded, and the plucked leaves cut)

Half a white cod stockfish head

Half a catfish head, well smoked and dry. (The smoked catfish head is broken up with one swift crack to the head with the ball of the hand. Your fingers must be spread wide and stiff. The gills of the fish are discarded. The head is rubbed with coarse salt and rinsed with warm water)

1 medium, smoked catfish body

2 cups shelled nkonko (beige, turban-shelled periwinkles)

1 cup fragrant white Ijaw crayfish or 1/2 cup ground smoked catfish belly (or both)

400g soft kanda (cowhide/pomo)

5 medium-sized snails, cleaned boiled each snail cut into halves

3–5 whole, medium-heat Scotch bonnets (depending on required heat, focus on aromatic rather than hot)

6 cups first-grade palm oil (lean cuisine is overrated. Best to focus on wonderful, oily fats and omega threes and sixes)

2–3 pints water for stock (depending on type of pot. This measurement suits my thirsty earthenware pots)

Ground dried Cameroonian peppers

Good sweet salt

Two inches of ginger root is my hidden ingredient in the stock. Afang purists think it is an abomination to cook soup with ginger root, but I don't understand why anyone in their right minds would snub ginger root and then cook with Maggi stock cubes. That is barefaced hypocrisy

Put 3 pints of water in an earthenware pot with the washed catfish head, washed stockfish head, cleaned and washed kanda, the 1/2 cup of ground fish, some Cameroonian pepper, a confident pinch of salt and one whole Scotch bonnet. (There are some people who don't want the intensity of the stockfish-head aroma but still want the depth of flavour it contributes. Do this: simmer the stockfish head on its own. After 30 minutes of cooking, drain the water, rinse the pot, put clean water in it, and then add the smoked catfish head and other ingredients.)

Allow the ingredients in the pot to boil, and then simmer for up to one hour, until the head of the stockfish has fallen apart and is gelatinous, and the kanda is very soft. In the meantime, boil the nkonko separately in another pot. Change the water in which it is boiling twice to get it thoroughly clean. Boil for about 10 minutes each time, drain the water completely and put the nkonko in the stockpot.

Cross Riverians don't remove any piece of the fish head from the stockpot. They leave in all the bones and even the gills. Part of the textural integrity of the purist's afang soup is hard fish-head bones, but I don't have the patience for licking bones. When it comes to soup, my idea of textual integrity is even terrain, not constant distraction. The typical Cross Riverian will also put in beef and goat meat. I find that quantity and variety of meat overwhelming.

Blend the rest of your Scotch bonnets with the white crayfish, and add the blend to the stock. Allow the stock to cook for another 20 minutes. You need to check the seasoning as you add the ingredients. Be careful not to add more water because the waterleaf will release a lot of water into the soup and the consistency will be ruined by too much liquid. Add the boiled snails.

Press the waterleaf into the stock and cover the pot. You may turn the heat down. Allow the waterleaf to be incorporated into the soup. This won't take 5 minutes. Press the julienned afang into the pot and close the lid again for another 5 minutes. Add your six cups of palm oil on top of the afang and this time close the pot tightly. The end of cooking is no more than 10 minutes away.

Stir the soup well, ensuring that the afang and palm oil are thoroughly combined. Quickly adjust the seasoning. Close the pot firmly and turn the heat off. The greens must not be overcooked. I like the twist of the Kachuan Eruan in Northern Boki, Cross River: they don't put their afang through the mill, and they add roasted groundnut paste.

I think of the woman who eats afang daily, and many women in Cross River do: luxurious quantities of barely processed saturated fats in palm oil; fatty heads of fish; wild, fresh greens with thousands of undocumented health benefits stolen from trees; complex carbs in the form of gari; no soft drinks, no greasy doughnuts, no city stress; lots of calming, drizzling rain, cool evenings, an outrageous amount of organic lovemaking … Aren't these what those fundamentalist nutritionists prescribe for improved hair growth? If we add a few dominant genes won't we effortlessly produce the sexy, carefree, full-bodied, 'hairy' Cross Riverian beauty of my husband's fantasies? Won't this soup put plenty of hair on anyone's legs, man or woman?

Between Ebà and Gari

In 2000, I walked into a buka in Enugu and asked for ebà. In my defence, I had been standing in one of the queues in the heat of the afternoon, in the confusion of the lunchtime rush hour, for about ten minutes. The people ahead of me, and in other queues were giving their orders to servers behind a long white laminate counter. Their plates of gari and soup, akpu and soup, were being handed over with the briskness of a buka that had been in the business of lunchtime swallow and soup for a long time.

The 'ebà' fell out of my mouth and more than a few people turned, knee-jerk, to look in my direction. My server looked askance, as if I just said something in Jalaa. It took me twenty prolonged seconds to make an embarrassed retreat. My use of the word 'ebà' was as unfortunate as standing in the palace of the Emir of Kano and shouting out, 'Aboki!'

'Gari!' I sent in hot pursuit of the ebà.

It was too late. My server gave me another look that said, *And you looked as sane as the next person.*

The man who drove me to the buka had no words of consolation for me. He was a generously upholstered man who liked to laugh, but he rolled around in my embarrassment. He said there is something the Igbos call someone like me, someone who comes from the part of Nigeria that I come from, walks into a buka in Eastern Nigeria and doesn't know to ask for gari instead of ebà. The word is 'ofe mmanu'. Or 'ndi ofe mmanu'.

Ndi ofe mmanu: one of the intellectually pretentious cloak-and-dagger, war-mongering, Scotch-bonnet gorging people who cook cardiac arrests with gallons of oil and call them peppery stews. We're talking about culinarily unsophisticated high-and-mighties. Not surreptitiously; they don't deserve that courtesy. Many Yorùbá people aren't familiar with the word ofe mmanu, but we know the equally disdainful 'ngbàtí-ngbàtí'. 'Ngbàtí' is the Yorùbá word for 'when'. The Yorùbá non-speaker, sitting on his spacecraft, listening in on a Yorùbá conversation, would hear a lot of the conjunction. The word does have something attention-grabbing about it. If an Igbo person wants to gossip in Igbo about a Yorùbá person and he wants that Yorùbá person to know he is talking about him, he will use the term ngbati-ngbati. The Yorùbá's ears will prick-up but she will probably not understand a word of what is said after the ngbati-ngbati.

It isn't because I am Yorùbá that I say ofe mmanu is a makeshift appellation, but because it's hypocritical. The difference between the ebà the Yorùbá eat and the gari the Igbo eat is only the degree of compactness determined by the amount of water added. Gari is often made off the hob, with boiling water and plenty of elbow grease. Ebà is made by adding the water to a smaller quantity of gari and allowing it to cook for a few moments.

The Yorùbá stew that the ebà accompanies is typically denigrated for being oily, but how, in comparison to Cross Riverian afang soup or edikaikong cooked in half an Eva water bottle of palm oil, is the Yorùbá pot of stew even commensurately oily? Our paltry three cooking spoons of groundnut oil per stew pot is lean cuisine in comparison. However, it is true that the Yorùbá's heavy reliance on stew for making every piece of starch palatable and lubricated is regarded by the rest of Nigeria as culinary sloth. Yes, we eat stew with everything. Yes, there are Nigerian men who will not marry Yorùbá women because they will have to have stew with absolutely everything. Perhaps it's because we eat stew daily and stew has to be cooked with oil, that we end up eating a lot of oil. But what is that oil in comparison to the quantity that Cross Riverians eat, with their plantain porridge and afang soups drowning in palm oil? They are the true ofe mmanus!

The Igbo, though, know exactly what they are doing by giving the Yorùbá the name 'ofe mmanu'. To argue that it doesn't fit only affirms the caricature. In consonance with their renowned shrewdness, they have earmarked sweeter names for the man from Calabar or Ikot-Ekpene: 'ndi imi nkita' is his nom de guerre, and it refers to that person whose nose is as cold as a dog's. The postscript is that the Efik and Ibibio's love of dog meat has caused an abnormality whereby their noses are cold to the touch. Naming someone or something is a way of overpowering the person or thing, of eating the person. The laughing driver in Enugu once explained to me that historical accusations of cannibalism were misunderstood: there were some enemies you needed to eat because it was an incontrovertible punctuation in their destruction. If your enemy was strong, you cooked and ate him, and you did it in company, to overcome him completely. If he was not so formidable, you owned him by naming him. 'Ndi imi nkita' is the slaughterhouse name given to a healthy dog in order to eat it.

The matter cannot end there. The Yorùbá are intellectual snobs, but a lot of the snobbery has nothing intellectual about it. We have tried very hard for very long to convince ourselves and everyone else that class and pedigree-consciousness is the same thing as intellectual precociousness. We believe, with quiet, strong resolve, that elbow grease is undignified and pen and paper is the route to the highest aspirations. God lives in universities from Mondays to Fridays and goes to church to meet us on Sundays. We don't care how well Bill Gates has done, he is *illiterate*. Illiteracy to a Yorùbá does not mean the inability to read or write; it means the man didn't go to university.

The Yorùbá are conclusively the crown princes of Nigeria. Our own name for the Igbo man is not in the stew, but in the 'swallow', in the movement of the starch down the oesophagus. 'Aj'òkuta-má-mumi' means, literally, the person who eats rocks and needs no water, no lubricating soup to move it along. In real terms it means a savage. We are always asking people, '*Who* is your father? *What* is your name?' And when we get a response, when we are told the name, we refuse to pronounce it properly.

'*Epo pupa gari Isobo £1.10…*' Isobo is the name that we call the Urhobo. Not because we can't say the letters in Urhobo but because we won't condescend to say their name properly.

The Yorùbá are always making class distinctions even among themselves. Even when there is no geographical factor we use words like 'ajebutter' (butter eater) and 'ajepáko' (wood eater) distinguishing refinement and crassness. We are obsessed with terms of reference, and we are the lords of culinary metaphors for defining class.

We join the Igbo in calling the Efik, Ibibio and Ondo (the last incidentally are our own kin) 'aj'ajá': dog eaters. We fell behind the Igbo in imaginative slurs for dog-eating so we make up our failure with facial expressions that get the full impact of our snobbery across. The Ondo will admit to eating dog but they will tell you that their dog of choice is bush dog, organic dog, vegetarian dog, whatever kind of dog it takes to get the attention off them and on to the real outsiders. Northern Cross Riverians will disdain the Ibibio from Akwa Ibom for the same reasons: 'Oh those Ibibio people will eat any kind of dog. Even the one that has been given its jabs!' An Ibibio man so discombobulated by the siege said to me, 'The dog that I eat only eats wheat not that other thing that dogs eat.' The Ondo want to have their dog and eat it too, quietly dining on dog in Ondo town yet retaining their rights to snub those people from Ore and upwards for other reasons.

We all have this kind of disdain for the same reason one might keep a gun in the house: it's for when an intruder comes. We never mean to use it. You love your Igbo in-laws but you want to keep the inane joke you can enjoy with your own people once their backs are turned. Sometimes you might crack these jokes in front of each other and laugh about it together. The jokes about food at least exhibit some self-effacement, because you are, at an infinitesimal level, acquiescing that your food is also peculiar; your okro (ilá alásèpo) smells too. You are being 'mindfully small-minded', for the good causes of joviality and building intimacy. You are being facetious and your self-administered higher scores on eating *better* are ultimately frivolous. The damage, if any, is a trifle. It isn't like those uncivilised *roast beefs* and *frog-eaters* who break heads open during Euro 2012 and then try to convince us that the

Euro channel means they are unprejudiced. It isn't India and Pakistan. Yorùbá and Igbo, we say on a sun-filled day, are brothers living in shared cosmopolitan spaces, sleeping in the same beds, working on the same portfolio at work etcetera, etcetera. Nigeria is one.

What makes disdaining otherness unique in Nigeria is the minefields of identity. Identification in Nigeria is an inflexible thing and for something so inflexible, so sure of itself, it is also rather nonsensical and volatile. At least with the roast beef and frog-eaters who share the European continent, a person can be a roast beef born in France and a frog-eater can be born in Somerton, Somerset. This can never happen in Nigeria. A Nigerian is *where his people come from*, not where he was born. A Nigerian is *what his people are*, never himself. Chiwetel Ejiofor the Nigerian–British/British–Nigerian movie star was asked by Ellen DeGeneres where he's from, and he guilelessly answered, 'London'. A deafening uproar went up across Nigeria: the correct answer, Chiwetel, is 'Enugu', and shame on you for trying to put on airs. London indeed!

Okere junction in Warri conscientiously showcases the contradictions. The Itshekiri and Urhobo have hated each other from antiquity, although most people will jump in with two feet and say it all started when the white colonialists came and put the Itshekiri over the Urhobo. Something about the Urhobo looking too intimidating with strong features, high cheekbones, black skin. From the informal history you would think every Urhobo man is so and every Itshekiri is otherwise. The Itshekiri till today have maintained the superiority complex, with the advantages, the strategic placements in corridors of power given to them by white colonialists. To this day, the Urhobo can't let go of the bitterness of being passed over, being disqualified from ruling. In recent times, the Olu of Warri lived on Okumagba land. Okumagba land is Urhobo land. Even though the Olu is monarch to both the Itshekiris and Urhobo, the Itshekiri insisted that he must be referred to either by the term Olu of Itshekiri or Olu of Sapele to showcase the continuing bias of Itshekiri superiority.

The Urhobo response: 'Is that so!' They ran the Olu off Okumagba land for the effrontery of wanting to be named only for the Itshekiris. Let him bear whatever name he wants especially as he is of no use to them and won't put a commensurate number of Urhobos in high positions of government. Whatever happens, the Olu can't maintain an upper hand for the Itshekiris and live on Urhobo land. So the Itshekiris and Urhobos procured new fuel for their old, longwinded attritions. They are willing to kill each other and they can't stand the sight or smell of each other. We believe them, until we visit Okere junction: as soon as the sun sets, as soon as the first strain of Emeka Morocco Maduka and his Minstrels hits the air, the pepper soup pot goes on the fire, and the sapele-water starts to flow, you'll find the Urhobo and the Itshekiri enthusiastically exercising each other's styloglossi, urgently seeking out miserable short-time rooms to sexually employ the angst and hatred. When day breaks, the hostility resumes, even in the broad daylight of modern marriages: a couple one half Itshekiri the other Urhobo, who left their villages behind thirty years ago, have been married for twenty years, have five university degrees between them. Every single quarrel they have will peak at the utterance of the words, 'Well they say the Urhobo and the Itshekiri should never marry.' Night falls and the hatred transmogrifies into unbridled passion. Night after night after night. Day in, day out.

When spouses are at each other's throats, everyone takes the sides *where they come from* and remembers to unsheathe the weapons that were kept polished for the intruder. You could never, ever trust those Igbo, who would come back from the dead if you waved new N1000 notes under their noses. They would sell their own grandmothers for money. And those Yorùbá: so filthy there isn't a clean glass to drink from in the whole goddamn house. When the daughter of a Yorùbá wants to marry the son of his good Igbo friend, they never sit down and philosophise that blood doesn't have a higher viscosity than camaraderie. They don't go over the nostalgic notes of their long-tested friendship from the Nigerian civil war. That will never work. In August 2013, the government of Lagos deported Igbos *back to where they come from*. Something about it felt right, otherwise there would have been a real uproar – like the one about Chiwetel Ejiofor saying he is British. Because we all stick to the indicators, whether they make sense or not, and treaties are intrinsically dull, Nigeria may yet divide along the lines of ebà and gari.

By the way, my in-laws are from Ikom LGA and Etung LGA in Cross River State respectively. But, as I was solicitously advised by a Yorùbá male relative, that is too much detail. Everyone from Ore in Ondo State up to Kwara is Igbo, and from Kwara going confidently north they are Mala. Insisting that my husband is not from Calabar but from Northern Cross River just complicates the issues of acceptance when I should have just left the matter well alone. Doesn't everyone know those Calabar/Igbo – whatever you want to insist they are – eat people! And don't even try to suggest that he might be in any way related to those notoriously promiscuous yam-growers, those Benue people, who offer their wives to guests in the name of hospitality. You don't want to be anywhere around Ugep after 6 p.m., standing on the side of the road and looking like a Yorùbá man! There is no questioning the fact that the five Yakurr communities eat people. You are only safe, ideologically and otherwise, in the south-west and only among your own people, who speak your language and eat your food.

The first time I made gari at the request of my mother-in-law, I put a little water in a pot and set it to boil. I got out a teacup and measured some gari into the boiling water. I was working hard to please her, although my overconfidence was about to get me killed. I stirred the gari into the boiling water, leaving it on the fire. I took it off the fire and turned it with the omorogun until it was nice and smooth. I put a slick of water in a round bowl, just to wet it. I put the gari in the bowl and rolled it around until it took the roundness of the bowl, forming a pretty mound. The kind you give to your husband when you are trying to make an effort, wave a white flag, or you know your soup is especially delicious and you want to show off. I presented the food to my mother-in-law.

She was unequivocal in her comments about my cooking. I was irritated; I thought we were playing for the same side. I did not understand what her problem was just as she did not understand mine. Now I am sure that her problem was that she had asked for gari and I had given her ebà. On the basis of those mixed wires, I was immediately written off as a bad cook. And the most outrageous thing a Cross Riverian man can do is marry a woman who can't make gari!

That refrain was playing loudly behind the disgust expressed over my food. As far as I was concerned, she was overreacting and I couldn't really understand what the fuss was about. I did not say anything about how my mother would call out from the next room, 'Leave that ebà on the fire, I didn't ask for ebà Igbo!' It was a tense moment, not one where I could be conciliatory by joking about prejudice. *Where I came from*, the desired end result of adding gari to boiling water was not a solid, but a smooth sludge. There was the issue of the quantity of gari that I made. In retrospect, I must have insulted my mother-in-law and left some suspicion of innate stinginess. When we made ebà *across the border* for a guest we did it with a subconscious calorie counter. You used it to pay a compliment to the eater. If the mound was too big, you were insinuating that your guest was a glutton. If it was cute and prettified, and she was a woman, even if she was a fat woman, you were complimenting her graceful mindful eating, and she might say something appreciative like, 'Oh, thank you, it is as if you read my mind that I didn't want a lot of ebà.'

My mother-in-law on the other side of the border was wondering if I was sending her the message, with my little hill in the bowl, that she was unwelcome in her son's house. Or if I was insinuating that her son was not a good provider and I needed to ration the gari. Or if I was hinting that she needed to be eating less food because she had a weight problem. All of the pieces fell into place when I was called aside on a later, relaxed day and gently admonished about generosity to guests and the necessity of always having food prepared and kept in a flask for whenever anyone dropped by. She went out and bought the food flask.

'Aj'òkuta má mu'mi', the Yorùbá title for anyone from Ore to Kwara, is probably more disingenuous than 'ofe mmanu'. I did not know this till I lived in Calabar and was ceremoniously introduced to the yellow gari made with palm oil. Yellow gari is made from cassava fermented for a short period. It is why you will hear of gari poisoning in the east and south-east of Nigeria but rarely among the Yorùbá, who ferment their white gari for a longer time. The yellow gari has palm oil added to even out the sourness of fermentation, make it smoother for swallowing and give an attractive yellowness. Cross Riverians, who are the real connoisseurs of soup, will eat yellow gari because there is no sourness competing with delicate flavours in the soup, but you won't find them drinking yellow gari, not if they have a choice. They drink the Yorùbá gari and consider it a delicacy.

We, the Yorùbá, eat the same gari both as ebà and for raw drinking. While producing gari, palm oil is added as a lubricant to help the 'rocks' pass comfortably down through the oesophagus to the stomach.

Isn't the real joke on the Yorùbá then, with their sour, hard, white gari ebà made without palm oil? Nothing worse than pointing one's finger and finding that there is an art to the eating of rocks, and you had the unsophisticated point of view all along. Not so high and mighty after all.

Ilá Cocoa

I love the sound of the words *ilá cocoa* – their resonance and soft sexiness, the way the 'cocoa' knocks twice on the roof of your mouth. I want to pretend I don't understand what they mean, that they are not Yorùbá words meaning soup made of young cocoa pods. They are, instead, the name of a beautiful country, or the perfect marriage between something sweet and something savoury.

I love the way food becomes animated when introduced to words. Even if you don't speak Yorùbá, there is an expectation of a treat when you hear 'ilá cocoa'. Instead of moving on to the mundane pounds and ounces necessary for the recipe, you want to camp at the words and find the engaging stories and muscular images that connect mind to emotions to gastric juices.

The story of ilá cocoa belongs to a man by the name of Festus Adétúlà, who insisted that his wife, Oyèbolá, never cook him okro soup in that lazy Yorùbá way. The Yorùbá cut up or grate okro pods, stir them into boiling water with salt and potash, and serve this briskly cooked okro with pepper stew and a choice of gari, pounded yam or fufu. This simple treatment of okro is scandalous to people from other parts of Nigeria, who dress up the vegetable with as many as ten other ingredients. Adétúlà considered it an abomination for a strong-brewed Owo man from Ibami Mose's farm to eat such spiritless food.

As a child approaching his adult years, Adétúlà's life moved seamlessly between work and hard work: from school to the farm and back to school. When he and his wife moved into their marital home, one of the first things he did was to plant his own cocoa trees. His wife thought he grew them for the childhood sweet treat of sucking on cocoa beans, or to beautify the garden, but he grew them for the nutritious, mucilaginous ilá cocoa. He taught his wife how to harvest twenty to twenty-five very young pods of cocoa. The green, grooved, elongated pods look like oversized okro pods, and perhaps this is what inspired the Yorùbá to cook them down into soup. The cocoa pods are wrapped and tied in glossy green cocoa leaves and steamed until the skin of the cocoa is soft. They are then mashed in a mortar, not with heavy pounding but with a measured, firm back-and-forth movement of the pestle. This produces a coarse mucilaginous mash of cocoa skin, beans and pulp.

In a pot, the stock for the ilá cocoa is made from ground pepper; chopped onions; boiled stockfish that flakes under the pressure of a fork; periwinkles; iru pete (fermented locust beans processed into a mushy wet consistency); ogìrì (fermented sesame seeds); and the holy grail of Yorùbá delicacies, the legendary eja osàn – a knife-shaped freshwater fish. This fish is so highly esteemed that the juju maestro King Sunny Adé immortalised it in song: 'Eja tútù Sokoyokoto ... Kí l'eléyi o o Eja osàn!'

Forty-two pieces of fragrant, smoked eja osan are presented by the groom to the bride's family during traditional Yorùbá weddings. Stewed eja osan is an undisputed aphrodisiac and a renowned husband-bewitching device. It's the official Yorùbá contemporary of Cross Riverian egome or Akwa Ibom ekpang nku kwo. Mrs. Oyèbolá Adétúlà uses the smoked eja osan.

Water is added to the stock ingredients and everything is brought to a boil. The mashed ilá cocoa is added to the stock with salt and a little palm oil. Shredded ugwu may be added at the end, just before the soup is taken off the fire.

This soup's ingredients are so dear that it is really only practical as a meal for one or two people. It must be served with authentic pounded yam made from yams grown specifically for pounding. They must be worked in a mortar and achieve a smooth, supple texture, otherwise, Mrs. Adétúlà says, her husband Festus would not eat it.

A few years ago, I met a Nigerian pastor who lived in Houston, Texas. He confided in me that there was no question of him coming back to live in Nigeria because he won't be able to buy his sausages. I was so astounded my mouth hung open in anticipation of the punchline. I can't resist contrasting the shallowness of living in a foreign country because of cheap sausages to the integrity of being opinionated about nutritious home-grown food. If Adétúlà had not turned his nose up at a dull bowl of okro soup, what sort of ilá cocoa story would we have to tell?

Nsala with Chicken

A Nigerian man is unfolding the details of cooking nsala soup. We are chit-chatting in spices: uda, uziza, ehuru, olima. There is no need to translate ingredients or the fine points of cooking. No need to say that olima are cayenne-red pods of grains of paradise. In the seven or so years since I began to write food, Google has become fluent in Nigerian condiments. For the record, this friend, this man talking nsala soup, speaks a different Nigerian language from mine.

Nsala soup is cooked with chicken, with love, or something akin to love, with lovemaking masquerading as contention. The soup has national character; an established personality. It's cooked with black fermented locust beans. Its base is silky stock coaxed diligently from fish-head bones melded with piquant, sweet and fragrant spices. The soup might 'be' regardless of the chicken, yet the chicken thickens the plot, enriches the soup and does both spectacularly. The spices will cross the blood–brain barrier, arousing emotions: hot ones, cool ones, ambiguous ones. If you suspect I'm paraphrasing an idealistically lavish soup, then you are right.

This Nigerian soup matter has not been loved-up enough, in my opinion. Think of the decades for which our food has belonged to the most fascinating person alive: the Nigerian. Our swallow and soup is that singular gem belonging to a nation of whiners. The way to identify the whiner's strong approval may be to mark moments of reverential silence: we never, ever whine about food. We whine about politics, soccer, bad roads, imported European beer (like anyone forced the stuff on us) and house of reps members, yes, but never about our food. There is, on the contrary, a drought of expression on our cuisine, strongly contrasted with reams and reams of words adorning the altars of other nationalities'. Yet there is real love in our relationship with food, deeply invested love and all the ramifications of that: the soft hum of energy generated by hard-working cabling between old married couples. I can rescue the luxurious beverage-in-outsized-mug quality of my words, the patriotic self-indulgence. I can convince all who argue against my idealistic lavishness with just one pot of nsala soup … with chicken.

My friend describes this soup in the context of spousal power struggles. Culturally, there are some things we both recognise as similar, universally Nigerian, even if we speak two different languages and those languages are deeply expressive of cultural differences. One similarity is the reticence in applying language to life: Nigerians have kept words away from describing food, as if speaking would diminish it. Here is a man born and raised in Delta State, bred to strive for pure reticence, with one of the keenest indigenous sensibilities I've encountered. So, in describing the soup it feels like he is saying too much, for a Nigerian man.

There is a complicating factor in the realness of the story. It is no allegory on food but a personal memory. He reminisces about night falling, hurrying between two villages, along hushed bush paths, carrying an irate chicken. The chicken's feet are tied together, its head hangs upside down, and it strains and complains throughout the twenty-minute distance. He has carried two others in the same way before, and has had to bring them back. The chicken is food and thus there is a disconnect – no consideration for its discomfort, no cultural footnotes for animal rights.

The village he is coming from is his grandmother's. The one at the end of the path is an in-law's. The chicken is being carried to settle a quarrel between an aunt and uncle. Their marriage is the sort that required the slaughtering of a whole farmhouse of chickens. The aunty has yet again offended her husband in a realm where husband is lord and master, where a compound can be made up of ten wives and fifty children, all serving the desires and enterprises of one man. Where women kneel to hand their lord and master his meals, on the best 'broken plates' (i.e. breakable plates) on an anxiously tidied tray. Women spend nights waiting their turn, their permission to be sexually reviewed, as dictated by a subliminal roster. Punishment is defined as losing one's place on the roster, and long years of programming means the exclusion hits home. It further solidifies one's dispensability. It overwhelms any thought or effective desire to outwit the system. No woman in that time and place wants to be a cultural outcast, so women always apologised to men because men were always right.

And yet Aunty was a repeat offender: mouthy, with the subtlest facial expressions, totally unaccommodating of any roster, real or imagined, featuring any other woman for lovemaking, cooking, washing of clothes or any other activity. She was apologetic about nothing. There had been some matter involving her husband and a girl in Lagos. No need to confirm whether the rumours were true. The girl was paid a visit by Aunty and given the sternest of warnings – death,

Sharia mutilations, pubic shavings, etc. – outlined in insane creative detail. It was only after the melodrama had faded, months later, that everyone clued in to the fact that Uncle had tired of the girl and let the knowledge of her existence slip, with full cognisance and confidence that Aunty would help him end the affair ... with a Dane gun.

It isn't difficult to visualise Uncle and Aunty's trip down to the village from Lagos on the day my friend ferried chickens to settle their quarrel: the transference of aggression to the steering wheel, the reckless flight of words contradicting necessary vigilance on the road, the haemorrhaging of time-honoured words.

'Ah-ah, am I, or am I not the head of this family? What I say goes.'
'You the man! But no, not a real man! No!'
'You will leave my house!'
'I will do no such thing! If you do not take care, you will leave your house.'

Aunty smugly served her words with seasoned nonchalance, with expensive engine-oil provocation, lubricating the argument. Outside the car, the day sparkled guilelessly. The elements were not supposed to be on her side. They were supposed to disintegrate in support of Uncle's cause. The reality of time and place was supposed to obey his birthright. Uncle was determined that he write the final chapter, put Aunty in her place once and for all. He might have married a younger woman, but none of them, *none of them*, would have survived the marriage. And if they did, they would not survive the living together after it. He was not going to be that man shamed by a woman whose dowry he had paid. And shame had degrees. His was soon going to be turned up to the fullest, if he did nothing. One day, he would find his head assaulted with rocks in front of his friends or children or colleagues from work, with words he would never be able to live down. 'There goes that man! Can you imagine what they said his wife answered him?'

After six hours on the road, Aunty and Uncle drove into the family compound. Uncle stepped out from the car, adjusted his trousers and made urgently towards the house. His plan was to enter the family house before Aunty had the chance to adjust her headtie and step out of the car. He said a quick word to his elder brother who had been standing outside to meet him. They turned and went to get their mother. They all came back out and stood with their backs to the door of the family house. Aunty limped delicately towards them. It had a little to do with the fact that her legs had gone to sleep. It had everything to do with milking the advantages of moving like she was fragile.

She smiled, they stared daggers. She curtsied delicately in greeting. They uh-huh'd in response. Even if she feigned nonchalance, it had to be dramatically toned down, because no matter how crazy you were, you never showed your in-laws barefaced defiance. Not unless you had made up your mind the marriage was over, and you had a man in the background somewhere, desperate to have you and your children. You kept the in-laws eternally wondering whether your husband was exaggerating the details of what had transpired. If absolutely necessary, you wept heartbreakingly to tip the scales, but before you did that, you fished for what they really knew of your quarrels.

'You cannot disrespect the one who holds the dowry on your head and expect to sleep in this compound. You will spend your night at your family compound. You can walk. You better head there before the sun sets.'

The correct answer from her was an unequivocal apology.

'Your husband says you dishonour and disrespect him,' said uncle's elder brother quietly. 'You insult him in private and pretend deference when in company. You say he is not a man. You said those words on your journey here. What would warrant such contempt?' Aunty agreed and kept the battle for another day, another private moment where she would make the fool pay. 'I admit to being hot-headed, and not thinking before I spoke. It was in the midst of a passionate quarrel that I said these words. I am sorry. It won't happen again.'

She moved on quickly to the penalty for her crimes, but Mama added, 'If he is not a man, you are the one who implanted your five children.'

Mama was the eternal snag. She didn't like the fact that the matter was about to be quickly packaged and dispatched. She saw through the insincere apology. It was one of many articulately phrased apologies. They would fine her a chicken. It was customary to do so if her quarrels with her husband had gone on after 6 p.m. of that day, and they had. Aunty would be made to go back to her parents' village, the neighbouring one, and send the chicken, along with negotiations of allowance to enter her husband's family house, via the young nephew

These special Ogbono seeds are a gift from a matriarch in Ebu, Delta State. The bush mangoes that they come from aren't green when ripened; rather they turn tan coloured. The mucilage generated by the seeds is subtle and sweet in aroma.

Sweet, steamed ripe plantains, served with ogbono soup, snails and chopped ugwu.

The cocoa pod bean, wrapped in thick white pulp, tastes like soursop or lychee and reminds me of the smoothness and creaminess of bananas. Biting on the bean releases a contrasting bitter taste.

Dawadawa, fermented locust beans molded into thick discs then sun dried or smoked lightly.

Dried Cameroonian peppers, which must be treated with the utmost respect. They are no respecter of persons. They are so hot they are lethal, yet beautifully aromatic.

Ogiri-isi (fermented castor oil or egusi seeds), a highly esteemed condiment with the unmistakable deep savouriness of fermentation and the texture and darkness of aged garlic.

The palm fruits are salty, heady, releasing a deep nutty flavour when you peel back the skin with your teeth.

A tablespoon of ground turmeric and fermented locust beans - not the purist's ideal combination.

Olima is one of two genres of grains of paradise ground with other spices for the Nsala Soup.

Ground small white Crossriverian crayfish, an ingredient as invaluable in cooking as salt or pepper.

One of my favourite condiment vendors in Marian market, Calabar selling everything that belongs in a soup pot from tinned tomatoes to hand shelled Egusi.

TOP: Sawa, Agodo, Sarapore. The Yorùbá specialise in smoking baby fish to delectableness.
BOTTOM: The best grade of stockfish in the market. The vendor Ijeoma has nicknamed it "glass cod" because of the vitreous complexion of the flesh on the inside of the fish.

Lime, yellow and red hot peppers dried so perfectly, they sound like beads when run through the fingers. Every home in the South of Nigeria has a container of ground hot peppers.

Dried multi-coloured chilies & milled red, yellow and green Cameroonian habaneros.

Punctiliously smoked prawns (Isa Opotopo, Ede pupa) from Garki market, Abuja. Their aroma is stunning, they are crisp and salty and difficult to stop eating. They are beyond expensive. The price of gold.

The perfect cold-stone weight for crushing pepper. The oyster shells are for sharpening the stones.

Orógùn kékeré for making small amounts of amala, igbako for serving the amala and ijabe for making ewedu.

Walnuts. Yorùbás call it 'Asala', and the people from Delta call it 'Ukpa'.

who had recently moved back to the village. Uncle's family would draw out the apology by complaining that the chicken wasn't big enough. They would send the messenger back and forth with chickens. But none of those things would draw real blood or humiliation, not from the likes of Aunty.

This was how my friend found himself carrying chickens on bush paths between two villages at night, his meal suspended until the matter had been settled. The third chicken was accepted and left at Uncle's village. My friend went back to get his grandmother and Aunty. The three approached Uncle's compound with kneeling, and the reiteration of apologies. It was all ceremonial, really. Everyone embraced and it was over, except that the chicken had to be cooked that night for Uncle. By Aunty. Cooked with nsala spices and served with pounded yam.

Nsala Chicken

1 whole, stressed, old layer chicken used to negotiate marital disputes

1 medium red onion (the onions in nsala lower the blood pressure)

4 medium-hot Scotch bonnets. (A fragrant yellow (Igbo) one can replace one of the four if available)

1 teaspoon uziza (cubeb peppercorns)

4 uda pods (selim peppers)

2 teaspoons ground white crayfish

2 ehuru seeds (calabash nutmeg)

1 teaspoon olima seeds

Half a teaspoon of alligator peppers (grains of paradise)

1 whole disc smoked dawadawa

6-8 cups fish stock

The chicken's complaints are silenced. It is cut into generous portions and placed in a large pot with pulverised peppers and onions. This pulverisation is the kind done with a hand stone mill that gets the essence out of every pepper seed. That's not its sole purpose: like the sound of the pounding of yams that will accompany the soup, the resonance of rolling stones in the quiet of the night, and the flexing of wrists, arms and waist in the grinding of pepper, are conciliatory images for a husband. These are images of a wife who is in her place. When she is done, after a bath, she will reinforce the imagery and motion in the dark, in the room.

The chicken for the nsala is slow-cooked with the 6–8 cups of fish stock. The uziza, uda, ehuru, olima and grains of paradise are crushed in a wooden hand mortar (nkpirite) and added to the chicken. So is the ground crayfish. Over medium heat, everything is brought to a boil. The heat is turned down to allow simmering for 20 minutes. A few spoons of the pounded yam are kept to thicken and whiten the soup.

'Isn't it all just foreplay?' I ask my friend. 'The whole thing? And isn't it a bit shameless to draw everyone into a quarrel that ends with the pounding of yam, the licking of soup, and tumbling into bed?' He shrugs and the reticence begins to set in. It makes me wonder if even men who agree to apply words to Nigerian life inevitably give in to weariness with words in the end. He rushes to give the story some trite conclusions.

'They say what makes marriage sweet is the real belligerence that ends in real lovemaking. If it were straightforward, it probably wouldn't be as interesting. I don't know. Haven't lived long enough.'

I ask him what happened when Aunty arrived at his grandmother's house without her husband, without her car. What did grandmother say when she saw Aunty approaching at that time of the evening on foot?

'Odiqua nma?'

There was no need to ask. You knew she was in trouble. She was always in trouble. And anyway, she didn't wait to enter the house before she started a monologue on that brainless husband of hers who ...[17]

---

[17] Aunty and Uncle now have nine children and many grandchildren, with their eldest daughter in her forties. Their quarrels remain ongoing and as recently as 2014 they again returned to the village to settle a year-long dispute.

Fermentation and Fornication

The Igbo call the prick of the pin, the pinnacle of wholehearted, home-made fermented locust beans, 'ogbein'. I had already chanced upon the subliminal drollery of the Igbo language. The words 'Ije kweuka tata' don't *really* mean 'Did you go to church today?' They mean 'Did you go to the house of doubt today?' Right now Igbo theologians are arguing back and forth about this syntactical entanglement: whether it is 'uno uka' (the house of doubt) or whether it is in fact 'uno nso' (the house of holiness). That is, whether the intention overrides the lingo and the contemporary generalised understanding of the words.

I wasn't surprised, therefore, to find a Mr Ogbein – Mr Fermented Locust Beans. I also encountered a Mr Akpu (Mr Cassava-Fufu), Mr Ukwa (Mr Breadfruit), Mrs Ugwu (Mrs Pumpkin Leaf), and a Ms Onuegbu (Ms Your-mouth-won't-kill-you) in the company of many other Igbo people bearing riddles for names with the same matter of factness as rising on Sunday morning to worship God in The House of Doubt.

Not even in the wastepaper basket of my most bizarre thoughts could I ever have paired the act of fornication with the fermentation of locust beans. It was Agi (short for Agnes), my neighbour's help and earnest advisor on honest dawadawa, who cautioned me that locust beans will not successfully ferment in the presence of a fornicator. It will disagree with the desired end, turn sour, grow mould, and give off an intensely offensive smell.

Agnes is like her name: so sincere that she often has no feel for a statement made tongue-in-cheek. So if she says that your dawadawa is doomed if a woman of loose virtue, or perhaps *lost virtue*, enters the kitchen while you are making it, then consider that statement irrefutable. It has an *Amen* behind it.

Agi's family can trace the making of dawadawa from virtuous woman to virtuous woman; that is, from handling by virginal girls and teenagers to handling by virtuous married women who only have sex with their husbands, down countless generations. Dawadawa categorically cannot be handled by even the ambiguously chaste. To show how much this requirement is taken to heart, regardless of the cloud of ambiguity, the rooms, out-rooms and cooking utensils relating to the sorting, boiling and fermenting of the beans must be distanced from any woman who is sexually active and unmarried.

I am, of course, firmly with the sceptics on this one. Agi's people must make their dawadawa on the moon if the preparation area is to be scrupulously free of the unchaste. What about the married woman fantasising about her husband's teenage brother? Is she chaste or is she fornicating? I also have to question the idea that dawadawa is offended by the unchaste woman but presumably not by the unchaste man.

I asked Agi about this. She shooed me away as if my question was the most stupid one she'd ever heard. But I got her. I caught her for a split, unwitting second where her face did something. Still, men don't make dawadawa so of course my question was stupid and naïve. An unchaste man, a fornicating man, is irrelevant because he won't be making the dawadawa. And if he is in the vicinity, it's unrelated to the locust beans. In essence, the relevant kind of fornication is the female kind of fornication. The ambiguity of chastity may not worry Agnes; it *needs must* worry the scientific sincerity of Obudu fermented beans. It certainly worries me because I have met many, many different definitions of fornication and I wonder which one applies to locust beans. If it is the Christian kind – and I believe 'fornication' was originally the property of ecclesiastical Latin – then intentions matter. As one Nigerian pastor said in transliterating Jesus's words, 'If you have done it in the laboratory of your heart ...' It is downhill or uphill from there, depending on whether you are for or against fornication.

Is kissing fornication?
For: (unambiguously) No.

Against: (Deep, extended rumination.)

Is regarding a woman with thoughts of fornication, fornication?

For: Of course not.

Against: Jesus says it is but ... all flesh is grass.

Is touching a woman's breast fornication?

For: Inside or outside her clothes? Maybe one can concede a PG13 kind of fornication but the nitpicking is pretty intense and impracticable.

Against: Well ... Not technically, because of course the reverse gear is still working at this stage.

Is touching a penis or vagina fornication?

For: Look is there penetration or not? And are we talking about men or women? I can tell you there is no man who will admit to you that touching a woman's vagina is fornication. That is farfetched.

Against: It is certainly going too far.

The word 'fornicate' is, in any case, like the word trafficate (that thing Nigerians do with a trafficator). It feels pretentious, like a word you can never put your back into using.

Agi is from the Boki tribe that lives in Obudu. The best dawadawa in Cross River State is from Obudu. There, dawadawa is so reverently handled that it can be eaten fresh (days after fermentation, that is) at room temperature without it being heated up in food or suspended over wood fires. It can be dispatched into soup without a second thought. The fermentation is so exceptionally done that it suggests something more than an expert hand; celibacy, perhaps?

Most of the fermented locust beans I had eaten before Agi's had an obstinate smell that you put up with because it was assumed that fermented locust beans smell bad. The truth is that locust beans fermented with integrity never smell bad. They shouldn't. Dawadawa can have the strong, invading aroma reminiscent of fermented foods like miso and Thai fish sauce, but unlike miso and fish sauce there is no commitment to quality control, no commitment to deciding that this is what good fermented locust beans smell like, so therefore it's a good smell.

The philistines are already trying to drag it down to a one-dimensional definition of aroma, but it will never be so. New terms of reference are needed for sophisticated circumstances. And dawadawa is sophisticated. However, having bought 'fresh' dawadawa, also known as iru pete, from Sura Market in Lagos; Dawadawa so shamelessly produced that it needed to be washed for sand and picked for stones. Anyone with marginally functioning taste buds understands that there is hardly any virtue left in washed dawadawa. Cooking with this Sura locust beans was made doubly traumatic by a plague of flies drawn by the smell, desperately trying to get in through the kitchen windows.

With Agi's dawadawa, you can smell the mustiness of fermentation, but it was also from hers that I first caught the strong suggestion of dark chocolate and saw the parallels in the preparation of chocolate and dawadawa. It makes sense that if fermentation enhances the smell of cocoa beans, then it can and should enhance that of locust beans. And it does, in the hands of the skilled (or is it the chaste?).

The locust-bean tree looks like the flame of the forest tree, producing long pods that explode when ripe, scattering dark brown beans that will germinate if left on the ground. The pods are harvested before they burst, put in a sack and beaten with sticks until the beans are released. The beans are boiled in a big pot with lots of water for the whole of the first day. Ashes from the cooking fire are added to the water to help darken the colour of the beans. On the second day, the fire is kept small; just enough to keep the pot warm. By this time, the beans should have swelled and opened, releasing beige-coloured insides from two outer coats, one dark brown and one translucent. The desired colour is dark brown or black, made possible by the addition of the ashes. The beans are drained and transferred to a mortar where the chaff is rubbed off, then transferred to a tray where the remaining chaff is meticulously picked out. The beans are washed and boiled again before being spread between pawpaw leaves for two days of fermentation. After fermentation, they are dried in the sun or hung high over a fire.

Dawadawa tends to go into my food at the very beginning, in hot palm oil. Hot, not smoking oil, because the idea is to add the aromatics of the beans to the aromatics of the palm oil and create a mouth-watering foundation for the soup, not burn the beans. In my ideal pot of soup, the layering of flavours and aromatics comes after this: smoked fish, hot peppers, bawa peppers, rehydrated stockfish, ground ogbono, ugwu.

I wonder why the fornicator's back should be spared the breaking work of dawadawa preparation, but be oiled with its medicinal properties (it lowers cholesterol and reduces blood pressure). Why would the chaste be required to do all the hard work, while the unchaste are not barred from gaining from it, eating as much of the dawadawa as they like? This was another stupid question, in Agi's estimation. According to her, I'm not a very smart *madam* for all the big bungalow and gardens that I live in. I'm certainly proof that not everything is commonsensical and that logic needs context. Agi is too polite to say these things but not too polite to express them in exasperation and condescending laughter.

Not everything can be scientifically explained. If Obudu produces some of the best fermented locust beans by far, then fine, we'll keep the fornicators away from the utensils. It makes a good story.

Rice in Many Guises

After long periods of eating rich spicy food, a simple bowl of white rice becomes excruciatingly appealing. I am always in search of the perfect basmati rice; the sort that you can steam briskly till you get single grains that bounce off the plate. It's true that white rice is not particularly nutritious or digestible, and draining rice when it is cooked instead of letting the rice absorb the water further depletes its nutritional value. Nevertheless, I tend to cook my rice by letting it soak in cold water for twenty minutes, rinsing it, then boiling it briskly and draining it.

It's the easiest way of getting each grain of rice to be a perfect, whole individual. If my rice is perfectly cooked, I find I can enjoy it with just a tablespoon of coconut oil, some yogurt, or home-made green pesto.

There is also something temperamentally appealing about a bowl of rice with green peas cooked in coconut milk. I love the colour combination of green and milky white, the smell of coconut accompanied by the sweet, bursting texture of briskly cooked peas, and the coolness of the dish in contrast to the heat of red pepper stew.

I once retained a rude and obnoxious cook for months on the merits of one rice dish that he cooked breathtakingly well. Well, the real reason was that my husband forbade me from sacking him, but once I had learnt the secret of the dish, he was promptly fired. The secret was the stock in which the rice was cooked. The cook's version was made with Maggi stock cubes, but I don't, won't cook with Maggi, so I made my own. It starts with a quarter of a chicken in about two pints of water, some garlic, ginger, fresh aromatic hot pepper and salt. Added to this is a generous pinch (and a half) of allspice, freshly ground cinnamon and some fish sauce.

This stock is brought to the boil and then the heat turned down. While the stock is simmering, cook 250g of mincemeat in a small, non-stick frying pan without any oil, salt or water. This means it must be cooked over very low heat and moved around to make sure it doesn't burn. If it is cooked properly, the water from the meat should keep the whole enterprise going without the need for any additional water.

When the mincemeat is cooked, it is added to the chicken stock and everything is simmered together for about an hour over very low heat, until the flesh of the chicken is falling off the bones.

The chicken is lifted from the stock, the flesh removed and returned to the pot. The bones discarded. Half a tin of sweetcorn and two tablespoons of coconut oil are added. The basmati rice, which has been soaking in cold water, is washed and put in the stock. The stock should stand above the rice by about half a finger's height. The seasoning can be adjusted here. The heat is turned down to the lowest possible flame until the stock has been absorbed and the rice is fluffy, the grains separate.

When we first came to live in Calabar, I was offered coconut rice. I had already begun to salivate at what I imagined would be a plate of rice cooked in coconut milk, served with goat meat stew. The rice arrived, and it was a bowl of muggy looking rice with no stew. It smelled predominantly of fish, not coconut and the smoked fish littering the face of the rice gave the impression of hard, smelly inedibility. There was nothing subtle about its look or smell so I was instantly put off. I was even less consoled when I learnt that I was in the presence of a Cross Riverian delicacy.

I created a more subtle interpretation that I thought might redeem it. One mature, sweet coconut is grated, washed with lukewarm water, and put through a sieve to give about two cups of coconut milk. One cup of washed long-grain rice (not basmati, as it is not sturdy enough) is added to the coconut milk, along with two finely chopped medium onions, some parboiled lean pork, some beef and its stock, or the flesh of an old layer chicken and its stock. Add some smoked catfish softened in the beef stock, some peeled, deveined fresh prawns, lots of chopped hot pepper, fish sauce, salt, and ground black pepper. The rice is simmered with all the ingredients until cooked. The strong fishy smell is avoided by excluding the smoked catfish.

Even this version I can only stand in small quantities, as I find it heavy and tiring on the palate. As offensive as the idea might seem to Cross Riverians, I think this dish might be much improved by a handful of raisins!

Fish Soups and Love Potions

River Oyono is a smoke-grey cloak animated by a strong wind. It is, in fact, only a small conceited river. It embraces the Atlantic Ocean for a passionate 24 km. Just before the open seas, there is an unusual meeting point of brackish and fresh seawater, creating an environment that provides stunning produce for the markets in Calabar. They say you will find fish there that you will not find anywhere else in the world. At five o'clock in the evening, as the sun is setting on Lagos Street, the local fish market comes alive. The crabs sit lethargically in stainless steel basins, while giant, whiskered catfish gasp for breath on worn wood tables that look distractingly like slabs of well-aged beef. Oversized prawns with moody blue-black armour glitter like lapis lazuli, seawater pulsating feebly under their carapaces. The price of baby tuna and sole is haggled and agreed on with an audacity that would make a Michelin-star chef in New York City catch his breath with shock and envy. Oysters are trampled as if they were bits of debris from a building site. I'm not exaggerating when I say they have no esteem here. If one were searching for seafood that connects the palate with sexual arousal – an aphrodisiac, a playful fetish – it would not be an oyster, not here.

I'm requesting the price of crabs, the female ones with coral caviar. I'm watching them closely to make sure they'll move. I watch the women's faces (we are mostly women at the market), charmed by an amplifying breeze. A storm is coming. It will be the perfect night for a hot, peppery, fragrant fish stew. All the stereotypes feel at home in this fish market. In full view are the 'winches' buying fish to take home, to cook for a man, to lure him away from his wife. Or the fish could be for a husband, to highlight his masculinity and satiate his sense of entitlement. For some reason, it is irrelevant when women cook fish for themselves.

How food becomes love potion is not an easily tackled subject. There are unspoken rules that govern the matter. The married woman who cooks soup so deliciously that the tongue is in danger of being bitten in half is a great cook, no contest, but the single woman who does the same is a 'winch'. It is universally understood and agreed that women do not perfect the art of cooking soup until they are past middle age and 'safe'. If they show any sign of prodigiousness before that time, they are suspect.

The Achatina fulica snail, dark brown or black, with its labia-like meat swathed in wilful mucilage, is what might suggest seduction rather than oysters. A man does not eat snails in okro soup cooked by just any woman. The mucilage is a significant half of the bone of contention. Mucilaginous soups like ogbono and okro are the stuff, the core, the depth, height, myth, truth and enigma of witchcraft. Or so we believe, and therefore the suggestively slimy soups featuring fish, snails and nfi (periwinkles, cooked in their shells and sucked out in the course of the meal), are the mediums and aphrodisiacs, the juju and fetishes of our sexual bewitchment or arousal or whatever you want to call it, because we freely interchange the terms. These are facts that no Nigerian can pretend not to know.

The archetypal businessman in Calabar is the civil servant, married with three children, two house-helps, a complicated and dependent extended family, two cars and a racy mistress with a large bottom who owns a small boutique. He closes work at about 4 p.m., and with so much free time on his hands, he would be ungrateful not to carouse in it. He is a devout Presbyterian, goes to church on Sundays, makes love to his wife once a month, visits his mistress once a week and fills the rest of his schedule with slender UniCal girls who have stomachs like chopping boards and skin smooth as processed shea-butter.

The antiquarian fattening rooms where women are still sent to grow love handles and learn the intricacies of how to pamper men's personalities into that of suckled babies might be on their way out, but that spirit of male entitlement to as many available women and young girls as are willing remains. Don't get me wrong; the man I am discussing is courteous, charming, and progressive in the number of languages he speaks. His English is impeccable. He is exposed to many cultures. His kin are fighting the Tivs on the borders with Benue State, he owns farming and fishing rights alongside Cameroonians, he might be smuggling goods from Douala, Bata and Malabo, and he is kinsman with the Igbo. He is, in fact, a kind of liberal gentleman with a long-standing sense of entitlement to women's constant attention, commitment and endless cooking sessions.

Women are indoctrinated from a young age into the mindset that men have all the advantages and, to be truly successful, a woman must somehow attach herself to a successful man, be it brother, husband, uncle, lover or sugar daddy. Enter that necessary artillery among artilleries: cooking. A woman must cook well; very, very well. Sex is a given, but it doesn't have to be outstanding sex. Sometimes the man wants a docile lover, but there is no compromise when it comes to food. A man will not marry a woman who cannot cook (a true abomination), nor will he emotionally desert a wife who can cook to play with a mistress who can't (a ridiculous proposition). A suitable wife must be a good cook, attractive, homely, God-fearing, and must come with a guarantee that she will bear children. A shrewd mistress must be a great cook; flatter diabolically; keep a scented, relaxed, undemanding second home where foot massages are spontaneously administered; know how to at least pretend some degree of sexual kinkiness; and know how to engage a man for as long as possible by whatever means necessary.

There is no land area in Nigeria that possesses the number, variation and quality of soups that Cross River State has. No state comes close. For the average Cross Riverian woman, cooking a pot of soup is a detailed, dedicated affair. Ekpang nku kwo, an Efik delicacy made from grated cocoyams rolled in pumpkin leaf and cooked like a porridge with at least ten other ingredients, is a case in point. It takes an early morning market visit, hours of patient rolling up of yams in leaf, and more than one set of hands to get a good pot of this going. It takes up the whole morning, and is not considered comparable in taste the next day. Most women go to the market or send to the market every day because they believe that refrigerators mar the taste of soup ingredients. There are ingredients that must be uncompromisingly fresh and are thus harvested daily: the ugwu (dark green open palms harvested in the morning) and the afang unwound from its symbiotic partner and shredded and pounded. Yesterday's soup is only eaten out of necessity and with an undercurrent of disdain.

It makes sense that men here still prefer women filled out, with big breasts and trembling backsides, in that way that requires the daily ingestion of healthy portions of gari and first-grade palm oil. The West's androgynous, starving goddesses parading catwalks and glossy magazine pages would not draw a reluctant glance from a Calabar man, or so they say.

Raw oysters cannot be our aphrodisiac because what they suggest in their mouthfeel, their look, and the viscosity of the liquid in which they are suspended is something close to a cultural abomination. The kiss that requires the opening of mouths, of tongues rolling around each other and the exchange of a slippery musky fluid is bad enough. I know men in my father's generation who would gag if the diagram of a French kiss were drawn for them. So better a knife is stuck in the gut and turned three hundred and sixty degrees than a typical Nigerian man be given a raw oyster to suck on.

When I came to Calabar, I discovered the self-effacing yet powerfully evocative fisherman's stew, made fashionable by restaurants like Thelma Bello's Le Chateau. The stew originated in the creeks of Cross River, where fishermen complement long nights of back-breaking work with breakfasts cooked and eaten on their boats. There'd be lit kerosene lanterns, the dawn breaking softly, birds tuning up, and air sweet enough to drink.

Aunty Thelma's version starts off with a little palm oil and chopped onions in a pot. The onions are not chopped too fine or large because they need to break down, thicken and give the stew body and weight. The onions are sautéed for a while, then blended fresh tomatoes and hot peppers are added.

Smoked catfish and crayfish, fresh periwinkles and oysters are steamed lightly in another pot. Keeping them separate maintains the textural integrity of the soup.

I have to contrast this to the original way in which the stew was cooked. Fishermen used the catch that wasn't sold to the market women on the beach by the end of the evening. By the morning of the next day, the fish was only good for two things: fisherman's stew (because you didn't waste what you had worked hard to catch) and for egusi soup as 'ebori'. Catfish was the perfect ebori. It swelled up and disintegrated, emphasising the paleness and contrast of the ground melon seeds. It thickened the soup and added depth to the flavour. By the morning of the next day, the fish had a strong aroma and the aroma of the onions glamorised that of the fish. This still happens in the creeks.

Thelma Bello's version eventually adds the steamed fish and shellfish to the stew. A little ground ogbono is constituted with hot water and also added. This immediately adds a visual shine and smoothness on the palate, but ogbono must always be allowed to boil sufficiently so that one does not get a stomach ache. Just before the pot is taken off the fire, chopped ntong (mint leaf) and iko (curry leaf) are sprinkled on the stew. It is served with pounded yam or hot gari. Cold-water gari is what a fisherman in the creeks would eat it with.

In the creek version, the strong fragrance of the fish is tempered by the sweet nuttiness of palm oil and the piquancy of ground hot pepper. The fisherman will typically finish his own modest version with a sprinkling of gari on the face of the soup.

The backbone of Cross Riverian cuisine is fish: fresh, dried, ground, whole, pounded, smoked in giant mud banks with great big burning mangrove trunks. Some are exposed to cool foreign temperatures and wind and imported thousands of miles from Norway as stockfish. Everything here is cooked with fish. Like the Thai nam pla (fish sauce), ground crayfish is the odorous main seasoning in all soups. Almost all dishes must be finished off with handfuls of ground crayfish. The head of the catfish is often ground up and used as seasoning. Many varieties of baby fish are ground fine for the same purpose. Ogbono, okro, edikaikong, afang, abak, ntutulikpo … name a soup eaten in Cross River and it will have some form of fish in it. On an average week, fights break out over fishing patches between the Ijaw, Bakassi fishermen and Cameroonian gendarmes. Politics might be the main business in Cross River, yet fish is one of the essential undercurrents and synergistic glues of life, food and sex.

The question is always posed – but only jocularly – about why the Cross Riverian's love of food and sex is so concentrated, their attention to the appetites so urgent. The superficial answers are that it is natural and common for rainforest/coastal people relaxed by sea air, cooling storms, and days of slow, drizzling rain to be that way. In April, the showers are interspersed with warm sunlight, humid days cool into stormy nights, Jacarandas and flame of the forest trees bud aggressively into lilac and red flowers, and everything lush and green is irresistible. It's completely propitious to lovemaking. It's said that forty weeks after the rainy April, hospitals are inundated with delivering mothers.

Some people say that the appetites are worshipped because one of the reigning spiritual principalities is the mammywater, to whose seductiveness, beauty and sexual prowess many matriarchs have pledged the allegiance of generations of their female descendants. Or they say it is cultural to keep a symbiotic relationship between men and women going because it ensures that everyone is taken care of: men support women economically, and women see to men's sexual and other needs, keeping the pillars of the world intact.

The real undercurrents, though, are the things left unsaid. The undrawn parallels are related to fish, mucilage, salt and saltiness. Trimethylamine, that compound found in stale rotting fish, is also found in gastric juices, in the female anatomy as a pheromone, and in smoked fish, a delicacy that is kept fresh over days and nights of reintroduction to lazy fires. Market women selling smoked fish take all their produce home at the end of each market day and put them on the fire, then bring them to the market again to repeat the process. It's hard, repetitive work that allows only three to four hours of sleep at night. The paradox is that the fish is kept 'fresh' in a roundabout, festering sort of way. To be sure, there is nothing fresh about it, but the word serves its purpose and is understood.

My point is that fisherman's stew, fish stew and fish soup are all a form of female pheromone soup. The smell of fish is constantly in the Cross Riverian's nostrils. Seawater, stale fish, salt, crayfish seasoning, smoked fish, stockfish: the aromatics are in the air, in the food ingested every day, in lingering smells on fingers used in place of crockery. It's ingrained in kitchen walls and upholstery and clothing and hair weaves. In a culture where the fire of the hob never goes out, and meals are languidly cooked for hours on end, reminders of sex and food are constantly being generated. This, for me, is the answer to the age-old riddle of the half-woman, half-fish mammywater: it's a symbol of unification of the appetites, and a sensual promise that they will be satisfied. It is the secret of the mammywater's power over men and why she can often lure them to destruction. It is why women pledge allegiance to the mammywater in a society where they are economically subservient to men. A woman has some kind of degree of power over a man if she knows how to satisfy his appetites for food and sex.

At least until someone with a more potent fish soup shows up, whose bottom trembles clockwise rather than anti-clockwise. Inevitably, boredom, the law of diminishing returns, the longing for greener pastures or unique twists to fish soups, or the restless sense of entitlement kicks in.

The mistress might end up on the back burner, consoled by her proprietorship of the small boutique, and small savings of cash gifts. The wife might see a minor, transient revival of the husband's libido and go for thanksgiving in church. The mistress might make a comeback if she knows her way around the darker stuff – gbelekokomiyo, kop mo mi, gbo temi, ibok ima: the love potions concocted by medicine men for the bending of the will. They are infused into mucilaginous soups, cooked with snails, or fish or whatever ... as if there is anything even remotely sexually attractive about a zombified man. Those who believe in and cook juju-infused fish soups also understand that it in time, its effect wears off. After all, everything pertaining to the appetites bows to the will of time.

Dead Man's Helmet

Questions about the republic of Biafra, about survival and comestibles, were surely going to bring up powerful ghosts. I knew I would hear many stories about gari and water, the sacrosanctity of the relationship of the two. Rarely would I hear about swallow and soup in the same sentence. Water plus gari would not only result in the swelling of processed cassava grains but ignite profound emotions. The soup would be a shadow in the background and there would be many still-lifes of an orange here, a coconut there, a glass of water that you drank with thanksgiving, and the last handful of gari, every grain counted.

I wanted to focus on the men's stories, which seems contradictory, but isn't at all, because the focus of food during war was not cooking but motion, and the necessity of forming a relationship with the bush through which you were moving, or the village to which you were displaced. It was about the keenness of mind to process survival, disconnected from the emotions of carrying children on your back and in your mind. It was the men who moved and starved *without distractions*. Motion and starvation formed a powerful alloy. I am in no way elevating their trauma above that of women, who had to starve and watch the children they were responsible for starve.

Men – as infiltrators, army captains, husbands, fathers, young men – had, at every point in time, to own a concrete, believable definition of themselves in the local parlance in order not to be abruptly shot. It was men who more vividly interacted on foot with spaces that metamorphosed with each step. First you were Nigerian, from the Eastern Region. Your country was the largest grower of cassava in the world. Then you were an islander from Biafra, a rebellious breakaway from the federation of Nigeria. From then on, and over the ensuing years, chairs, beds and cooking pots disappeared from your definition of possessions. They were no longer the familiar things you moved around. Your small possessions gradually went too, every time you were compelled to move and keep moving.

The cassava farms remained, growing tall and more influential than men. The rain came down and they produced tubers. Their owners died, fled, moved on. Other people moved in and took refuge on the farms, among tubers that were poisonous on first interaction. They could not be owners. Men moved horizontally, haphazardly, sometimes taking residence under the soil and staying there. The cassava moved vertically and when it grew horizontally, it was shelter, refuge, home, food, keeper of secrets. If men had opportunity and time and a few weeks or months of rest, they could harvest the cassava and make gari, and they would do so with great respect. They did not have the air of ownership about them. It was in this time and space that the truth of men's relationship with the land emerged and remained. Men did not own the land; the land owned them.

What follows is the story of a friend whose grandfather walked through the bush and found a Dead Man's Helmet.

During the war my grandfather lived in Lagos. He'd fled Asaba through the bush, because the men of Asaba were being murdered. He spent a long time making his way on foot. When he got to Lagos, he had to be not-Igbo there. Don't go to where my people come from, where my people are and say that we are Igbos. They will not laugh it off like Lagosians do. They will be offended. Till he died he spoke Yorùbá fluently, better than the Yorùbá speak it. Many of my relatives do. You can hear the Yorùbá words peeping through the Ebu. My grandparents become Lagosians in Lagos. There they witnessed Igbos losing their homes even in a supposedly neutral city. You left your house in the care of neighbours who you had known for all your adult life and came back to be told, by the same person, to your face, that he didn't know who you were, that you left nothing in his care. He told this lie to your wife and children.

If you had your wits about you when you were leaving Asaba, you carried gari on you when you left a home you may never return to, even if you carried nothing else. You'd inevitably find a dead man's helmet in the bush, on a dead man's head. On a dead Biafran soldier. You'd be sorry for the man; that could be you. You'd be afraid. But you would be grateful for the helmet. You took it off his head with great reverence, if there was a whole head to talk of, and it became your pot and plate and bowl.

You dared not make a fire. You would never be that foolish. If it rained, you had water or there would be a stream in answer to your prayers. You made cold-water gari with water from the stream or rainwater or you made something close to the gari in peacetime by using hot urine. You ate the gari by itself, and sent a prayer of thanksgiving up through the roof of the forest. If you found a snail underfoot, ah, you had a feast. It wasn't the flesh of the snail you were after; you wanted the mucilage it was carrying in its home. If you had cold-water gari and snail's mucilage, you had swallow and soup.

In a dream, I once saw a snail walking up a friend's back. It meant death, of course. Although my friend did not die until months later, his fate was already sealed like the tracks of snail mucilage along the ground. A live man would never have a snail walk up his back.

My father-in-law, Ebak Ogbe, was a refugee secretary in Biafra during the war. In peacetime he was a council secretary for Ikom Local Government Area. This is his own story from the war:

I had taught in the Presbyterian school in Nde Mission for going on two years. My brother-in-law, Chief Okpokam, was a politician, a member of the Eastern House of Assembly, the inspector of schools under the Roman Catholic Mission, and the chairman of Ikom Local Government Area. He told me there was a vacancy in the council, which had decided to train their own secretary to the local government rather than depend on the government for seconded staff.

When the war started I was still in the service of the local government. The war was already raging in Opobo, close to Ogoni, where I was stationed. It was a matter of crossing a creek or something. When fighting crossed from Opobo into Ogoni, it became a matter of every man for himself and God for us all. I came to the office and picked up what I could.

I had just been conducting a meeting in a school compound in Uiakara, Ogoni, when the federal troops/planes came on a bombing mission. They strafed the whole area; everybody had to take cover. I think there were a few casualties. When I was going from the Bori headquarters to that meeting, I had to ask my sanitary inspector, who had a motorcycle, to give me a lift, because it was not safe to drive my car, a light grey Peugeot 403. He took me on his bike to the meeting and at that meeting the federal troops strafed everywhere and we had to take cover in an uncompleted building. As soon as the planes went away, we cut the meeting short. I told the young man to drive. He would watch the road, I would watch the sky. Whenever there was danger in the sky, I would warn him and we would take cover.

We drove like that until we got back to Bori, only to hear that that same plane had thrown a bomb near the motor park in Okporo, Ogoni. One young man from Boki, Mr Ochubiri, was sitting in a restaurant and drinking beer when the plane strafed. It broke down the wall the young man was sitting behind, and the wall hit his back and he died. He just died like that, from the way he was hit. Thereafter, the divisional officer, who happened to be a man from Cross River, Mr Aquaisua, said that we had to move. The place had become unsafe. Federal troops were entering and they would not be friendly to us. Bori was the headquarters of the government of Biafra. The federal troops bombed such strategic government offices and then declared the administration changed on the spot. The people become Nigerians, no longer Biafrans.

By the time we got to the council headquarters, this air raid had taken place and Ochubiri was one of the casualties.

Meanwhile, I was being sent out on scouting missions by the divisional officer. One day, after an air raid, I came back to find that my wife and children were not in the house. They had taken cover at the cassava farm nearby. My wife said that she could no longer stay in that place so we had to move, taking whatever we could carry in my car.

So we moved and imposed ourselves on her cousin/uncle Mr Mfongang. He had a small family and they were living in Rainbow Town in Port Harcourt. Occasionally the residents of the town would have to do what we called 'combing', because we suspected there were Nigerian infiltrators coming to spy on us. Sometimes they caught a young man like that and if he could not give a good account of himself, he would be killed.

Sometimes he was not an infiltrator. If you could not give a good account of yourself and no one in the area knew you well ... And you couldn't know everybody in Biafra. Biafra was a country, if you like. So Nigerian government soldiers – spies – were sent in. We stayed in Rainbow Town with our in-law for almost a year. By this time the federal troops had liberated ... The federal government used the word 'liberated' because they felt that, in Biafra, you were under bondage, so no matter how harshly you were treated by them, they were liberating you. We heard about what was happening in Aba. I had carried my box and all my valuables, and sent them to my brother Charles who was working in Aba, because we thought Aba was safer than Ogoni, but all those things just perished there because it wasn't long before Aba was 'liberated' and he too had to run for his life. All my things, my whole library, which was in the sitting room, our bed, everything ...

Port Harcourt was shaking. Every now and then you would hear the pomporompopom, as early as seven in the morning. Every man had to go for combing. Go to the bush and see if you could find anyone not known to the people in that area. So we did that for several weeks, until Port Harcourt finally fell and we ran, along with our hosts, Mr and Mrs Mfongang and their children. All of us (including our two children and my wife's brother) piled into my car. We were running towards Owerri and that meant dropping even those things we managed to bring from our station. Only the most vital things were taken. Each person had about two or three items.

You should have seen the stampede when people were escaping Port Harcourt. Most people were walking. They had abandoned their property from one stage to another. You abandoned this, abandoned that, or it was stolen or seized by force. So there were many people who walked from then on. The few of us who managed to go by car couldn't really move because the whole road was jam-packed. On the road, nobody cared about you. We managed like that. At noon that day we arrived in Owerri, which the federal troops had not yet entered. We sat there, stayed there and in the open there like that, we prepared and cooked a meal. Gari or something.

Mr Mfongang's friend, an Igbo man who was a native there, helped us. He brought us food items from the locality. You had nowhere to move into to do the cooking. This was actually in the village of Iho, about eight miles from Owerri. We cooked whatever it was, I don't know, and ate and continued. Sometimes we saw the dead bodies of Biafran soldiers on the roadside.

Iho was the home of [a friend of the] Mfongangs. He took us there as refugees and gave us two small rooms. The natives searched our luggage because we were coming from liberated areas and were suspected of having possibly helped federal troops to succeed. In Iho, from time to time, different groups would come and search our things, so you had to keep your small belongings open for searches all of the time. Shortly after they went, another group came again to search.

For a time, my wife traded. She would go to market and buy a few things to cook and sell. We survived like this until one man from my clan, my village, called James Nzan Okpuruwu, found out we were in Iho. He was the secretary of the whole church mission in Umuokpukpara. The man in charge of the mission was Canon Onubugu. The headquarters were close to Anara junction in Mbano, where the road to Okigwe comes to that junction and continues to Owerri. James Nzan discovered us and arranged for us to come over to his station and stay in the school compound.

The schools were not functioning. The teachers had gone to wherever their homes were and their houses were vacant. The school grounds became refugee camps. James gave us a room. The Mfongangs also had one room. Several other families were there. After some time, we found we were incompatible with the Mfongangs, so we decided to move out. James Nzan helped us to move and find another house near to his station, where the Canon himself was living in a big compound. I had a place where I could park my car. We covered it with palm leaves so that federal troops would not fly over and see it and bomb the place. That is where we stayed until the war ended.

When we were in Umuokpukpara, the provincial secretary, Mr Ogbu, decided that the secretaries who had been displaced from their different stations in Port Harcourt province should be deployed so that they could be useful while they were there. So while my family was staying in Umuokpukpara, the provincial secretary decided that I should go to a place inside the forest called Eche. My job there was buying gari from refugees and distributing it to the war front, using salt as a motivator for the refugees' production of gari.

There was no salt to buy. It would be loaded in trailers and driven down and distributed to us secretaries in different locations. They would give you a few bags, because salt was extremely scarce and expensive. Government traded with the people in salt. You, the council secretary, informed the refugees, who were there in hundreds, that for every quantity of gari they sold to you, you would sell salt to them at the controlled price of £1.

In other words, you sell me a quantity of gari and you qualify for a cup of salt. We collected the gari and stacked it. At the appointed time, the trailer would come round and they knew how they distributed it to the soldiers at the war front. Refugees were given the freedom to harvest cassava wherever they could find it, make gari and sell it. The owners had run away or ...

The refugee camps had camp managers. When relief materials, like bales of stockfish or whatever, were distributed to the camps, the camp manager would take control of it and share it according to the families living in the school compound. You would queue and pick up your rations.

To get from Umuokpukpara to Eche you had to enter down down down and drive through bush roads. When you reached Eche, the first section was called Ogida, Eche. You came in from Ogida Eche to a camp where many refugees were staying. But my station was to be across the river and I could not get my car across. So I parked the car, covered it with grass and palm leaves, and crossed to Owu, Eche. There I stayed and worked. From time to time, on weekends, I would cross the river, take the car and drive down to see my family at Umuopkupkara. You crossed the river by canoe.

One day, a senior civil servant based at Olu sent a message that he was coming to address us. On that day, I told the man who was helping me, Jonah Ekpiken, that I was crossing to attend that lecture. I left him and crossed by canoe from Owu to Ogida where my car was. On arriving, instead of seeing signs of the man announced to come, the place was deserted. I learnt that, during the previous night, trucks had been used to evacuate the orphanage and take relief materials from Ogida to Olu. There was no possibility of the man coming. I had to stay and send a message to Jonah Ekpiken instructing him to pack up our little luggage in Owu and cross over by canoe to meet me in Ogida. We would head back to Umuokpukpara.

We could not leave for Umuokpukpara by car during the day because of its light colour, so we waited until sundown. By this time there was a crowd of refugees escaping to safer areas and it was again difficult to drive with the pedestrian traffic. People were moving towards Olu and other areas. All the time, you could hear federal planes overhead.

We got to a village close to Owerri, just a few miles from Umuokpukpara, where my family was. Suddenly we heard loud gunshots from the direction we were headed, and people in front of us started to turn back. We tried to follow the refugees running on foot through a bush track going towards the Port Harcourt–Owerri road. We reached a stream that had had a wooden bridge before, but the bridge had rotted away. There was no way of crossing that stream, so I drove the car back to a compound near the village we had left behind. The village itself was deserted. We saw an elderly man sitting down. I still remember his name: Nlemanze Onu. He said people had fled the village because of the war, and he was alone in his compound. We left the car with him, locked it, and pocketed the key.

With me was one assistant divisional officer, Julius Nwasomba; my house boy from Eche; and Jonah Ekpiken who was very timid and afraid. I was wearing rubber slippers because, in the intense trauma of that situation, I had left my shoes in the car. We joined the refugees on foot and kept trekking until we burst out on the Port Harcourt–Owerri road. When we got there, there was a Biafran army officer driving his car. He asked us who we were. We told him we were refugees coming out of Eche, going to Owerri. He told us we couldn't go there because his men were laying an ambush there and would shoot and kill us. So we crossed the road and continued along a bush track until we reached a village where we saw soldiers from Umuokpukpara. We knew one army officer; he was kind to us, and brought some coconuts that we broke and drank the water. That gave us some energy.

The journey from that village to Umuokpukpara was hard, especially because I had no shoes on my feet. There was a point where we were so dirty and had nothing to drink. The house boy walked ahead. Nwasomba had parted from us and was finding his way towards his own family, as had Jonah Ekpiken, the cashier. I had become very weak. The boy would walk some distance and come back and check on me, walk ahead and come back and check on me. It got to a point where I had to take pineapple peelings somebody had left on the ground to quench my thirst. People saw us and suspected us, asked us where we were going. I had to mention the names of prominent people who were living in Umuokpukpara so they believed me. If I were an infiltrator, I would not know so much about the place.

During my father-in-law's chronicling of the war years, I only heard the mention of soup once. I mean a real mention of soup. He successfully made his way back to Umuokpukpara from Eche and towards the end of the war, he entertained a suggestion by an elderly woman who lived in the school compound with them that he go back and find his car. He left his wife and family in Umuokpukpara and travelled on foot with his wife's brother Ajom towards Owerri. They had with them *a deep container of soup.*

I went back to search out Nlemanze Onu and my car. I was anxious to get the car back, and set out on foot to retrieve it. After I left Umuokpukpara, the government in Ikom sent a man called Christopher Etta in a Land Rover to locate all the camps where Ikom refugees could be found. He offered to take my wife home to Ikom and she had to make a decision about leaving, about going back without me. Everybody in Umuokpukpara was going back to their villages but she stayed behind because they would have asked her where her husband was and she would not have been able to give them a concrete answer.

We found the village and the old man, Nlemanze Onu, but not my car. The car was gone and Nlemanze Onu pretended not to know who I was. My wife's brother was furious and said I should have driven the car against the rocks and destroyed it instead of leaving it behind. We lost the car anyway. By the time I got back to Umuokpukpara, my wife and my children had left for Ikom. Only my wife's sister Rose, and a lady called Magdalene were there. Phillip Efiong had declared the surrender of Biafra to the federal government. The war had ended.

However, there were still young Nigerian soldiers straggling around. They wanted to harass the two girls. Rose and Magdalene were hiding somewhere in the house and when it was clear the soldiers would begin to comb the house, they burst out to the backyard. The soldiers chased them and they ran into the bush. They couldn't catch them. The soldiers came back and took me to the bathroom of the house, told me to lie down, said they were going to shoot me. I think they presumed that one of the ladies was my wife and whatever they did to them, my death would be their cover. Eventually, they just took my watch and my transistor radio ...

Peppered Snails

I once had an informal *toaster* in Obáfemi Awólowo University nicknamed Buscopan. The term 'toaster' for a university lad was as transparent and as precarious as Pyrex in its intentions. You heard it and you knew that you and all the females in first year were marked for the gridiron. There was no equivocality to the word, not really, yet for some primitive reason, when you sat with your newly acquired friends tallying the number of roasting forks at the end of which you were suspended and turning above the fire, you felt privileged, and wanted more butter slathered on to facilitate the roasting, or toasting.

The toasters were always on tenterhooks, waiting for the next instalment of Jambites or Jambitos. The term called to mind Doritos: imported snacks that you did not think too highly of. You ate them when the opportunity presented itself, or when you were at a social gathering and had nothing more virtuous to eat. 'Jambite' was an appellation that included both men and women, boys and girls, who had been admitted into the university that year based on Joint Admissions and Matriculation Board scores. The ruse was simple enough: female Jambites were suya for university lads – toasters – who would spend hours, days, weeks, sometimes even years oiling, basting, seasoning, toasting, roasting, grilling their chosen Jambito or Jambitos. The way the repast was treated when it was finally served up was completely contradictory, completely belying the focus, dedication and time invested in the toasting.

From the Jambito's point of view, there was usually a song and dance, some longwindedness to signing the agreement to be eaten. If you drew out the toasting, it announced your virginity loudly or – if there was no virginity on offer – your organicness, nutritional virtue.

There were those infamous toasters who spent extravagant amounts of time perfecting their cooking skills. You knew them by their academic 'carry overs'. Some of these lads had spent ten years studying a four-year course. They'd begun to sound like Felix Liberty's 'Ngozi' on turntable. You wished the university would give them a ceremonial degree in culinary arts and set them free.

Buscopan was not a sophisticated toaster. On the contrary, he was always tipsy, too happy, a little too close and touchy-feely. When his face was this far away from yours, then you could smell the Guldar beer that accompanied pounded yam and goat meat. The name 'Buscopan' was a nudge and a wink to the happy drunk who made you laugh when you spent your evenings sitting at the beer parlour. His friends gave him the name, which was the brand name of the tiny white pill that you were given for menstrual cramps at the sickbay in secondary school. The lads kept 90 per cent of the joke inaccessible. It was surely something that was more prurient than funny.

Buscopan had an exquisite musical ear. He could play a few musical instruments, and played the church organ by instinct, with precision, confidence, beauty and nuance. You would never reconcile the drunk with the instinctive brilliance, never. If he was sober and could distinguish hymn 501 from

105, then you were roused by his playing from the depths of your soul to the tips of your split ends. Buscopan's social ineptness seemed very much in line with his brilliance. He spoke his mind without ever doing the sums. He gave me *a look* one day and said, in Yorùbá, 'Màá yí e l'áta.'

He stressed every consonant in the saying. In order to really explain these words I have to go back to the beginning and first make clear why I italicised 'toaster' when I mentioned Buscopan. Anyone toasting a girl in 1989 would not use the words 'Màá yí e l'áta'. They are not words you used for nice girls. They are not words you used for un-nice girls either because, in 1989, every girl wanted to be nice and part of the toasting was a presumption that the girl you were toasting was nice. When you toasted a girl, you told her you wanted to introduce her to your mother. You told her she was beautiful and you loved the way her lips parted and closed when she ate. You took her to New Buka to eat dodgy Chinese instead of Old Buka to eat pounded yam and soup. You wore a cravat in the boiling heat to impress her and you spent all your allowance buying her rice and dodo at Forks and Fingers. You took her on excursion to Erì Ìjesà just to position her under a small waterfall and say, 'Wet becomes you.' Yes, another toaster actually said that to me.

'Cook me in some hot pepper' is what Màá yí e l'áta means. In fact it is more explicit than that, because the word 'cook' cleans up the proclamation considerably. The closer word, though awkward, is 'turn', and Nigerians often use it in place of the word 'stir'.

Why did he want to turn me in pepper, you might ask. It was for no other reason than to eat me. And when you eat something called 'yíláta', a common prefix for peppered chicken or peppered snails, you suffered. To understand the popularity of the yíláta, at the Palms Mall in Lagos you could, until recently, get two different kinds of chicken yíláta from two restaurants right next to each other. We called it the battle of the yílátas. A winner was never formally declared. When you ate yíláta, your nose ran, your eyes watered, you got hot under the collar and everywhere else. You wept and fanned yourself in vain from the effects of the quantities of pepper applied to the yíláta. You laughed at your own stupidity. You drank glasses of water and your temperature soared dangerously. But underneath the pepper, the snails or chicken or ram was so delicious, you couldn't help continuing to eat and suffer. Even if you were sitting in the most expensive restaurant, your suffering *manifested* in the most undignified way.

By using this imagery of eating pepper and meat, Buscopan was suggesting an emotive, life-threatening experience, if not a love affair.

These days, I cannot eat peppered snails without thinking of Buscopan. My neighbour in Calabar taught me a simple, delicious recipe. I have to put the simplicity in perspective because preparing snails for cooking is not easy. It only really becomes simple after the cleaning of the snails, which can be quite harrowing in the removing of stubborn mucilage.

It's important to always choose the small snails, the bite-size ones. It must be possible to put a whole snail in your mouth and have lots of space for chewing it.

Sometimes it is hard to tell if the snails are alive when they are being purchased especially if they are sold out of a container or basket. It is best when snails are bought off the bare-floor: the live snails will move and the dead ones will be obvious. Snails die wrapping parts of their shell into their flesh, so when you cook and eat them, you can feel the shards of shell between your teeth.

Always buy large pieces of alum for cleaning the snails because smaller pieces will make your job twice as hard. Coarse salt is also good for washing snails, but one still needs the alum to get squeaky-clean snails.

During washing, go over the snails again and discard any that have shrivelled entrails or visible broken pieces of shell in the skin. Both are signs that the snail was dead on purchase. My neighbour always insisted on cutting off the faces of the snails because she claimed they gave her nightmares. Personally, I have never seen a face on a snail in all my years of eating them. Maybe I'm too distracted.

The snails are boiled with salt, a little ginger and garlic, until they are al dente, not soft. Also not chewy; it's a difficult balance at first. The sensation of biting on a well-cooked snail is almost crunch-like. This is another advantage of using smaller snails: they are easier to cook to this texture. The pepper for the snails is a mixture of onions, tomatoes and small aromatic hot peppers. The onions are cut in long slivers, the tomatoes roughly chopped. The hot peppers are chopped very fine.

Pour a generous layer of oil into the bottom of a pot over high heat. Throw in the onions, tomatoes and peppers and sauté, stirring all the time. You can turn the heat down and cook the mixture until it resembles a sauce, until the tomatoes soften to salsa. Add the tomato puree and season.

Throw the snails in the pot and stir – turn – until they are well coated. The snails are served on their own or with a bowl of basmati rice soaked for twenty minutes, washed then briskly steamed. The rice is enhanced with a generous tablespoon of coconut oil.

I could eat the combination of peppered snails and basmati rice day in and day out, year in and year out, and in my sleep. Delicious.

Unfortunately, I was the butt of rude jokes for many semesters after Buscopan's offer, made in a loud voice in a public place. Whenever his friends saw me, they shouted at the top of their lungs, 'Màá yí e l'áta!' I think this announcement followed me till I left Obáfemi Awólowo University in 1993.

Buscopan did not get to live long; he ran into a tragic incident with vigilantes on his own doorstep. He took his brilliance and music and social awkwardness with him and we all missed him.

He might have read this and had a good laugh. He might be reading this and having a good laugh.

Ram Testicle Suya

The suya stalls on Bogobiri Street, Calabar are only prominent in the darkness. In the daytime, Samuel Bill's Qua Iboe church dominates the view. It is a pristine redbrick backdrop behind one long row of sooty stalls. In the daytime there is also a market around the church named for the street. On the face of the street are men in immaculate babanriga and woven skullcaps perched handsomely on the sides of their heads, smelling of spicy perfumes that make you think of incense and leather slippers. The men are mobile bureau de change. They call out an invitation as you pass: 'Dollar?'

The history of the street is that government gave the Bogobiri fathers all the land around the mosque to settle their families after they migrated to Cross River State from the north. The mosque is across the main road from where the bureau de change men are stationed. There is an alcove that you walk into to buy mudus of tuwo shinkafa, jeero (sorghum), guinea corn, sweet potatoes, white corn for ogi, Irish potatoes and yams. On the floor in front of the entrance to a warehouse that extends into the back of the alcove, is a large spread of blackcurrant-coloured sorrel leaves air-drying on old rice bags. There are recycled paint buckets of finely ground, luminescent Moringa leaves tied in cellophane. On rickety shelves against the walls are faded boxes of bottled aphrodisiacs and locally brewed pheromones. On a Friday, Bogobiri becomes the site of a gorgeous festival. It is only prayer day for the Muslims, but all the little girls dress up in pretty blue shifts with matching hijabs, and special-occasion shoes and sandals. Their eyes are heavily lined with black danjere. The boys wear freshly pressed white babanriga and look just like their fathers.

At night, the church disappears and the suya stalls emerge in the illumination of dozens of hanging light bulbs. I'm mesmerised by the sparkle of curved, wicked-looking knives rising and falling silently against meat, murky rivers of oil pooled on damp newsprint, thick smoke unfurling to meet soot-black stall roofs, and naked bulbs hanging as if on long, desiccated ram's intestines. Everything is black and smoke and sepia, and a heavy fog of meat-scented smoke overhangs the whole area.

The meat is piled in chaotic heaps, red in some parts, glossy brown in others, all of it continuously dipped and squirted with oil. This is not Lagos, where meat is tidily presented in meticulous rows at Ikoyi Hotel suya spot or the University of Suya (rows of suya stalls) in Akéréle, Surulere, so as not to offend your sensibilities. I'm standing in front of one particular stall, looking down at a table of black towels of tripe; long, thick, rippling intestines, large and small; kidneys; livers …

And ka'aiki … ka'abuna … dat ting …

It doesn't seem to have a formal name but it is a serious delicacy and if you don't buy it quickly, someone will swiftly beat you to it. I mean the ram's penis.

My friend Michael Mukolu's stories drew me to this place. He once stood negotiating the price of the ka'aiki and the testicles but when he momentarily hesitated or as his attention wandered for a split second, someone came up stealthily behind him and motioned to the suya man. This person just had to point and the ram's penis was swiftly transferred to the barbecue mesh over glimmering coals, turned from side to side, cut up, garnished with groundnut-flavoured pepper and raw onions, and wrapped in old newspaper. There! That's what happens when you negotiate leisurely over a rare commodity.

Mr Mukolu came back without the ram's penis, but with the testicles and delicious black tripe shaki that was tender with brittle frills. I feasted on the tripe, but the sponginess of the testicles put me off. By the time he had polished them off though, oohing and ahhing over them, I wished I had at least tried one piece. Talking about meat and sensibilities, I realise how superficial my finicky distinctions are: if I can eat tripe, then why not testicles?

A few nights later, Mr Mukolu, his wife and I drove back to Bogobiri, determined to secure all the relevant body parts for research. I resolved to shelve my impractical sensibilities and regard all parts of the animal's anatomy as fit for consumption. In the car, Mr Mukolu talked about a man he once saw at a suya spot, crunching with deep concentration on the cartilaginous ears of a cow. The man's own ears were humongous – so humongous that Mr Mukolu began to imagine that his ears were a clue to his love of eating cow's ears. In other words, could one not safely conclude that if you were in the habit of eating unusual animal parts as suya, especially if you ate them with enthusiasm, then your own corresponding parts would begin to testify to your habits? And if a man loved to eat ram testicles, surely his testicles would soon begin to showcase this strong preference?

Oh, it was all hilarious until we reached Mr. Mukolu's favoured stall, became irrationally tongue-tied and started motioning with our eyes and whispering and using words like 'ka'aiki' and 'dat ting'. If we were not careful the same thing that happened a few nights ago would repeat itself. Someone who spoke fluent sign language, or had no qualms saying 'penis' would come along and buy our research material.

'Dat ting no dey?'

'E dey!'

There were no testicles, but the penis sat there next to a large intestine and kidneys attached to a flat wall of flesh. The vendor and his assistant stood wide-eyed and comfortable while the smoke made our eyes water. He was generous, offering samples of tripe, topside, and lumpy intestine in a small metal bowl. We negotiated and renegotiated. We could afford to. The usual crowd of young men fondling scantily dressed young women and wooing them with meat had not begun to build. Nor had the testicle enthusiasts with their sign language arrived. I wondered about the acute aroma of raw red onions that accompanied suya, if it wasn't a deterrent to the wooing process. I surely would not toast a girl with suya and onions if I were dying to kiss her full on the mouth later.

My opinion of ram penis suya? Overrated, spongy, fatty, like cheap sausage. A layer of smoky, oily, crispy skin around a globule of fat. Not my cup of tea at all. Perhaps because I had no corresponding parts to motivate me. There has to be a significant male associative state of mind attached to eating penises. There are those men who eat it because they like to eat it, and because there is just one unit of it among four limbs, ribs, thighs, etc.; it's a delicacy because of its scarcity. And then there are those men who eat it because they are men and it enhances their sense of masculinity and virility. In other words, it makes their psychological penises bigger. All I have to say is that they are welcome to have it all.

Ka'aiki

Dat ting,

Tout.

Ewà Olóyin

Someone might well ask how Heinz baked beans have offended me. My answer would be that I really don't know. I just cannot stand baked beans. Nothing affronts my taste buds like baked beans, although, if I wanted to be longwinded and fair, I would make a list that had Liquorice Allsorts at the top. In second place would be eko-tútù, that breakfast fare my mother would not stop proposing when I was a child, irrespective of the fact that I was unequivocal about my hatred of it.

Eko-tútù is white corn fermented in clay pots over two to three days. The corn is ground and filtered using clean white cloth to get a smooth paste. The paste is covered with water, then slowly poured into boiled water and briskly stirred to get a pottage. The pottage is divided among pieces of banana leaves, arranged in a kolobo and allowed to cool completely. It is usually served with stewed greens, or with water-yam pottage (ìkokore), as the Ijebu love to eat it.

There are few things as beautiful as eko-tútù presented in fresh banana leaves. The white of the finished patty is ravishing. The aroma of corn and fresh leaf, along with the textural softness and wobbliness, makes eko-tútù the epitome of comfort food. To crown all these virtues, eko is temperamentally cooler than a cucumber. In the opinion of my taste buds, it is best eaten with hot food: pepper-hot, heat-hot. The contrast of hot and cold is a lovely complexity for the palate and tongue. It feels like there's dancing going on in your mouth. Then there's the sourness of the fermentation that cleans your palate for the next mouthful. But eko itself, in cold milk with sugar, like my mother used to serve it, drowns and dies and becomes a white, smelly, nauseating bog.

Baked beans rank as number three, after eko-tútù in milk, on my list of foods I will never love. This means that if I were starving to death, I would pass on the eko-tútù in milk but eat baked beans with gratitude and you wouldn't hear a word from me. It is important to testify that I will eat almost anything because, as a child, I had to eat what I was given and be grateful for it.

With baked beans, there is a progression of affronts from visual to olfactory to the red mess spreading across my tongue. The only time I ever enjoyed eating baked beans was in 1998 when a friend rinsed them (thoroughly) under a tap, stewed them with ground, dried hot pepper and onions, and served them on a plate of steamed rice. Of course, by virtue of that process, they had ceased to be baked beans. Occasionally, I revisit them to try to understand the reason for their world-renowned personality. Then I have to go through that process of psychologically forcing my way past the tin dressed in green.

To my native mind, there is an irrefutable acceptance of what the green of banana leaves (ewé-eko) and Thaumatococcus daniellii (ewé-eran) contribute to the food they unveil. The green of thaumatococcus and of banana leaves is more than packaging. It is aromatics and flavour. It is outstanding presentation. It is contrasting colour to clean the eyes and stimulate the mind. When you eat with your hands from ewé-eko or ewé-eran, there is an added dimension of aromatics transferred to your fingers and inhaled as the hand is lifted to the mouth and proximal to the nostrils.

On the other hand, I do not understand why a tin of baked beans is green. Or not green per se; more annoyingly, it is turquoise, and that turquoise is trademarked. Nothing about that turquoise tin prompts me to expect something delicious. For those people who salivate at the sight of a tin of baked beans, I can only imagine that it is from years of mental association with something that I cannot in any way associate.

After the struggle with the tin opener, and that first look, there is the honest-to-God, paramount affront of those revolting little air bubbles on the face of the beans; that phlegmatic expression from decades of British smugness about its own self-estimation. There, right there, is Fortnum & Mason in Piccadilly genealogy, Boston, Massachusetts ancestry, uppity family members with names like tinned toasted scorpions and goose foie gras: a world so distant, I can't think of it as just the United Kingdom on the continent next door. It is millions of miles out of the orbit of my taste buds.

Then from the look of it to the smell; what can I associate with that smell? It is an important question because I love the smell of cooking honey beans (Ewà Olóyin), especially when there is some fragrant yellow (Igbo) pepper, ginger, onions, cumin and bay leaves in the boiling water. Now there's a homely smell, raising the expectation of a satisfying meal from the core of the stomach and the mind. Here is association worth an appraisal. The aroma follows you from room to room to room, grabbing the man walking past the house by his collar. But the smell of baked beans ... there is nothing to redeem it. It is only through sheer force of will that I can continue after opening the can to put the beans in a small pot and place it on the hob.

Let no one suggest that I eat baked beans without warming them first. The two types of heat are not a cultural preference; they are a necessity without which the baked beans are completely unpalatable. Even if I could forgo the heat that is pepper, I certainly could not do so the temperature. Even now, I can recall perfectly the feeling of revulsion at watching someone piling baked beans straight from a tin onto a piece of toast. With a little heat, the baked beans sputter and churn in the way that thick messes do, and I can turn it out onto a plate.

The next question is, what to eat it with?

I don't want to eat it!

I won't eat it!

Back to the other beans, with the perfumed yellow pepper. Olóyin is the highest grade of bean available in Nigeria. A pot of them will feed four men, and the reference to men here is purposive. I have not met a Nigerian man who does not love his beans. Not baked beans, but Ewà Olóyin cooked with palm oil and ripe plantains. If I did not live in Nigeria, and if I had not tested this premise over and over and found it 100 per cent kosher, I would doubt it. I would call it a generalisation. It is not.

Ewà Olóyin

4 cups olóyin (honey) beans, picked for small stones and chaff, washed thoroughly, and soaked overnight

2 fresh lemongrass stalks, bulbous ends bruised to release the aromatics, folded and tied to form a neat wreath

1 tablespoon balsamic vinegar

½ teaspoon toasted whole cumin seeds (optional)

2 yellow Scotch bonnets, 2 tatase peppers, and
1 leek, all blended with a quarter cup of water

½ cup best-grade palm oil

¼ cup fresh beef stock

2 ripe plantains cut into half-inch rounds

Himalayan crystals

A pinch of fresh grated ginger root

Enough water for an elongated boil

Put the beans, lemongrass, balsamic vinegar and water in a big earthenware pot. Set to boil for 15 minutes. Drain all the water, rinse the beans thoroughly, cover with fresh water and set to boil again. You may leave the lemongrass in for the duration of the cooking or take it out now. I leave it in because I sometimes have problems digesting cooked beans. The combination of lemongrass and vinegar helps to counteract the bloating that may result from eating legumes. I use balsamic vinegar because its sweetness enhances the natural honey flavour of the beans. The balsamic vinegar flavour stays far in the background because most of it is gone with the first rinse.

The second boiling includes the cumin seeds and the grated ginger. The beans are cooked diligently until textural perfection is reached. This means that, when you bite a bean, it slides, its skin shifts and then it yields and becomes mush. The bean can't miss one of these steps. It must be as texturally sensual as two hands sliding against each other. Water must be added carefully during cooking because you don't want to drown the beans and then throw the water away when you are preparing to add the condiments towards the end of cooking. I usually stay close to the cooking beans and add water as is needed. The ideal height of water over the beans is about an inch.

Why am I not using a steam cooker? I love my earthenware pots. Some of them are at least four years old and layered with flavour because the pots are porous. I use them whenever I can. Also, at the end of the cooking process, the burning at the bottom of earthenware pots adds a necessary last burst of flavour enhancement.

When the beans are perfectly soft, put in the salt, blended peppers, stock and palm oil. Some extra slivers of onion won't go amiss here; they add a lovely textural angle to the finished beans. At this point, the beans have about 20 minutes left to cook. I agree with those people who secretly add a teaspoon of honey. It might not be traditional, but it adds value. However, I find that my plantains add as much sweetness as I need. The beans should simmer over low heat until an inevitable layer of burning coats the bottom of the pot and adds the aroma, until the plantains are velvety soft, and the rich smell of palm oil and beans is pure torture.

The height and peak of decadence is an accompanying plate of fried plantains, but there is also one accompaniment that should be tried by all, even if it's just once in a lifetime, and that includes those unfortunate gluten-intolerant people. One must step outside one's house and comfort zone, hail the woman hawking pale, brick-shaped loaves of bread sweating unhealthily under cellophane, and buy one without questioning its bromate content. Get a bread knife and cut across the top of it. Carve out the soft insides of the loaf without making holes in the crust. Fill it with cooked beans. Fill it to the brim and indulge.

Bush Cuisine

The lecturers' bungalows at Obáfemi Awólowo University had long fluorescent bulbs under the eaves above their front doors. As you drove through the streets at night, they snagged at your vision from between trees and tall patches of bush. I knew a lecturer who particularly looked forward to the beginning of the rains in March because the first rains brought rain termites with oversized silver gauze wings, burrowing out from the ground. Fishing for termites needed hardly any effort. A fluorescent bulb is the bait. A bowl of water is set out at night, near the light. All that's needed is the stingiest of showers and, in the morning, the surface of the water in the bowl will be black and silver with drowned termites.

This ritual is perfect for a Friday night because, on a Saturday morning, one can leisurely bring out the frying pan, add a little oil, and briskly toss the termites in it. Less is more. The excess oil is drawn out with absorbent kitchen paper, and the termites are transferred to a clean bowl. Two tablespoons of tinned sweetcorn is all the accompaniment needed for the termites. You will need all your fingers, because the wings that have not fallen off with the back-and-forth of the spatula have to be extracted manually. You would also feel pretentious eating termites with a fork. The fingers on the freer hand will offer one or two niblets of corn to the fingers offering the termites to the mouth.

I stumbled on the lecturer's longwinded meal one afternoon at her house (it went on and on and on; she kept getting up to do other things then resuming the meal after each interlude). Well it wasn't so much a meal so much as a snack, analogous to eating a bowl of boiled groundnuts; a nonchalant entertainment of the mouth and fingers. Feeding a craving rather than the stomach. At first, I was horrified at the recognition of whole black termites and yellow kernels in the bowl in her lap, but there was something about the way she sat and ate this fare: a ladylike interaction between the fingers, termites and sweetcorn, each placed just at the lips so that the words could flow unobstructed, and the small morsels were drawn into the mouth in a disinterested sort of way. Her leg hung over one arm of the chair, swinging like a pendulum keeping sedated time.

I think I was partly intrigued by the fact that she offered none of it to either me, who was staring like a child in the marketplace, or her daughter, who had brought me to the house. It is culturally appropriate to offer your food to visitors if they arrive in the middle of your meal. If you don't want to, you cover the meal and put it under your bed. However, I was her daughter's guest, not hers and she was in her house and it was Saturday so I really had no right to any kind of effusive welcome, or entertainment.

We sat long enough that the hand movement, the pendulous leg, and the drawl of her speech made me ravenous for the trinkets she was juggling. I was close enough to put my hand in that bowl if she turned away for just one second. We didn't get even a glass of water at the lecturer's house, but I left with an enduring inquisitiveness about eating winged termites. I just lacked the guts to fish for my own with a light bulb and a bowl.

I lived in a boys' quarters room facing a random stretch of bush in Ife, with squirrels scrambling up and down the trees and electrical poles in broad daylight. Not once did I think of harnessing my 300 mcg of testosterone and going after the squirrels. Not even when my friends came round and wondered aloud why bushmeat was crossing my front yard with such audacity. Something about the ruralness of Ife-town, its early winding down of pepper-soup joints and amateur plays at the pit-theatre, inspired all manner of delinquent cravings and plans to hunt down meat. It wouldn't be for a meal because there was food at your residence halls, or you could buy a real meal at a restaurant or a buka if you didn't want to cook. If you wanted to sit down to a bowl of beef or sticks of suya, you didn't need to hunt to get them.

It was the spirit of the fluorescent bulb and bowl, of the hunt, that made my friends drive a Volkswagen Pescaccia called Amoke at breakneck speed up and down the university roads in the middle of the night, aiming the tyres at the heads of squirrels and cane rats. Amoke was an old car that we speculated was used in the Nigerian civil war. It had to be parked on a slope to get the engine going in the morning, but in the middle of the night when it was called upon to chase down bushmeat it became another being entirely, with full-on headlights, killer instincts and testosterone running through its engine. Needless to say, the driver and passengers were all men.

In 2008, my family took a road trip from Calabar to Itigidi. We drove through the village of Ugep and our driver, a friend of the family, noted that Ugep was renowned for its 'cutting grass'.

'Grass cutter', I corrected.

No, 'cutting grass', he insisted.

It was the beginning of a witty introduction to the many different types of bushmeat available in Cross River State. More illuminatingly, it was an eye-opener to the near lack of discrimination in what is classified as meat. The eclectic delicacy called bushmeat is expertly hunted by men who disparage the use of guns, because a cane rat with Dane gun pellets in its belly is a signboard for an inferior hunter. Bushmeat is so expensive, it is eaten with barefaced snobbery. In Ikom, Northern Cross River, the most esteemed dish on the menu is egome, a combination of green plantains, palm oil and smoked bushmeat. If an Ikom woman wants to acquire another woman's husband, she does it via egome, not by ekpang nku kwo, fish pepper soup and scripture. Most Lagosians are too modish to be offered rat on a menu without being completely put off. They eat it all right, but it cannot be called anything more specific than bushmeat. In Cross River State, however, people refer to 'cutting grass' as 'big rat' with ease and savoir faire while it's sitting on their plates, not only when it's an animal scurrying around in the bush.

Chuku-chuku beef is the local parlance for porcupine. Chuku-chuku is the onomatopoeic word for the porcupine quills that are burnt off and sold to hairdressers for making perfect lines for hair braids. Other bushmeat includes monkeys, drills, squirrels, antelope, bats, snakes (which are called 'floor-ropes' so that they don't come when you don't want them), civet cats, the futambo or Hausa girl (deer), and 'kata beef', which I persistently requested a description of and had no success whatsoever in visualising. There was no joy with Google either. On the border of Cameroon, one can buy smoked elephant and gorilla meat. Cameroon bushmeat is charismatically catholic, broadminded and inclusive of crickets and tadpoles.

My next-door neighbour Andrew Dunn in Sacramento, Calabar is the country director for the Wildlife Conservation Foundation in Calabar and Cameroon. He would often come round to have coffee with condensed milk and we would talk about his work in the bush. One of the Foundation's top success stories is the exchange of gorilla hunters' guns for beehives, of hunter adrenaline for apiarian even-temperedness. It is a drop in the bucket of efforts to rescue endangered species from the time-honoured Cross Riverian palate. You can still buy smoked baby sharks in Henshaw Beach Market and near-extinct drills smoked on stakes in the bush. One of the most popular eating points in Calabar is Atimbo, a line of individual shops with names such as Atimbo Galilee, Uncle Taste and See, and Shade 9, all selling bushmeat and steamed plantains served with okro, palm wine tapped from the top of the tree, obadale palm wine (tapped from cutting down the whole tree) or ukot (fermented palm wine).

You would never know what the bushmeat you were eating was. You'd recognise the gaminess of the meat, you'd see the synthetic twine used to tie parts of it together during cooking and notice the distinct pinkness of cooked pieces, but everything else would be concealed under a sauce of greens and palm oil. You might well be eating a near-extinct Hausa girl and not know it. Often, when Andrew left my house for his, Sylvie, his Cameroonian wife, came round and together we planned the day's pot of extinct species soup. *One's enemies shall be members of one's household.*

She was complicit in my initiation to stewed porcupine. Someone who had no idea who I was and was trying to butter up my civil-servant husband gave me one at the end of the year; an early Christmas gift. It was sent round to the house with the confidence with which you give an expensive, universally desirable gift. It looked like a large, long-legged rabbit with a painful death expression on its long-toothed face. I kept my mind open only by not looking at it for long stretches of time, by not really looking at it at all. I gave it to Uduak, the help, who was sneering to take it round to the Dunns.

It was a near successful coup on my sensitivity. I warned that I didn't want to see the head in the stew, so Uduak ecstatically kept it for her own stew. A few hours later, a porcupine meat stew was on my kitchen counter, delivered from Sylvie Dunn's kitchen. It smelled absolutely delicious, but Uduak and Sylvie had left the fingers and fingernails on the appendages of the stewed porcupine. It looked like it was writing a letter when it died. They also left on hairs as thick and black as embroidery thread. The nail in the coffin was the texture of the porcupine's skin: like cooked leather. I kept thinking *Rat!* as I ate the meat and I resolved never to eat another piece of chuku-chuku beef.

Mid-2013 I got another gift of chuku-chuku beef. The skilled porcupine hunter had used a trap not a gun. You can tell from the resourceful building of traps from bits of wood, and the attention to detail in the stretching of the skin across the stakes for smoking, that procuring and preparing this meat is a way of life, and the product of hard-earned skills. The hunter understands that he can't get too close to the prey. If he tries, he is going to be sprayed with porcupine quills, so he creates a respectful trap. He kills the animal in the trap, and carries it to the village with the other bush animals he has caught.

The meat is gutted, cleaned, washed and prepared for smoking. It is stretched as taut as a tent across an intricate network of small twigs and thick, strong aromatic tree branches. This stretching is done so expertly it looks like a mechanical procedure. The skill to do this, and do it well by hand, is remarkable to watch. The meat is smoked continuously, considerately, over a close fire and a distant one, for days, until a buyer comes along. It is sold for a princely sum that represents the work. My small one cost about N4,000. It arrived with a dense aroma of meat, wood smoke, burning, cooking, gaminess and 'freshness'. Even the stakes used to stretch the meat smelled delicious.

I decided to cook this one myself, and make stock that I could then use for soup. After about an hour of slow cooking in stock, the meat expanded to reveal three layers of flesh – the dark outer skin with the taste and consistency of ham rind; a pink, salty middle layer with bite; and a white, delicate inner layer. All three layers peeled away in delicious strips. The porcupine gave the stock a heady, smoky aroma and deepened its flavour. If chuku-chuku beef were not such expensive fare, it would be great on the daily menu.

The most interesting aspect of the bush menu is the mischievous nose-thumbing from Cross Riverians towards conservationists like Andrew Dunn, who are trying to take things off the menu and getting no commitment from the locals. The minute you bring the topic up, an impish aroma rises from the Cross Riverian. Conservationists are not concerned about winged termites or cane rats, but about the rare species of floor-ropes, civets, some species of porcupine, drills, monkeys, and the beautiful Hausa girl. The aroma of the attitude is defiance against the uppity white man who thinks he knows everything. The laws against eating drills have only made the experience of eating them more exquisite. The reality of Cross Riverians driving their rainforest wildlife to extinction by satisfying their cravings for rarefied meat is tragic, but there is no way you can suppress a smile when the unswerving answer to 'But what does it taste like?' is a resounding 'Very sweet!'

Between a Trophy and a Wife

There's nothing I hate like that venerated, swaggering, empty-headed title of 'Island big boy', or 'Island big girl'. It refers to a man or woman who works and lives in Ikoyi, Victoria Island, Victoria Island extension, along Lekki-Epe expressway, grudgingly Ajah and not one kilometre past Badore. They can afford a certain lifestyle that is way above and beyond the means of 90 per cent of Nigerians.

The Island is also the hub of a kind of social dining, for nowhere else in the entirety of Nigeria can one view, purchase or eat such a rarefied variety of exotic, overpriced food and drink: sushi, fresh or frozen dim sum, smoked salmon and chorizo, organic, eco-friendly rice milk, quinoa and amaranth, dainty seedless grapes, roasted and seasoned seaweed, Armand de Brignac's Ace of Spades, and gourmet fair-trade coffee worth an arm, a leg and a vital organ. You'll find pink and white Himalayan crystal salt, oolong tea worth $80 and some of the best chocolates and cheeses money can buy.

Island restaurant food can be cooked exceptionally well – not hit and miss, not experimental cuisine by some brilliant Nigerian apprentice chef. Well maybe, but at some point in your meal, some fair-skinned fellow from an unheard-of province in Myanmar – head chef to you – will pop his head round the restaurant's kitchen door for your benefit, so *you'll know* he has been imported and they must pay him a humongous salary, part of which you will soon be contributing to.

It is incongruous and fascinating to add up the number of butter croissants, farmed salmon and N500 tomatoes eaten in one day on Lagos Island. Incongruous, because an island tends to be either a terrifyingly desolate (even if breathtakingly beautiful) patch of real estate, where basic necessities are life-threateningly scarce; or at the other extreme, a decadent destination like Ibiza, where real life is perpetually suspended and tourist dollars, drugs and sex keep the economy buzzing, if indeed 'economy' is the appropriate word.

We are obviously not like the former island and as for the latter, I imagine that in Ibiza they have 'light' (i.e. constant electricity, running water, and health insurance), and all the grooving, happy people do not find their partying obstinately interrupted by PHCN and the *beep beep beep* of inverters.

Lagos Island is one of the most incongruous pieces of terra firma in the world, a unique pod of time and place where one can live in a N100-million home without reliable basic amenities, around the corner from a rubbish dump. One's neighbour will be a man in a shabby babanriga who lives in a shack selling boxes of matches, sticks of cigarettes, tom-toms, and family-size Indomie noodles out of his flexible living space. You'll snub him as you drive out of your gates, and not answer his greetings, but on the night when your fridge is unexpectedly bare because your million-naira job won't let you keep on top of supermarket trips, you'll send out to him for a family-size packet of noodles, a tin of Derica tomato puree (the queen of tinned tomato purees), three eggs and a tin of Titus sardines. He'll send the items to you with the words 'no change', and you'll get the real message which is,

I'm keeping your change and if you don't like it, return my noodles, my tin of Derica and my eggs and go to bed without satisfying your bullshit hunger.

Here we are, after all, eating South African leg of lamb, prosciutto and Camembert and we might as well be doing so by candlelight; not romantic or aromatherapeutic candlelight, but the other kind that every single Nigerian, without discrimination, cannot deny knowing about – the Abela kind that necessitates keeping cheaply manufactured candles at your bedside just in case the electricity goes, the generator doesn't work, and the inverter develops a problem. In 2014, on Lagos Island, the humble candle is the only source of illumination guaranteed not to fail the Island big girl.

I enjoy social dining but I sometimes resent the fact that the availability of foreign and novel foods has nothing to do with me. I understand that in most countries, the ability to buy foreign foods is initially immigration-centric, expanding as the indigenous palate does so. But the expansion feels stunted here. Nigeria has a many-tentacled insularity that keeps the food prices high and the Nigerian snobs elevated. Lagos Island's relationship with the food belonging to South Asia, Lebanon and Liberia is a compromise with chaos, and a wasted opportunity. Regardless of how long peoples have lived here, we have never incorporated their food into our culture, and barely even acknowledge it. We are accused of going to other people's countries and looking for Nigerian bukas there, so it's not surprising that when the foreign food lands on our doorstep, our relationship with it is awkward. Consider that fascinating market at Jakande, the one next to the Lekki Art Market, where you can buy fresh pak choi, frail coriander and orange pumpkins. Like a slap in the face, like being put in one's place, in one's own country for that matter, it's called 'white man's market' and will remain the white man's market for a long time to come. Many specialty supermarkets are for expats who live in clusters in Ikoyi and Victoria Island. And when Nigerians go to white man's market and try to buy pak choi, frail coriander and orange pumpkins, the traders will sternly ask you why on earth you are buying them! The reprimand is an accusation of pompousness: *So your own food is not good enough for you abi?* You can read it in their tone and questions.

There is something very play-pretend to our eating out at foreign restaurants. We do it in the capacity of Island big boys and girls, in an almost weary well-what-can-one-do manner that suggests our hearts are really, really not in the whole enterprise, as if we are obligated to play the role of oily ajebutters to show we are current and trendy. I wonder what the real point of being an Island big girl or Island big boy with so much disposable income is, if the best one can do is pretend. I urge the reader to compare our enthusiasm for eating foie gras at Villa Medici to eating hot amala, gbegiri/ ewedu and small-small meat served between 8 a.m. and 10 a.m. sharp at a buka on Okánlàwon Àjàyí Street at Alhaji Masha in Súrùlérè. I happen to know some Island big boys who keep to this Saturday-morning deadline without fail and God help the person who tries to stand in their way.

Our eating of foreign versus local food is like the difference between acquiring a trophy wife and committing to the love of one's life even if there's no trendiness to commend her. There is absolutely nothing wrong with admitting one just wants one's own food and nothing to do with all the mede-mede on offer and there is everything to be commended in the embracing of the curries of the Indians who have lived in Lagos for fifty years and the cooking of Liberian beans torborgee.

The Secret Ingredient of
My Secret Ingredient Soup

Elderly Nigerian women who have made an art of cooking often give me a look when I show enthusiasm for something they have made. If I say, 'This is delicious, how did you cook it?', a wall comes up, and I'm not sure why.

Is it boredom or disdain? Or that it's just not cultural to talk recipes? The conversation tends to end on a detached, 'It's just egúsí soup' or 'It's just ìkokore', with an attitude that says take it or leave it; this fuss you are making is a little unseemly. No one has ever leaned over and whispered conspiratorially, like Mr. Ping to his son Po in *Kung Fu Panda*, 'The secret ingredient of my secret ingredient soup is …'

I think it might be the dearth of Nigerian cookbooks and the fact that we mostly cook how our mothers taught us to cook. All Nigerian mothers, without exception, would rather be strung up and quartered than have their daughters defined by those two grave words: *cannot cook*.

Nigerian women of my mother's generation mostly cook with the mindset that this is what well-raised women do to keep their households running smoothly and their husbands happy. It is a functional art and therefore most of their generation are not watching the BBC food channel and obsessing about whether cos is preferable to arugula. If it is true that women take pride in their discomfort, time and secrets in the kitchen the same way men can sometimes take pride in painful machismo, then perhaps the attitude is a rebuke for my unseemly behaviour.

Yet all egúsí soups are certainly not the same. There are those people who cook egúsí you are happy to eat, and there are those who cook egúsí that has you weeping with joy. The details, the techniques, the quirks and the secret ingredients are there, but they are not being compared at tea parties. Rather, there is a dignified nonchalance typical of women who cook in my mother's generation. They are not on show; they are just cooking.

I have often mentioned cutting plantains against one's palm as opposed to cutting it against a chopping board. When I did so in front of a non-Nigerian friend, she said it was irresponsible and dangerous to do this when one could simply cut them on a board. I had to explain to her that if you cut plantains on a board in Nigeria, you were a wimp. In the same vein, I find myself pretending to elder Nigerian women that my cookbooks are purely for reference or to make the house look like it belongs to someone who loves food. I don't tell them that I cook out of them because they would disapprove strongly. You can't cook if you are cooking out of a cookbook.

The secret cannot be neatly processed into pages of recipes either. It is part of the person called 'olowo síbí': literally 'hands for spoons'. It is like if you asked a woman what she does in bed to keep her husband happy and she was unable to tell you because it's not line-by-line, precept upon precept. It's been so meticulously woven into the embraces and kisses that there is a need to stop and think, but you shouldn't be asking her such questions anyway, so she peremptorily slams the louvres shut. She might not be literate either and so her memory would do the work of paper. I am amazed at the amount of detail so-called illiterates keep in their heads: they are the ones who go to the market with fifty items to buy and remember every single one. An illiterate woman's mind will have subconsciously arranged the facts of sexual pleasure or Nigerian cooking and taught them to her fingers. The difficulty, therefore, is getting the secret out from the subconscious, from the very bottom of the soup pot of the virtuoso cook.

I cannot express how much I fear the words, 'There is no recipe. It's just the way I cook it!' It means you have to eat humble pie and take time out to travel to Kotangora if necessary to watch the cooking being done and extract the minute details yourself. And you have to watch carefully, or else you might miss something. And these women are often watching you like a hawk. They note every thread of inappropriateness and penalise you.

'How are you holding the serving spoon?'

'Are you left handed or right handed?'

'You always scoop the soup towards you and never away from you.'

I once told Mumsie the fish seller that I would rather she cut off the head of the catfish I was buying than pay N5,000 for the whole fish. In the process of negotiating, she had mentioned that the head of my fish alone was N1,500. If that's so, I said, then cut the head off and sell me the rest of the fish.

She was scandalised. How could I talk about the head of catfish in such an irreverent manner? And I reached a conclusion that still plays out in my head like an epiphany: *the secret ingredient of the Nigerian secret ingredient soup is fish head.*

Fish head is the secret ingredient in ekpang nku kwo and in afang and in edikaikong. Furthermore, ground, smoked fish head is the secret of that coy pot of soup with no meat in sight. How come it is so delicious? Certainly not Maggi; the answer is fish. And if it's not a ground, smoked, oily fish head releasing all its flavour into the soup, then it's crayfish.

That same day of the fish-head negotiations, I heard a discussion about waterleaf and how one must always use the smallest leafed variety in cooking afang, so as not to drown the soup in the vegetable's water.

Another woman came to the fish stall and declared that her fish never goes in the freezer otherwise its taste is ruined. While listening to all of these gems, I wished I could be present in every incidental context where secrets were freely exchanged, in those places where these uptight elderly women forgot themselves and were carried away in the pride of the moment.

I remember cajoling my Aunty Thelma to tell me how she gets her fisherman's stew to move like velvet. Because I didn't watch her cook it, that process never really fell into place. Eventually, after interacting with other soups from Cross River State, I learnt that the trick is in the chopped onions melting into a thickness, plus a little ogbono added almost at the end.

I have to acknowledge that I have my work cut out for me. I'm on a mission to put onto paper all the secret ingredients of secret soup so that everyone can share in it.

Molará's Jollof Beans

I've read that the word 'jollof' is another way of saying 'Wollof' or 'Wolof', one of the languages spoken in Gambia and Senegal and a minute part of Mauritania. It originally stood for a combined dish of rice and fish called *benachin* or *ceebu jen* in Wolof.

If I were asked what jollof means, I would propose that it means 'enjoyment'. That is what it means here sometimes, hence the colloquial word 'jollofing'. The other meaning needs the word rice, for the ubiquitous red-faced rice dish served at every social Nigerian event and sold at every fast food joint. The enjoyment and the rice are connected because you will, without fail, get a plate of jollof rice at any Nigerian party. Parties and jollof rice are siblings. At the very least, you will be within your rights to ask for a plate of jollof rice and meat if you don't see it anywhere at the party.

The only real similarity between our jollof rice and the original Wolof version is that it is cooked slowly in a suspension containing tomatoes, tomato paste, onions and hot peppers. The Wolof version is more elaborate, cooked with spices and different kinds of meat. I would hate to say that many Nigerian jollof rices are pretenders, because that would go against my own principle of audacious and persistent tweaking of recipes. Nigerian jollof rice is approximately what it is and its red face has paid its dues in party attendance and decades of Nigerian home-cooking. I have also tasted many delicious versions, none of them claiming to be the official West African chargé d'affaires. The best, without exception, is cooked outside over firewood.

I was thrilled when I went to visit my brother and his family some years ago and my sister-in-law, who I'm not flattering but is really lovely in that salt-of-the-earth fashion, cooked something called jollof beans. I was immediately enthralled. The word 'jollof' is already so gastronomically familiar that putting it in front of 'beans' just makes all my salivary glands go into overdrive. I love the fact that the recipe is like a family heirloom taught to Lará by her mother who was taught it by her own aunt forty-five years ago. If I were Lará, I would never give away such a recipe without making the asker beg and grovel for it.

The first premise, obviously, is beans: light brown, small, glossy honey beans that the Yoruba call ewa olóyin because they say it has a superior sweetish accent to it and it cooks quickly (in terms of cooking beans). If one can't buy the olóyin, the next in preference is olo 1, which is the first of three grades in the darker brown-eyed beans. Then there is olo 2 and olo 3. Lará's preference is olo 2 because there's no need to break the bank to have delicious jollof beans and one can save the difference in price. There is also a trendy, unclassified grade from Kano: not quite white yet not quite brown, and not even available in Lagos, Oyingbo, Iddo, Ìkotún or Mile 12 markets. You will only find it in Abuja. I myself had no clue that beans had grades until a friend of the family who 'knows her beans', gave me a summary on the mind-taxing negotiation of grades of Nigerian beans. Last year, she brought back an unfamiliar speckled specie from Abuja and declared them, 'don't quote me – Boko Haram beans'.

As with distinguishing between hand-shelled and machine-shelled egusi, I rely on a friend to help me buy beans. Nothing stops a dishonest vendor from switching the beans if you don't know the difference. The ewa olóyin is quite fair-faced compared with the three olo grades, but distinguishing between olo 1, 2 and 3 isn't as straightforward as it sounds.

The beans for the jollof are picked for stones and chaff and soaked for some minutes. The skin is washed off as if one were making moin-moin or akara, so that only the white under-skin of the beans remains. The beans are placed in a pot with just enough water to cover them and cooked over medium heat until soft. Thereafter, a blend of hot peppers, tomatoes and whole onions is added. Alternatively, ground dried pepper, diced onions, and a little tinned tomato puree can be used. Other ingredients are fresh shrimp, pieces of smoked mackerel, chicken stock, a little vegetable oil, and salt. All these are mixed well with the beans and returned to the hob for about ten minutes. The end product should not be waterlogged or thick. The total cooking time is about thirty-five minutes.

Lará lists Maggi as one of her ingredients, but I don't see why home-made stock, added as part of the water allowance at the beginning and then again when all the other ingredients are added to the beans, won't do significantly better than Maggi.

When she gave me the recipe, I remembered an old, forgotten passion for smoked mackerel from the market, wrapped in greasy old newspaper, the smell so gorgeous that the fish never quite makes it home to where it was intended for cooking vegetable soup. I would, of course, always give myself a stomach ache, since the handling of the smoked fish in the market is never quite as hygienic as one would like and the fish needs to be heated to make it safe for consumption.

I must make a last reference to onions and the magical textural touch they give to food. It was Aunty Thelma who gave me an old-hand secret about finely chopping or blending onions and how making a decision for either determines whether the stew or soup to which they are added is velvety or just plain smooth. One would imagine that blended onions give a velvety texture, but it is actually the finely chopped onions that break down into velvety, bubbling soup. I'm still trying to figure out the chemistry behind that.

So there is MoLará's understated but highly successful jollof beans with melted down onions, the dazzling smell of smoked Titus fish and the extravagance of fresh shrimp, eaten with dodo or soft bread rolls (Lará's suggestion). I would eat it with a confident sprinkling of sour white Ìjebu gari.

A Twitter uproar ensued in June 2014 when the photograph of white-faced jollof rice appeared on UK Tesco's website. It was interesting to note that the protests were about complexion. If the rice was red, most Nigerians would have snorted at the strips of charred red sweet peppers and decorative parsley on the rice and moved on.

I sent a message to Senegalese chef Pierre Thiam on his 'Blue fish with red rice and vegetables' recipe in his book *Yolele! Recipes from the Heart of Senegal*. Was this red rice close to the original jollof rice? He confirmed that it was, with 'some minor variations'. It gave me the confidence to propose that jollof means red from tomatoes, especially from tomato paste. If this ingredient is present, everything else is forgivable. And, based on the evidence, I think it makes sense to stretch the

definition of jollof to include variations. I can't resist quoting
from the head-notes on Pierre Thiam's recipe.

Often there will be a coating of browned rice on the
bottom (khogn), stuck thanks to the sugary thickness
of the tomato paste in the sauce. Because those
dregs are so delicious, they become the cook's prize,
a fitting reward for a hard day's work, which she
may or may not choose to share.[18]

Incidentally this intense browning is the secret to Nigerian
jollof anything. The party jollof rice firewood aroma is the
perfume of burning pepper, tomatoes and rice.

---

[18] Pierre Thiam, *Yolele! Recipes from the Heart of Senegal* (New York: Lake
Isle Press, 2008), 125.

The Marketplace

'Ofong isin N150 today!'

I'm in the market again, shopping for food. I love and hate
the process. As soon as I step out of the car I am bombarded
by deafening static, heavy breathing and revolving chronicles
on polyester blouses and considerately worn second-hand
brassieres. The bras are swinging from nails in the beam of
a stall in the carpark opposite the entrance to the produce
section of the market. The second-hand-clothes man selling
his wares over the loudspeaker wants the bras to catch your
eye. He wants you to feel the loudspeaker quickening your
heartbeat with dense sound. Today's special offer is one yard
of wrapper for N150.

I shop in the market inwardly grousing that the world
wholeheartedly belongs to extroverts, and introverts are
marginalised. Market shopping is an unequivocally extroverted
affair: the swagger, wit and pretence of casualness, the false
sociability and the endless superficial repetition of 'How's
your family?' when I couldn't sufficiently care. If I don't ask
the vendor how his day is, how his wife and children are, and
how his weekend was, he will take offence and consider me
too abrupt to be given a good price. If I ask those needful
questions I will immediately be rewarded with blinding smiles
and reciprocal queries. Not that he's invested in the enquiries

about my family either; these are simply the preliminary rules of market negotiations: ceremonial, desultory, straining. I am too slow to skilfully calculate whether I am hearing an absolute truth, a half-truth or a blatant lie. I take every word to heart, then upstairs to the lab for slow analyses until I am overwhelmed. I sometimes employ shouting, a legitimate part of the marketplace's lingua franca. If someone yells at you and you don't yell back, you are a pushover and you will pay for it when it's time to negotiate the cost of the commodity. In contrast, there is something soothing about supermarket aisles and their aloofness, about the allowance for inward negotiation of choices.

I much prefer to go to Marian Market with my neighbour who I call 'Local Government Chairman'. She is tall and heavy-boned with glossy, inky skin. She walks slowly with her shoulders held back, rolling one buttock then the other buttock like perfectly synchronised cogs. She brushes her teeth hard on market days. With primed flashing smiles, she wraps the vendors round her finger and chops every price they offer in thirds. She walks through the market like she owns it.

When we first used to go to the market together, I would trail behind her and pretend I was her mute relation from Cameroon. It gave my brain the freedom to really negotiate the sights and sounds. I was trying to cultivate that necessary organic relationship with food and the accompanying skill or common sense that allows one to recognise good fresh produce that has not been tampered with, force-ripened or presented to hide rot or decay. It's a skill I believe is becoming obsolete because it isn't necessary to buy food at the market anymore. The supermarket's cool aisles are an option.

A young lady who I sometimes send to the market always astounds me by bringing back the freshest, most delicious produce at considerably lower prices, and has a feel for the market and its food that I don't have even in an elementary capacity. She can keep her head against the loud tide of smells, conversations and confusing banter, somehow project her mind into every tomato, yam and green leaf and know if it is the best to eat or the absolute worst. She has a relationship with food that is significantly more cultured than my weekly urban-mute visits to the market.

As much as I hate the sweltering, loud, smelly assault on the senses that is the marketplace, on Thursdays you will find me standing in front of Mumsie's smoked and dried fish stall. My head will almost be level with her roof of suspended stockfish, worth as much as the plaster-of-Paris ceiling in my house. Mumsie will stand to the right of a table piled high with smoked, impaled shine-nose, rolled up catfish and piles of shimmering crayfish. On the wall behind her, the letters YHWH are scrawled, and around her neck she wears a Catholic scapular. Fish hooks rescued from the mouths of Norwegian stockfish are arranged on the top of the YHWH wall. They are resold expensively to the local fishermen.

Local Government Chairman wants to kiss the shine-nose fish full in the mouth to find out whether its belly is fresh. She holds its head in one hand, the tail in the other and kisses it for a split second, then opens her mouth and inhales to taste if the air from the fish's belly is fresh. She is performing because she knows everyone at Mumsie's fish stall is watching her. Everyone seems to have stopped to hear her verdict on the kiss. The shine-nose, which the Efik call 'edeng', is a large fish with a blunt, protruding nose. It makes sense to cut it up before smoking it, but the Efiks give it to their in-laws at weddings, and they want to make an impression with the size and length of the fish, so Mumsie won't cut them up for smoking.

There is a woman who has been standing on the other side of the stall talking to one of Mumsie's daughters. They are engrossed in the conversation, but it is in Efik and I can't understand what they are both so invested in. She's got her hair stylishly swept up on one side, held up with a pretty pin. Everyone either comes to the market dressed to the nines or in their nightgowns with headscarves. The in-betweeners like me stand out. I often find myself staring into faces with mascara, eyeliner, eyeshadow and bright pink streaks on cheekbones. I stand behind someone with a false Hermes bag and high heels, who whispers something at the condiment woman in an accent that goes with her bag. There's even a woman in a black gown that she has to hold above the mud.

Mumsie's daughter and the woman with the pretty hairpin have been at the conversation for about thirty minutes. Mumsie whispers that she is negotiating the price of a head of smoked catfish, the same one that I often put down and tell her to cut if it will reduce the price of the rest of the fish. She laughs as she cuts into the belly of a smoked shine-nose with a bright orange saw, and I beg her to sell me a piece of the belly that is falling apart. It is a clean, white fish that comes apart like a revelation, with the smell of smoke and cooked fish percolating from the cutting, moistness tempering the parting of the layers, a brown strip of skin precariously holding it all together. Even the fish bones look like they belong in your mouth. Mumsie raises her eyebrows, secures the pieces of fish with rubber bands and declares that that one piece of the belly I want (surely because I want it, and I am visibly salivating) is worth the price of one whole smoked catfish.

'WHY?'

'Fish no dey!' she says, wrinkling her nose.

It is another inherent part of the market lingo. There is fish everywhere but there is no fish. Smooth okro, hairy okro with cactus-like pins, pink okro, stubby okro, slim okro but *okro no dey*. Orange hills of carrots catch your eye from left and right as you walk the dark corridors where the fresh-produce sellers converge ... yet *carrot no dey*. The meaning of 'E no dey!' is plain. It is rarely ever about whether the item one is attempting to buy is in or out of season. It is more likely that a scarcity has been declared by the produce vendors in order to get the best sale price.

And anyway, Mumsie says, the belly of edeng is expensive by virtue of the way it makes a pot of okro soup sublime. 'Aye!' she exclaims jerking her shoulders up and down to drive the enticement home.

A small elderly man, who Mumsie's daughters call 'Ete Nuak Nuak Nuak' because he wanders the length and breath of the Marian Market to save N50 on a purchase, is having an argument with Ijeoma, Mumsie's older daughter. She wants to sell him a bowl of crayfish for N900, and he won't pay more than N800 for it.

'Let me look at it, wait wait!' he says to her, turning the bowl round on its bottom as it sits on the table. He inspects it closely as if he can tell the weight just by looking. 'Today na die go. I for carry coffin for head come. Make it snappy Mbok,' he says under his breath.

'OK Bro!' she says laughing sheepishly. Now he's talking to himself.

'800'

'900'

'800'

'Nyeneke!'

Mumsie doesn't even have the energy to banter today. On the days when she is determined to empty your pockets, you'll hear:

'Fish don go husband house.'

'E don marry.'

'Fish don buy wrapper.'

'E wan born pickin.'

Often I find myself beyond incredulous, standing and listening to market vendors talking, reassuring myself the story must be true; no one would go out of their way to say something so impossible unless it were true. Once, a goat vendor followed me through the market in an attempt to convince me that his he-goat – which only looked slightly bigger than a puppy – was a good buy. He told me that I was not to worry; once the goat had been fed and watered it would increase in size and become comparable to any other goat in the market. He followed me for twenty minutes and I believe if he had followed me for twenty more, I would have bought the inflatable goat.

If you ask too insistently, Mumsie won't sell the fish at all. She will ramble on about how the Ijaw men who fish have all disappeared into thin air, not one of them to be seen on the beach, not one fishing boat in sight. How all the fishwives got to the beach at Ekang and you could hear a pin drop. 'One has to be careful in light of the struggle for prime fishing spots between the Cameroonians and the Nigerians.'

You will hear longwinded tales about Governor Imoke's logging bans and how the onunu wood that burns sweet, lasting smoke is now, by policy, unharvestable. The wood grows out of the Calabar River and is hard enough to harvest as is. Your ears will be full and your mind reeling with details of impromptu battles between Cameroonian gendarmeries, Ijaw fishermen and fish sellers on the sands of the beach. You will see, in clear detail, blood and Heineken beer flowing and evaporating in the sand and sun. Mumsie says the sellers pay fishermen for the fish, and they must agree to be taxed in cans of Heineken for the privilege of having fish sold to them.

This is the thing about the marketplace: its confusion and animation can be addictive. The inspiration it gifts is unparalleled, and certainly not available on antiseptic supermarket shelves. I lived almost forty years and had no clue about the incidental delicacy that is the belly of a shine-nose. One day I was in the market and, in an organic moment, I was introduced to imperfectly smoked fish, one part dry the other moist. For this imperfection, one pays, and pays rapturously, because of what it will do to okro soup when it enters it. On another day, and never again, I found coral crayfish so expensive I flinched at the price. I discovered fresh red bush pepper berries, harvested from the forest, heavy on stalks before being dried into the black, sullen pellets we all know as black pepper. There was edible, ferociously addictive native chalk the colour of onyx on the outside, grey dust on the inside: a true enigma when it tastes like one is eating sand and there is a risk of getting lead poisoning. There are local pink apples shaped like bells that disappeared off my radar at some distant point in childhood.

As I price a baby barracuda at Mumsie's stall, a woman passes behind me and asks, 'What are you cooking?' You can't be rude and tell her to mind her business, you must answer and do so politely.

'I'm not sure,' I say. I'm really not sure. She looks me over intently, my face, my clothes, my hands, hair and shoes, because women don't go to a market in Calabar in faded green corduroys and black t-shirts, and they don't admit to not being sure what they are cooking. 'I will make stew with it,' I say, so she will go away.

'Stew? Why stew when you can make pepper soup?' Cross Riverian women can be unfairly contemptuous of stew. I won't mention that I am Yorùbá, because that will help convince her of my confusion in the market, and my laziness. She's already concluded that I'm useless; the suggestion of pepper soup is child's play, a tap on the wrist and encouragement to do better next time. 'My children won't eat stew you know. Put the barracuda in lots of water with pepper soup spices, with hot pepper, salt. Just leave it to boil and simmer well. You can put a drop of palm oil in then put some cut efirin (bush basil) in at the end, then serve it with boiled rice.'

I thank her and file the recipe.

I make a promise to myself to brush up my market lingo, pay more attention to my clothes when I'm going to the market by myself, tie a headscarf because it immediately makes me respectable, and take one of my children with me because women wearing wedding rings and dragging surly children make market vendors absurdly happy. They give you extra everything for the child's soup – extra okro, extra carrots, extra fish – in the midst of the 'E no dey' scarcity.

The Marina (Henshaw Beach) Market is a cheaper market with beautiful views from the road. You can see the Atlantic Ocean from the entrance: boats gliding in the distance, brightly coloured umbrellas in clusters at the bottom of the slope you have to climb to reach the market. In this market you'll find all kinds of crayfish: elegant, fair-faced, dark, red, fine-beads, white, scruffy. There are a dozen different species of garden-egg; the season is ending so they are like turmeric light bulbs. A blue moped passes you going up the slope with soft-drink bottles jingling on its back. A woman with the complexion of light butterscotch sits on the floor tying afang leaves together. The smell of a mountain of rubber slippers evokes memories of those treacherous Cortina school shoes that rubbed your heels raw.

In this market I stand out more, make more mistakes. I'm an easier target because I leave home for the market with that mindset that I won't change myself to influence the price, and I won't edit my descriptions of produce in shapes and colours. The words 'round', 'square', 'oval', 'red', 'green' and 'black' mean completely different things in the market. Many of the words for shapes don't mean anything to people selling in the market – they are the language of preschool rooms they never visited and numeracy lessons they never took – yet this is the rudimentary way I was taught to describe things.

Going to the market to look for red bananas will end up a wasted trip unless you practise rules like never ever saying the word 'red' to refer to a colour but only as a description of a level of ripeness. Red is my favourite colour. I like using the word red. I have a rule of wearing something red every day. At home I have a chair draped with red chenille that the average Calabar man won't sit on when he visits us because he thinks the redness of the cloth is indicative of something ominous. Saying 'red' means you want ripe produce. 'Green' means unripe, unless you are referring to bananas and plantains, where black plantains mean unripe and not overripe as you would imagine. The word 'yellow' never, ever comes up when you are talking about bananas and plantains. If you insist on talking colours when you are referring to onions, red onions are called purple onions. White onions are not 'white', they are 'Hausa' onions or, 'Spanish' onions. Yellow corn isn't 'yellow' when it's ripe; it's 'red'.

I love the marketplace but it doesn't love me. It's out of my league. It's smarter than I am. Impatient of my slowness. Many times, I will go to the supermarket and buy fresh produce from the fruit and vegetable stall erected outside their front doors. I'll do that because I just want to see a white tag that says 'N100'. I don't want to haggle or fight. I don't want to hear a thirty-minute story of how a man bought a smoked catfish, took it home, kissed it and it turned into a woman who he considered marrying but changed his mind about on account of her nagging. He took her back to the market and demanded his money back but the fish vendor said, 'What! After you've kissed the fish and done all kinds of things with her?' So a huge fight broke out in the market that morning ... In other words, and by virtue of the fight that took down many market stalls, 'Fish no dey.'

Safe as Stews

If I were asked to describe the typical Nigerian palate in barefaced generalisations, I would say we enjoy foods that generate stomach fullness and familiarity, especially the safe, stodgy goodwill of dense starches and lubricating grease. 'Safe' is a key word, both in terms of feeling protected from danger and feeling a reassuring familiarity with food.

I once hired a man called Muri Fini to take care of my garden. He had lived on Lagos Island his whole life, and every day he woke up and ate his soft white bread accompanied by fried eggs and milky tea. For lunch, he had a bowl of rice and peppery stew, and at night he had his heaviest meal: èbà and efo rírò or àmàlà and ewédú with stew. At Easter, he had beans frejon and deep-fried croaker, but not because he was Christian. He was, in fact, devoutly Muslim. He ate it because he was a true Lagos Islander, and it was fashionable to eat frejon and fish at Easter if you were from there.

The frejon and croaker were the only meals that ever differed from his daily routine. The highlights of his meals were as much meat as he could afford, and all of it was present in the anatomy of the cow. If he could eat generous portions of tripe (shàkì), cow intestines decoratively plaited and stewed, cowhide (ponmo), cow leg (bokoto), oxtail (ìrù-eran), lungs, liver and tongue, then he was eating like a king. He is one of the most physically strong men I have ever met, so if you talked about nutrition, balanced meals, he would scoff. Muri once fell down three storeys. He went to hospital a couple of times, drank many self-prescribed doses of Alabukun, and recovered promptly. Nutrition was for wimps, and Muri was no wimp. Experimenting with food was completely off his radar.

While Muri was working for me, my mother-in-law came to stay from Calabar. She is of the unwavering belief that you must offer anyone who enters your house a proper meal. Not chin-chin and cold Coca-Cola, but rice and stew with beef at the very least. She attempted to nudge me out of my kitchen; I suppose that's what mother-in-laws do to reassure themselves they have acquired a daughter rather than lost a son, and because the woman who rules the hearth, rules the house. It would have been culturally appropriate for me to have moved graciously over and out rather than wait for her nudging, but I have never been culturally obedient.

She offered Muri some food. Muri agreed with visible excitement, not giving a second thought to what this meal would be. What was he expecting? Probably a bowl of rice and stew with beef. She handed him a generous helping of gari and afia efere – white soup.

He took the food and thanked her. My mother-in-law and I went upstairs to do other things. We came down about fifteen minutes later to find that Muri had left the food on the table and absconded.

It was mean-spirited to gloat but I did it anyway. If her generosity in giving my staff food was meant to show me up in my urban stinginess, it had failed. My poor mother-in-law was offended and confused by this behaviour. When you were approached with such generosity, you went out of your way to clean the bowl. You left not a morsel behind. You washed the dishes. You grovelled in thanks. It was the way.

Why had he not just declined the offer of food? Because he was eager to eat and he trusted me enough to agree to eat the food we were planning to have. Unfortunately, the white soup was so completely removed from anything he had eaten in his life that instead of inspiring hunger or curiosity, it inspired fear, distrust and revulsion. I could not, of course, tell her that he had made up his mind about her based on that one bowl of soup. It was unfair but that was the way it was. He had decided he couldn't trust her. Not when she had given him something white, not red. Aromatic, not peppery.

If you consider Muri's classically superstitious 'Isale Eko' Yorùbá upbringing, with over twenty years of eating red stews, then you could empathise with his reaction to the alien yam-thickened off-white countenance of afia efere, and the never-before-encountered aroma of the tetrapleura tetraptera pod. Muri knew he would be coming back to work in a couple of days, so leaving the food, walking out of the compound and going home showed how completely destabilised he was. There was nothing rational about the way he had dealt with the situation. In Calabar, a serving of afia efere was not something you would be offered every day. It is one of the Efik's most esteemed soups, and my mother-in-law had offered it with all the associated fanfare.

When I demanded an explanation a few days later when he turned up for work, he shuffled his feet and mumbled something about never having seen that sort of something or the other before. He was so embarrassed that it would have been cruel to continue to probe. I have said that Muri was very strong physically; he could work extended hours and clear a field in a way that suggested he'd grown up doing physically demanding work, farm labourer's work. Whenever you sighted a snake, Muri was the one you called, and he came with his chest out, drunk on being our saviour. For such a man to run at the sight of a bowl of white soup was hilarious.

The incident happened before I moved to Calabar and I offered all kinds of incentives to get Muri to move with me to work there. He resolutely refused. A few years later, he confided the reasons for his refusal: *those Igbo people* were a different world; the Yorùbá did not go that way. What would he eat when he got there? More pertinently, would someone see him and decide that he was worth eating? I only laugh when Yorùbá people say things like that because it's important to make them feel at ease to continue to talk. If you reprimand them with even a facial expression (especially as my husband was *one of those Igbo people*), then they clam up. They were, in fact, already beating themselves up. Especially people like Muri, who were conscious of their too-brief excursions through school, barely able to read or write. But if you talked long enough, perhaps they would rethink the deep-seated prejudices about people next door, the people they were rubbing shoulders with every day in Lagos. Perhaps they would rethink their irrational fears of *Obe Íbò* – soups from the east and south south.

Though Muri's case is funny, not life threatening, I have also heard the tragic story of a fifty-year-old Nigerian woman with crippling arthritis, eating red stews made from tomatoes, tatase (mild red peppers), onions and rodo (hot peppers) every day even though she had been given medical advice that tomatoes and peppers (which are in the nightshade family) sometimes cause or aggravate inflammation and rheumatoid arthritis. She might get substantial pain relief if she did not eat her daily stews, but she refused to stop. Any Nigerian, whatever their age, might react with the same initial disbelief and anger. How could you be a Nigerian of Yorùbá descent and not eat stew? Not eat steaming, peppery, red jollof rice? Or ofada? Or goat stew? What is the use of living then? Stew is our safety net for hunger. Stew with everything. Stew is safe. There is nothing as safe as stews.

I have had people write to tell me how unimaginably alien they find the idea of cooking a stew with coconut milk or fish sauce. It makes sense, because a Nigerian stew needs to accompany everything from ebà, gari and semovita to beans, so a coconut-milk stew is a mighty leap for the Nigerian imagination or palate. Still, I wonder about the Yorùbá running from Efik soups and the unfamiliarity that we smugly hold up as a defence when confronted with food from different parts of our own country. There is residual wisdom in being able to exclude onions and tomatoes from your food if you have food sensitivities. The Obe Íbò have excelled at this for a long time.

I wonder that we are not dying of curiosity about Tiv cuisine and uncommon hot peppers that grow in remote areas of Yenogoa. Or why our 'national cuisine' is so restricted. If the typical Nigerian had to choose between not eating stew and death, would he really choose to die?

A Pot from Efak Satan

I braved Efak Satan in Watt Market for the sake of made-in-Nigeria cookware; for intuitive, heavyweight, shallow, two-sizes-fit-all pots made from black clay, with curvaceous bottoms, porous matte glazes and gratuitous, beautifying scarification. The pots have a long list of commendations yet their lids don't quite survive the galloping drive home from the market.

Efak Satan means Satan Street. It's a ramshackle corridor in Calabar's Watt Market, with the natural lights mellowed in the shadows of old buildings that are a collage of wood stalls and ancient concrete. Cobbled stones flake under your feet. To get there you go past the cloth vendors, all men, standing too close. They won't touch you like in Lagos markets, but they might as well be. Just after them is the head of the corridor, like an accidental door into another world. There is nothing natural about the progression of wares as you enter Efak Satan. From leftover cuts of imported fabric, the rejects of the rejects bought off smugglers' trawlers, you progress suddenly to recycled paint buckets filled to the brim with hundreds of dried baby chameleons. Efak Satan is full of bizarre things: suspended baby gourds, manillas, oninis, cowries, white wooden dolls with red painted lips awaiting concrete nails and malice. There are animal skulls and shabby containers labelled 'Dápadà [return-to-sender] perfume' and 'Holistic brain tonic'.

In front of the biggest stall in Efak Satan, I stand staring into the wide-open eye of a casqued-hornbill, a forest timekeeper who, until its decapitation, announced in nasal booms that it was 6 a.m., 12 noon, 3 p.m. It seems doubtable that he is dead, a silenced clock, desiccated with impossible expertise. His eyelashes are stunning, black strands of glossy silk; of course he will blink at any moment. Aunty Thelma, who volunteered to take me into this corridor, asks the owner of the hornbill head if the street is really called Efak Satan. She knows it is but she is looking for an answer for my essay. The vendor's eyes disengage from ours, moving slowly over our heads. He replies so languidly you can hear his mind ticking through the seconds. It isn't called Efak Satan; it's called Efak Ikpok Eto (Back-of-the-tree Street) he tells us. I walk around the tree in my mind just to be sure where the back is.

When we moved into our house in Sacramento estate in Calabar, it was one of ten houses canopied by trees as old as I was, some older. Three years later, the landlady came along and began to cut down the trees one by one. We heard she said the trees walked around at night. Walked around the sleeping people. In the daytime they stood perfectly still and cast sinister shadows. I'd heard of trees walking before. Or rather, I had heard people accuse trees of walking, of uprooting their feet and putting them back down around sleeping men. But I also heard they hadn't corrupted themselves, that it was men with blades making incisions, rubbing concoctions into the wounds and asking forbidden questions of the trees: 'Sir, who went this way?' It was men who crossed the boundaries. And as soon as the trees learnt to converse with men and agreed to speak, they were chopped down.

This was what I meant about this Satan fellow for whom the street in the market was named: the ominousness of invisibility. There was the false modesty of only having one little corridor in the whole of Calabar named after him, but not really named after him because the vendors refuse to admit it. There's a sly manipulation of light and shade involved in sending the visitor out on a roundabout mission to find the back of a tree. You could only find the back at night, in dreams, when the trees were walking around you.

Among other wares in the man's stall were pieces of something like orange Styrofoam, like packaged cheese sticks opened out into a clay dish. I prompted Aunty Thelma to ask what they were for. The man answered that they were for the worship of Anansa the temperamental water goddess, colloquially called mammywata.

I wasn't a neophyte when it came to wandering around markets and stumbling into strange, unscripted encounters in an otherwise unexceptional day. There are many reminders of Watt Market's Efak Satan on Lagos Island. I once turned to see a snake's head on the most prominent shelf of a plain market stall, the snake's mouth propped open as wide as a doorway. His eyes delighted as if he were posing for National Geographic. The seller was nonchalant, as if a snake's head is something you grow next to lemongrass in the back garden. When I went to Efak Satan I was already used to these breath-snatchers, intense snags in the already high-strung material of market- places. And I was really, *really* desperate to find my pot made from sand, water, heat and integrity, to discover in it new opinions on flavour.

That said, I still found the trip deeply unnerving. You see, my mother's family worshiped Èsù Láàlú, who the English language translated to 'Satan' many generations ago. A few generations closer, my forebears decided that Èsù was not some short, ugly, ambiguously male stone figure elevated in the town centre of Ìgbájo to whom worship was offered, and on whose behalf festivities with food and drink were organised. What really happened between innocent dancing and full-grown resolve on the light and shade of the matter is undocumented, but in the end, my mother's family felt that Èsù's lack of commitment to good or evil, black or white, light or dark was increasingly *disconcerting* in a world of concrete good and evil. They decided that 'mischievous' was too disingenuous a word to describe his personality or the idea of bending light and dark as a pastime. The point is that my mother's family deserted Èsù's altars; agreed to his being Satan. I am not sure how he feels about this. I would therefore never have braved Efak Satan in Calabar's Watt Market if my quest for the pot did not absolutely necessitate it. Without compelling reasons, I would not be hanging out on a street named after Èsù Láàlú.

The local pot that drove me there was one of which I have always innately known. I *knew* that it existed and I *knew* that it was designed, without question, by Nigerians and had a long intimate relationship with our soup. I knew it must be capable of all kinds of wonderful and unusual things. I had already learnt that it sat proudly on or inside a naked fire, in the midst of robust firewood flames. It was going to sit even more proudly on my hob. I heard it got fatter and more confident with time and use. It inhaled air and exhaled flavour and aroma, even when it was not working. The pots were already sold to my imagination. The problem was approaching the dreamlike fringe where it was sold, and allowing my mind to be invaded by wares like snake heads, oil for stopping demons and red cam-wood dust in cellophane swinging like silent wind chimes.

My son was the one who inspired me to finally get up and find the pot. By 6 a.m. every morning he would have a spatula in his hand, demanding freshly cooked food. He'd do so again at noon, 3 p.m. and 7 p.m. He really did wield that spatula; I'm not making it up. He held it in one hand and gripped the seat of my jeans with the other and I'm not sure whether he was threatening me with cooking implements, or hinting strongly that I should have been holding a spatula at all times to give him the psychological comfort of knowing that food was almost ready. I was the surly buka attendant and he was the customer holding up the utensil to indicate impatience. Anyway, the problem was his physical and cognitive sensitivity to all sorts of things, and we had to take account of what pots did to his food when heat was applied to them. He needed an organic pot that inhaled and exhaled only food, water and flavour.

For long enough, like most people, we took it for granted that when we bought any pot for cooking, the manufacturer was guaranteeing us that he had our best interests at heart, and that he had used the safest, most ethical materials. Of course there was never any such guarantee. We subconsciously made it up because it was necessary to get on with buying the pots we needed. However, a N10,000, imported, non-stick pan will spontaneously exude those chemicals that have been used to make it non-stick. This effect of the cooking pan or pot only seems to get questioned when food allergies and sensitivities are in the mix, but it wasn't always thus. There was a time – and there are still some places – in Nigeria Where people understood that the pot's contribution to the food matters intrinsically. Villagers who cook with locally made earthenware pots will tell you that the fabric and the porosity of the pots undoubtedly enhance the soups.

The organic local pot is constructed using only clay, water and heat, and those three words bring to mind the delicious images associated with groundnuts being roasted in heated sand. The sand is the medium for cooking. It's the real pot, whatever other container the sand is in. There is enough constitutional distance between the sand and the container, enough filter in the nature, movement and heat resistance of sand to make the container irrelevant. The heat imprints the smell of fired sand deep into the very core of the nuts, and their skins are turned to salty parchment. I suppose it's not an appropriate snack for the asthmatic, but it's illicitly aromatic, pica-delectable and just honest-to-God gorgeous. The aroma rises up into the top of the nasal cavity where it lingers and smothers.

The local pot is built with the help of an old-hand, old-world manuscript with intricate details on the movement of firewood-heat through earth and water. The pot manipulates heat to perfection. Its bottom is never flat like the oyinbo pot. Like the idealised Nigerian woman, it has a voluptuous bottom. It dips into a valley and curves upwards. It topples easily and dances like a top on a flat surface. Jollof rice in a native pot is first scorched for flavour at the bottom and then the heat moves up and around the pot, building gradually but confidently, cooking the rice and pepper to perfection. The scorched rice at the bottom is flavour and aroma and a protective skin for the sousing of the rice above.

The intelligence of the pot includes the circular movement of dissipating heat as it reaches the outward curves of the rims. I am amazed that we have forgotten this amazing piece of equipment that has so much integrity, so much necessity, inventiveness and cleverness. It has so many secret rooms and stories that the imported pot appears dishonest, ostentatious and distant in comparison. On too many occasions have I grabbed my pot straight from the fire and put it under the rush of cold tap water. I have broken a few imported earthenware dishes and pots in this absent-minded way, and they don't break elegantly. You hear the cracking across the pot's fibre like the world is ending. On the other hand, the local pot harbours heat so uniquely, so effectively that the cold tap water glides off its skin, causing nothing but impetuous sizzling, kissing of teeth.

In the open market you will find either the atrociously ugly Tower Aluminium pots that look like they were made by prison labour, or imported stainless steel or non-stick pots. The idea of a non-stick pan might well be a marketing scam. The Chinese have long established that all you need to make a pan non-stick is some oil and heat. And if the food sticks, it tastes better. Anyone whose taste buds are alive knows that the bottom of the pot, that part that experiences the full blast of heat, gets the best marks for flavour.

Ìkòkò tí ó j'ata o, ìdí re a gbóná (The pot that wants to eat pepper will allow its bottom to get very hot indeed).

My online research into unglazed earthenware pots turned up the suggestion that one never cook strong flavours in unglazed earthenware pots. Nigerian cooking wisdom dictates doing exactly that. Our native pots are seasoned with strong flavours over time. My pots are seasoned with rainwater and blistering sunlight. They're left out in the night air to inhale and exhale. The native pot ages like a living thing and fattens up with flavour. A new native pot must make obeisance to a year-old native pot. They are not in the same league.

I once put some stockfish in my newish pot with some water and set it to boil on the hob. A few minutes later, some guests came in and started to demand the details of the feast I was putting together. I explained that there was no feast, just stockfish and water, but they kept insisting until I had to let them look inside the pot. What was generating the smell was not the food but the pot, and the aroma was from just two nights of cooking ogbono soup. Now the pot smells of ogbono soup whether one is cooking it or not. The area in which it is kept smells of ogbono soup. In a year, the pot will be ogbono soup through and through. This very intrusion of the pot on food and food on the pot, this synergistic relationship between pot and food is fundamental in the layering of flavours in Nigerian food. We are not afraid of strong flavours, strong aromas or intense heat. The combined aromatics of firewood, dawadawa, stockfish, smoked fish, and scent leaf are not going to turn their nose up at a pot that absorbs strong flavours.

The Yorùbá's version of saying 'blah blah blah' is the words 'Ìgbá, àwo, Ìkòkò baba ìsasùn'. It literally translates to a selection of cooking and eating implements: pots and pans. I suppose it means the movement of pots and pans: noise. I have to remove the 'Ìsásùn', the local pot, from that trivialising list. It has been disregarded for long enough. In my house, it is the king of cookware.

Bibliography

'A Comprehensive Guide to Vegetables' in *South African Cookbook* (Heritage Publishing, 2006).

Adesokan, Akin. 'Ibadan, Soutin and the Puzzle of Bower's Tower', *African Cities Reader*, 1 (2009).

Barry, Michael. *Exotic Food the Crafty Way.* Norwich: Jarrold Publishing, 1996.

Donaldson, Enid. *The Real Taste of Jamaica.* Illinois: Warwick Publishing, 1996.

Kusa, Femi. 'Natural Remedies for Sound Body and Mind', *The Nation*, 14 January 2010.

Mitter, Siddhartha. 'Free Okra: Rescuing a vegetable from a slimy stereotype', *The Oxford American*, 49, 2005.

Takano, Junji. 'Health Benefits of Okra', www.pyroenergen.com, last accessed 20 March 2016.

Thiam, Pierre. *Yolele! Recipes From the Heart of Senegal.* New York, Lake Isle Press, 2008.

Usigan, Ysolt. 'Ugly foods you should be eating', *Shape*, www.shape.com, last accessed 13 January 2016.

Williams, Lizzie. *Nigeria: The Bradt Travel Guide.* England Bradt Travel Guides, 2012.

Acknowledgements

My highest acknowledgement must go to Bibi Bakare-Yusuf, the vegan Nigerian who edited my stories and set a high standard that produced a good book. Without her, *Longthroat Memoirs* the book would not exist, the subtitle 'Sex, Soup and Nigerian Taste Buds' would not be present, and I would not have had the courage to finish and polish what started as a collection of food articles with faint literary sparkle.

Amma Ogan treated my weekly articles with such respect she made me doubt my unsophistication.

Many of the recipes are not my own. The jollof rice and puff-puff recipes belong to my sister, Tósìn Ògúnbánjo, while the twist of adding pepper to puff-puffs was learnt from an elderly lady called Mama Rose. My afang soup is a cross between Rose Odok's (my help in Calabar) and Aunty Thelma's (Thelma Bello's) recipes. Aunty Thelma also owns my fisherman's stew and ekpang nku kwo recipes. I learnt to cook ntutulikpo soup in her kitchen. My ogbono soup was first taught to me by Michael Mukolu, whose stories and strong, observant Nigerian intuition helped me interpret many riddles. When Elizabeth Nkem Jinanwa came to Calabar she taught me how to make kunu zaki and two types of oseani. The jollof beans recipe belongs to my 'one and only salt-of-the-earth sister-in-law' Omolará Aríbisálà who learnt it from her mother, Mrs.

Múyìwá Osìmókun. My vinaigrette was taught to me by Barbara Page-Phillips in Somerton, Somerset, and Barbara must be especially thanked because she gave me an entire cottage to write in for seven whole months. I was introduced to ekoki by Elizabeth Ekpiken Akan, and ila cocoa by Mrs. Bolá Osìnbódù Adétúlà. I have an obe-isapa recipe that belongs to Bámidélé Adémolá-Olátejú and I am in the process of loving her up for the following recipes: ewe coco, groundnut soup and tuwo made from Japanese rice. Mrs. Bolá Osìnbódù Adétúlà has also promised me a recipe for efo made from efirin. I mustn't forget Ebùn Feludu's ìrù stew and ram cooked with yogurt. I could go on … *Longthroat Memoirs* would be Cup-a-Soup minestrone without all their wonderful recipes. Thank you!

Last but not least, to Lauren Smith who copy-edited *Longthroat Memoirs* and made my head fly off my neck in rage a few times too. Well done you.

Last but not least, grateful acknowledgment of Kólá Túbòsún's crucial additions of tone-markings to Yoruba words, and Kate Haines' keen perceptive proofreading.